REDUNDANCY AND PATERNALIST CAPITALISM

REDUNDANCY
AND
PATERNALIST CAPITALISM

A Study in the Sociology of Work

by
RODERICK MARTIN
and
R. H. FRYER

LONDON · GEORGE ALLEN & UNWIN LTD
RUSKIN HOUSE MUSEUM STREET

First published in 1973

© George Allen & Unwin Ltd 1973

ISBN 0 04 301053 9

Printed in Great Britain
in 11 *point Times Roman type*
by Unwin Brothers Limited
Woking and London

ACKNOWLEDGEMENTS

The following study would not have been possible without the financial assistance of the Social Science Research Council. We are grateful to the Council for the grant of £1498 to the senior author, Roderick Martin, in 1968–9; this was used to enable R. H. Fryer to work full time on the project for twelve months. We are also grateful to the Faculty of Social Studies, University of Oxford, and especially the Department of Social and Administrative Studies, and to the University of Manchester Institute of Science and Technology for small grants for equipment and special purposes. Trinity College, Oxford, provided facilities for typing both an initial draft of the book and the final manuscript.

Our major debt, however, is to the people of Casterton, especially the former employees of Casterton Mills; their co-operation in answering questions and in providing other forms of assistance was exemplary. We are especially grateful to the personnel manager of Casterton Mills, for making available to us a list of former employees, to the sample of respondents themselves, and to the numerous local officials who provided ungrudgingly the information we requested repeatedly. The need to preserve confidentiality, not ingratitude, is the reason for their anonymity.

We would also like to thank those who read through and commented upon an early draft of the manuscript, especially Professor John Eldridge of the University of Bradford; his critical comments proved invaluable in refining our analysis. Mr John Goldthorpe and Dr A. H. Halsey also provided helpful comments on matters of both substance and style. Mr Colin Ackerley, now of Croydon College of Technology, and Mr Greg Bamber, now of the Commission of Industrial

7

Relations, and Ann Fryer all provided valuable assistance with the collection of the data.

This book is the final result of a joint project. Fryer was mainly responsible for the field work, and for some of the data analysis; Martin was mainly responsible for coding the questionnaires, analysing the bulk of the data, and writing the manuscript.

January 1972   *Trinity College, Oxford*

NOTE

Casterton and Casterton Mills are fictitious names. All place-names which could have been used to establish its real identity have been changed.

PREFACE

Sociology, as C. Wright Mills stressed, should be concerned with private problems and public issues. Redundancy, the process whereby workers whose jobs disappear are dismissed, is both: a pressing personal problem for the workers involved, and a major issue for policy makers concerned to minimise the suffering caused by economic and technological changes. During the two years 1967 and 1968 in which the redundancy we describe was announced and carried out half a million men and women in Great Britain received redundancy payments under the official redundancy payments scheme totalling over £100 millions, and a further million people who were ineligible for the receipt of government money are estimated to have lost their jobs through redundancy. Over 446,000 workers received redundancy pay between October 1970 and October 1971.

What follows is an account of the attitudes and experiences of a few of these people. In January 1967 the management of Casterton Mills (the name we have given to the plant in our research), a large manufacturing plant located in a medium-sized industrial town in the North of England, announced that they were going to cut their labour force by 1500 people over the following three years. Their target was achieved in less than two years; a labour force of 2500 was reduced to just over a thousand by restrictions on recruitment, natural wastage, and redundancy. During this period of two years nearly a tenth of the occupied population of Casterton changed jobs, became unemployed, registered as sick, or retired as a result of this decision. Seven hundred and thirty-four (619 males) hourly paid employees, manual workers, and 322 (183 males) monthly paid employees, non-manual workers, left Casterton Mills between the beginning of February 1967 and the end of

9

November 1968: we interviewed a one in three sample of male manual leavers (voluntary and involuntary), and a two in three sample of male non-manual leavers. This data provides the basis for most of our discussion below.

We have tried to explain the meaning of the redundancy at Casterton Mills both for the employees directly concerned and for the community as a whole. The Mills had been the largest employers in the town for over a hundred years, and its owners had played a central role in the development of the community. The redundancy was thus not simply a personal shock for those workers involved, but also a serious disruption of the taken-for-granted world of the community as a whole. The meaning of the redundancy can therefore only be understood in the light of the recent history of the community, and the employment relations of what we have termed 'paternalist capitalism'; the structure and culture of paternalist capitalism form an essential background to the events at the Mills in 1967 and 1968. At the same time the redundancy was a 'key event' in the development of the community, and therefore provides a way of laying bare the basic elements of paternalist capitalism, and the strains it was subjected to in the late 1960s.

Although we do not claim that Casterton, and the redundancy at Casterton Mills, were 'typical', we do believe that examination of events there significantly illuminates the general problem of redundancy: we have examined the general through the particular. In doing so we hope that we have increased the understanding of the problems of redundancy, the meaning of work and non-work in contemporary Britain, and the complex reality which lies hidden beneath the generic term 'industrial society'.

CONTENTS

1 INTRODUCTION: UNEMPLOYMENT IN A FULL-EMPLOYMENT ECONOMY

Since the Second World War the major countries of the developed world have pledged themselves to joint and individual action to secure full employment. As Article 55 of the United Nations Charter declares, 'with a view to the creation of the conditions of stability and well being which are necessary for peaceful and friendly relations among nations . . .' the United Nations shall promote: higher standards of living, full employment, and conditions of economic and social progress . . .'. In Britain the Coalition Government's acceptance of Beveridge's key 1944 White Paper on Employment Policy set the tone for successive post-war administrations: both Labour and Conservative parties have agreed that the war against unemployment should be waged with the intelligence and energy previously devoted to the war against Hitler.[1] In the United States the 1946 Employment Act committed the Federal Government to taking measures to 'establish conditions under which there will be afforded useful employment opportunities, including self-employment, for those able, willing and seeking to work, and to promote maximum employment, production, and purchasing power'.[2] Similar undertakings to preserve full employment were given by other capitalist governments, and

---

[1] '. . . if, as has been done, a nationally directed effort can be made to reduce unemployment to the disappearing point in order that the nation may survive, let no one say that an equally comprehensive plan is not possible to remove economic anxiety and promote the well being of the people in normal times. We must organise against the encroachments of the internal enemy with the same determination we have displayed in confounding an external one' E. Shinwell, *The Britain I Want*, Macdonald and Co., 1943, p. 48.

[2] Quoted in A. M. Ross, *Unemployment and the American Economy*, New York: John Wiley and Son, 1964, p. 18.

unemployment has been officially abolished in socialist countries.

Despite this commitment unemployment and the fear of unemployment remain primary sources of tension in contemporary Western society. 'Full employment' remains an aspiration, a slogan, rather than a reality, in Britain as elsewhere. Since 1945 the annual national average rate of unemployment has fluctuated between 1·6 and 3·7 per cent in the United Kingdom, between 2·8 and 6·6 per cent in the United States, and between 6·3 and 8·2 per cent in Italy. These proportions, perhaps small in comparison with the levels experienced in the inter-war years, represent substantial sectors of the population: in August 1971 929,000 workers were out of work in the United Kingdom. In limited geographical areas, like the Highlands of Scotland, the central and eastern valleys of South Wales, Northern Ireland, Tennessee and West Virginia in the United States, full employment is not even a realistic aspiration: in the 1960s and 1970s parts of Scotland, Wales and Northern Ireland have experienced unemployment levels of 10 per cent and more. Moreover, the fear of redundancy and unemployment hangs over far larger sections of the labour force, particularly those employed in industries experiencing long-term economic difficulties, like coal mining, the railways, the docks, and ship-building, contributing significantly to the acute industrial relations problems of those industries. And even in prosperous industries, like engineering, periodic lay-offs due to cyclical and seasonal fluctuations in the level of demand undermine the attractions of high hourly earnings or loose piece-work rates.

Labour economists rather than sociologists have provided the major explanations for the continuance of unemployment. Building upon the work of Beveridge, they have focused upon six sets of factors: fluctuations in the level of aggregate demand; changes in the direction of demand; changes in the processes of production (especially technology); individual incapacities (e.g. illness); geographical and occupational obstacles to labour mobility (e.g. the inflexibility of the housing market, trade union restrictions upon entry into occupations); and market friction due to the inadequate coordination of leaving and entering jobs. Especially important are the first three sets of factors: the level

14

of aggregate demand; the direction of demand; and technological change.

The role of the level of aggregate demand in the determination of unemployment levels has been the subject of intense controversy, mainly in the United States: little work has been done in Britain. According to the 'aggregationists', rises in the level of effective demand (by consumers at home and abroad, by government, and for investment) have failed to match increases in output potential resulting from new investment, expansion of the labour force, and increased productivity: 'the rate of growth in final demand has been low relative to the actual and normal rates of growth in potential supply made possible by increases in capital stock, labour force, and productivity'.[3] Such deficiency in the level of aggregate demand was largely responsible for the high level of unemployment experienced in Britain in the inter-war period: exports declined due to a structural change in the pattern of world trade to Britain's disadvantage, whilst domestic demand did not rise enough to take up the slack. Since 1945 the impact of the level of aggregate demand upon unemployment levels has varied. Between 1945 and 1966 a long-term investment boom, the relative scarcity of labour compared with capital, topped out with Keynesian style government intervention when required (as in 1954–5, 1958–9, and 1962–3), helped to maintain a high level of aggregate demand and a low level of unemployment.[4] Since the economic crisis of 1964–6 the political obtrusiveness of balance of payments problems and a faster rate of inflation than other industrial countries have led to a squeeze on domestic consumption, a drop in investment, and an increase in the number of unemployed from 300,000 in 1966 to over 900,000 at the present time, mid–1971. However, the present unresponsiveness of the level of unemployment to an increase

[3] U.S. Congress, Joint Economic Committee, Subcommittee on Economic Statistics, *Higher Unemployment Rates, 1957–1960: Structural Transformation or Inadequate Demand*, Washington: U.S. Government Printing Office, 1961.
[4] R. C. O. Matthews, 'Why has Britain had Full Employment since the War', *Economic Journal*, Vol. 78, 1968, pp. 555–69: cf. J. C. R. Dow, *The Management of the British Economy, 1945–60*, Cambridge: Cambridge University Press, 1964, pp. 92–4.

in exports and a limited managed expansion in domestic demand, and the persistance (and even widening) of regional differences in the level of unemployment, suggests that the increase in unemployment since 1966 is not simply due to a deficiency in the level of aggregate demand but also to long-term changes in the direction of demand.

Since the Second World War there have been sharp changes in consumer preferences; for example there has been a sharp decline in the demand for coal, cotton textiles, and railways, with a parallel increase in the demand for oil, artificial fibres, and motor vehicles. These large shifts in consumer demand have resulted in significant changes in the industrial distribution of the occupied labour force, with redundancies and substantial unemployment in the contracting industries. The number of workers employed in the coal-mining industry dropped from 788,100 to 427,500, in textiles from 1,031,400 to 750,000, and on the railways from 503,900 to 293,100 between 1954 and 1968. Despite restrictions on recruitment, stemming in part from declining wages relative to other industries, and 'natural wastage', substantial redundancies have occurred; 60,000 redundancies are believed to have occurred in the cotton textile industry alone in the late 1950s as a result of the reorganisation of the industry. Even this high rate of contraction has not been able to prevent substantial unemployment. In May 1968, when the national average rate of unemployment was 2·5 per cent (unadjusted for seasonal variations), unemployment was 4·2 per cent in coal mining, 2·3 per cent on the railways (which has traditionally had a low level of unemployment because of its relatively coherent structure), and 1·7 per cent in textiles (where the unemployment statistics are particularly inaccurate because of the exclusion of substantial numbers of female workers from the unemployment insurance scheme, and their consequent failure to register with the employment exchange). Such changes in the pattern of demand have been responsible for the problem of regional unemployment which has persisted since the 1920s, and has been a serious political problem since the early 1960s: the decline of coal mining (and ship building) in West Central Scotland, North East England, South Wales, and parts of Lancashire, the decline of cotton textiles in

16

Lancashire, and other changes discussed by Gavin McCrone in his useful survey of the problem in his *Regional Policy in Britain*.[5]

The contribution of technological change to the level of unemployment is unknown; there is no systematic data available relating changes in the level of industrial productivity to changes in the level of industrial employment. It is unlikely that technological change has yet made a significant contribution to unemployment levels; a Swedish study revealed only a very weak correlation between changes in productivity and changes in unemployment levels.[6] Increasing productivity has been associated with declining unemployment, for capital investment is obviously more likely in expanding sectors of the economy, where employment is relatively secure (as in the oil refining or chemicals industry). However, it is easy to be too optimistic. Intra-company transfers, restrictions on recruitment, and natural wastage may successfully absorb workers displaced by improvements in technology (as Hunter, Reid, and Boddy have shown); but the permanent reduction in employment opportunities exerts a cumulative effect upon the level of unemployment, limiting the subsequent employment prospects of new entrants to the labour force, and leading to increased unemployment in the long run (as is shown by our research at Casterton).[7] Moreover, the absorption of labour displaced by technological innovation has hitherto been accompanied by a high level of aggregate demand, by a long-term expansion in the labour-intensive service sector of the economy, and by the cheapness of labour relative to capital: as the level of aggregate demand declines, the service sector reaches saturation point, and the cost of labour relative to capital increases, technological unemployment will increase. Gilpatrick's tentative conclusion on the impact of technological change upon employment trends in the United States probably applies equally to Britain: 'The

[5] G. McCrone, *Regional Policy in Britain*, George Allen & Unwin, 1969.

[6] Ed. S. K. Anderman, *Trade Unions and Technological Change*, George Allen & Unwin, 1967, pp. 85–6.

[7] L. C. Hunter, G. L. Reid, D. Boddy, *Labour Problems of Technological Change*, George Allen & Unwin, 1970, Chapter 12.

clearest danger from [technological unemployment] appears to be in agriculture [no longer so in Britain] mining and utilities, since . . . the skills involved would not appear to be easily transferred. . . . In those industries where productivity continues to outpace output, workers will have to find sufficient and suitable jobs in industries where output outpaces productivity. Only government appears to have performed strongly as a consistent source of new employment.'[8]

Changes in the level of aggregate demand, in the direction of demand, and in the processes of production are the major causes of unemployment, whilst frictional unemployment, due to the imperfect coordination of job leaving and job entering, is of less significance. Personal incapacities (ill health, mental subnormality, etc.), and personal and institutional barriers to mobility – the major factors traditionally examined by sociologists – effect partly the level and partly the incidence of unemployment. It was estimated in 1964 that 143,000 men (60 per cent of the men wholly unemployed at the time) were out of work through personal difficulties – although this is probably an over-estimate, for it was based upon returns made by local employment exchange managers, who are inclined to emphasise the personal rather than the situational difficulties of their clients in areas of high unemployment.[9] This group included a variable core of 'unemployables' (e.g. vagrants), together with the personally incompetent (e.g. chronically bad time-keepers), and the physically and psychologically handicapped, taken on only in periods of labour shortage and dismissed as soon as possible.[10] Among the major personal obstacles to mobility are custom, ignorance, housing problems, and kinship ties; among the major institutional barriers are those erected by professional associations and trade unions to restrict entry and to maintain income levels – what the Webbs

[8] E. G. Gilpatrick, *Structural Unemployment and Aggregate Demand: A Study of Employment and Unemployment in the United States, 1948–64,* Baltimore: The John Hopkins Press, 1966, p. 55.

[9] *Ministry of Labour Gazette, 1966,* p. 156.

[10] For the psychological problems associated with work see W. S. Neff, *Work and Human Behaviour,* New York: Atherton Press, 1968. Chapter 13, 'The Psychopathology of Work'.

succinctly described as 'the Device of the Restriction of Numbers'.[11] We return to such barriers in Chapter 8.

The level of unemployment in industrial society is thus determined by five sets of factors – the level of aggregate demand, the pattern of demand, the rate of technological change, the personal characteristics of the population (age and sex distribution for example), and the efficiency of the labour market institutions – whose relative significance varies over time and space. There is an 'irreducible minimum' level of unemployment, due partly to the existence of a core of 'unemployables' and partly to the time spent moving from one job to another. Above this minimum level the major determinant is the level of aggregate demand.

During periods of high levels of aggregate demand, as in Britain in the early 1960s, workers who lose their jobs through changes in consumer preferences or technological change are relatively quickly reabsorbed: the average length of time out of work is relatively short – between 1961 and 1967 61·2 per cent of workers registered as unemployed for under a week were in work again within four weeks.[12] Regional employment problems appear manageable, partly because even the sensitive industries concentrated in depressed areas share in the general prosperity, and partly because firms are willing to consider relocation during periods of expansion. The definition of 'unemployable' is loosened, and workers possessing poor sickness records find it relatively easy to obtain work. The major barriers to full employment are personal and institutional barriers to mobility. During periods of declining aggregate demand, as in Britain since 1966, a similar cumulative process occurs; there is little slack to take up workers dismissed because of changes in consumer choice or technological progress; regional employment problems become acute (as in the North-East in 1970–71); the definition of 'unemployable' is tightened,

---

[11] S. and B. Webb, *Industrial Democracy* (1920 edn.), Longmans, 1920, p. 560.

[12] R. F. Fowler, *Duration of Unemployment on the Register of Wholly Unemployed*, Studies in Official Statistics, Research Series No. 1, H.M.S.O., 1968, p. 8.

and the effective size of the labour force diminishes – as the decline in the participation rate for men since 1968 reveals. The result is a disproportionate increase in unemployment, and a lengthening in the average length of time out of work.

Analysis in these terms – perhaps expressed with more reservations – constitutes the core of current discussions of unemployment in labour economics. Labour, as one of the factors of production, responds to the laws of supply and demand; changes in the level and distribution of demand for goods, and by derivation for labour, cause changes in the supply – an immediate change in employment levels, and a gradual change in the occupational and industrial distribution of the labour force.[13] In the long run, *ceteris paribus*, changes in the occupational and industrial structure restore a new equilibrium point for employment levels: declining earnings lead to differential wastage rates, and to differential recruitment of new entrants to the labour force. Unemployment due to changes in the level of demand can be reduced by taking measures to stimulate demand, for example by fiscal and monetary policy; unemployment due to changes in the pattern of demand will disappear automatically through the operation of the market mechanism. Such an analysis shows clearly the major factors governing overall changes in the level of unemployment, and provides guidance for the formulation of economic policy at the macro-level. Following from this analysis, manipulation of the level of aggregate demand, together with regional investment incentives and measures to improve the institutions of the labour market, have therefore been the major techniques used to maintain full employment in both Britain and the United States since the Second World War.

This analysis is problematic even in its own terms. As Gilpatrick has shown, the distinction between 'aggregate demand' and 'structural' unemployment is analytically crude and empirically difficult to measure, for the categories are not clearly differentiated: 'structural and demand unemployment

[13] D. Wedderburn, 'Redundancy', in ed. D. Pym, *Industrial Society: Social Sciences in Management*, Harmondsworth: Penguin Books Ltd., 1968, p. 77.

are so inter-related as to defy dichotomous enumeration'.[14] The distinction is primarily useful as a policy guide and legitimator – although it has lead to uncertainty over policy formulation, as the heated controversy over the effectiveness of the Kennedy income tax cut in 1963 showed. Moreover, in Britain it is doubtful whether the manipulation of the level of aggregate demand can create and maintain full employment without setting up strong inflationary pressures, leading to domestic discontent and serious balance of payments problems. However, we are not concerned to enter into the disputes of the political economists; we are concerned with the limitations rather than the inadequacies of the economic analysis of unemployment.

The presupposition of the economic analysis of employment problems in labour market terms is that behaviour can be explained *as if* economic considerations were paramount. As Hunter and Reid write in their study of *Urban Worker Mobility*: 'An economic model of mobility can explain why employees change jobs, industries, or occupations; and the process of allocation by which labour is distributed, or distributes itself, between alternative uses is broadly controlled by supply and demand, costs and returns.' 'Flows of labour between occupations can be explained in theoretical terms either by a scheme of occupation systems [as in L. Broom and J. H. Smith's paper on 'Bridging Occupations'] or, more conventionally, by a consideration of the costs and returns involved in movement.'[15] Hence personal attachment to a given geographical area is an irrational emotion, an 'obstacle' to be overcome by providing information about opportunities elsewhere, by providing assistance with movement, and by improving the institutions designed to facilitate the working of the labour market (for example by improving coordination between Local Employment Exchanges). However, economic analysis in market terms becomes at best opaque, at worst self-contradictory, when it explicitly faces the problem of the relationship between economic and non-economic factors: 'social and institutional factors are

[14] E. G. Gilpatrick, *op. cit.*, p. 215.
[15] L. C. Hunter and G. L. Reid, *Urban Worker Mobility*, Paris: O.E.C.D., 1968, p. 123, 97: cf. L. Broom and J. H. Smith, Bridging Occupations, *British Journal of Sociology*, 1963, pp. 321–34.

very important in underpinning and *shaping* the economic forces which *basically determine* mobility' (our italics).[16]

Instead of viewing the labour market as a mechanism for the adjustment of disequilibrium between labour supply and labour demand, we view it as an arena within which individuals attempt to satisfy material, psychological, social, and cultural needs, and achieve personal goals, within the perceived limits of a specifiable occupational structure, whether national or local. Hence the explanation for patterns of mobility or immobility following redundancy lies in the occupational preferences of the labour force, moulded by family, educational, and previous occupational socialisation, norms, expectations, and the perceived opportunities provided by a given level of labour demand. Hence the lack of geographical mobility is not simply due to ignorance, obtuseness, and inertia – although these do play a part. Rather, individuals are located within an organic structure, composed of kin and friends, customs and places; for many workers these are more significant than a high level of income, or even in some circumstances a job at all. Geographical immobility cannot be explained in terms of the laws of supply and demand, nor, in view of the generality of immobility, is it enough to push it aside into a residual category of 'social' factors (see below, Chapter 8). Understanding behaviour within the labour market involves understanding the meaning of work, and of jobs, and of the relation between these and social structure (as in Chapter 3 below). For some workers the loss of a job is a minor matter, a further incident in an erratic work career involving frequent job changes; for other workers it may involve the destruction of a whole identity, requiring a complete reconstruction. In short, understanding redundancy and unemployment requires understanding the social behaviour of human beings, not markets.

Hence, at one level, analysis in terms of levels and patterns of labour demand constitutes an explanation of redundancy, of why people lose their jobs and sometimes become unemployed. However, at another level, it is inadequate, explaining why unemployment rises by x per cent, but not why Smith

[16] Hunter and Reid, *op. cit.*, p. 123.

rather than Jones loses his job; and the incidence is as interesting as the level. Moreover, at the individual level, economic pressures exercise varying degrees of constraint upon managers making decisions about dismissals; on some rare occasions the pressures may leave little room for manoeuvre, on other occasions they may allow considerable discretion, leaving managers free to dismiss whom they wish, and when. We attempt to show the variable significance of economic and other constraints in Chapter 5.

Finally, the consequences of losing a job and becoming unemployed are not simply economic, although of course the economic consequences, both for the individual and for society (through the further reduction in effective demand), are serious. Sociologists have hitherto focused upon the social consequences of unemployment – for personal social integration, for family life, for leisure activities – and upon the 'culture' of the unemployed. For the unemployed develop their own subculture, with its own distinctive way of life, its own norms and values, its own argot, even its own timetable – the unemployed tend to go to bed late and to get up late. As the Pilgrim Trust report noted in the late 1930s, 'the unemployed [live] in an all-pervading atmosphere of football pools, greyhounds, and horses'; by the 1960s, especially in the United States, the major foci of concern had become television and sex.[17] The long-term unemployed naturally adapt to their situation, becoming lethargic, alternately authoritarian and submissive, self-preoccupied, and in general ill-adapted to the requirements of future employment; as one employer interviewed by Beveridge remarked, 'we have always found, as to the artisan, that, if he happens to be out of work for three months he is never the same man again. He becomes demoralised.'[18] It is hardly surprising that the best indicator of the length of time an unemployed worker will take to get a job is the length of time

[17] The Pilgrim Trust, *Men Without Work*, Cambridge: Cambridge University Press, 1938, p. 98; P. Jacobs, 'Unemployment as a Way of Life', in ed. A. M. Ross, *Employment Policy and the Labour Market*, Berkeley and Los Angeles: University of California Press, 1966.

[18] W. H. Beveridge, *Unemployment—A Problem of Industry*, Longmans, 1930, p. 139.

he has been out of work; the longer he has been unemployed the longer he is likely to remain unemployed in the future.[19]

In short, the conventional economic analysis of unemployment possesses validity in its own terms, and at its own level, the level of the labour *market*. Changes in the level and direction of demand, in technology, in the composition of the labour force, and in the efficiency of market institutions determine variations in the level of unemployment. Yet analysis in these terms is incomplete, providing the basis for the formulation of economic policy at the macro-level (although recent experience suggests that it is a shaky basis) but not for *understanding* the behaviour of the redundant and the unemployed. Analysis in market terms requires supplementing with analysis of the process whereby individuals lose their jobs, the incidence of such redundancy, its consequences, and the meaning of such changes for all concerned. As Max Weber and many other social scientists have stressed, explanations in the social sciences should be valid at the level of meaning, both for the actors concerned and for the observer, not simply at the level of prediction, or policy formulation.[20] It is with such meanings that we are primarily concerned.

The social and personal meaning of the loss of jobs cannot be encapsulated in discussion at the level of generality common amongst labour economists: a full analysis requires an understanding of the whole situation, of the meaning of work and jobs for the workers concerned, of the processes of managerial decision-making, as well as of the direct consequences of dismissal, possible only at the micro-level. It requires sociological imagination, not economic analysis. This is particularly so when the model of rational economic man is patently inappropriate, when workers behave in 'irrational' ways. Understanding redundancy involves understanding the redundant, their norms, values, and customary patterns of behaviour. These, in turn, are moulded by their historical experiences, both personal

---

[19] *Department of Employment and Productivity Gazette*, 1968, pp. 627–8. Between 1961 and 1965 workers who had been out of work for 52 weeks could anticipate spending a further 59 weeks unemployed.

[20] M. Weber, *The Methodology of the Social Sciences*, Glencoe: The Free Press, 1949.

and collective. The remainder of this study is an exploration of these issues in depth, focusing upon one group of workers who left one factory at one particular time. We do not claim that they and their experiences were typical, for there is no information upon which to assess typicality; we do claim that their experience is enlightening and instructive. Only future research will show how typical the events at Casterton Mills were.

2 PATERNALIST CAPITALISM: POLITICS AND SOCIAL CLASS

Individual beliefs, expectations, and behaviour are moulded by group norms and values, and the physical and social environment within which they occur, and present norms, values, and environments cannot be explained without reference to history. Accordingly, the redundancy at Casterton Mills must be located within the context of the overall historical development of the community, the specific event only becoming meaningful, in the fullest sense, within the context of the whole.[1] More specifically, we hope to show how the salient features of Casterton's economic and demographic development, especially the evolving mutually dependent relationship between the Mills and the town, conditioned workers' attitudes towards politics, social class, work and the firm.

Casterton's geographical isolation, well-established commerical and kinship ties with surrounding rural areas, demographic stagnation, imbalanced occupational structure, low educational level, and emotional as well as economic dependence upon a limited number of employers, especially the Mills, sustained a complex structure of paternalist capitalism, together with its supporting array of attitudes, until the redundancy. This was characterised by authoritarianism, tempered with generosity, on the part of the Mills, and deference, tinged with resentment, on the part of the employed – a combination of attributes familiar from Lane and Roberts' study of Pilkingtons.[2] As Lane and Roberts comment: 'Pilkingtons' dominance

---

[1] As in the last, and best, volume in Warner's classic Yankee City series: W. L. Warner and J. O. Low, *The Modern Factory: The Strike—A Social Analysis*, New Haven: Yale University Press, 1947.

[2] A. Lane and K. Roberts, *Strike at Pilkingtons*, Collins/Fontana, 1971, p. 31.

26

is dominance of the labour market. It is not just that no other employer of male labour can afford to pay very much less than Pilkingtons, it is also a question of the people's feeling of dependence upon Pilkingtons. Nothing can be done to offend the firm too much, for, who knows (?), they may pack their machines and take them somewhere else. In this situation people are likely to develop contradictory attitudes: an exaggerated deference on the one hand and a dull resentment on the other.' Casterton was, in this respect, very similar to St Helens. A community's economic development largely determines its social structure; its economic and social structure mould and focus the attitudes of its inhabitants; these attitudes, in their turn, help to maintain the pre-existing structure. We hope to show how this circle of causality operated in Casterton.

I

Casterton's geographical isolation survived until the development of a national motorway network in the late 1960s, substantially reducing travelling time between Casterton and the major population centres of the industrial North; some respondents alleged that its emotional isolation continues. As one 57-year-old supervisor commented, 'there are a lot of people who think that if they move out of Casterton they are going to fall off the end of the world'. The town is situated on the outer fringe of the industrial North, with a substantial belt of rich agricultural land between it and its nearest neighbour, Ashton; there are no important towns to the north – the town is at the end of the line. Perceived distance was even greater than actual distance; the major industrial towns of Yorkshire and Lancashire were regarded as a different, more grubby world from which they were glad to be cut off.[3]

Despite this isolation Casterton is an old established town, two prominent buildings surviving as symbols of medieval prosperity. But the town fell into decay in the sixteenth century, and Camden commented laconically in his *Miscellany*, 'the

[3] Compare the stress on amenity, below p. 158.

town at this day is not very well peopled nor much frequented'; most of the medieval town was destroyed by fire at the end of the seventeenth century. After a short cycle of prosperity and decay in the eighteenth century, which has left few memorials, the real foundations of the modern community were laid in the nineteenth century with the development of the floor-coverings industry in the area. The city was outside the mainstream of nineteenth-century industrialisation, and there was little significant development of textiles, mining, or engineering within the area; but it benefited from a secondary effect of industrialisation, the boom in urban house-building. Beginning in the late 1840s Casterton became the centre of the floor-coverings industry, and Casterton Mills one of the largest manufacturers of consumer durable goods in Britain; at the turn of the century over 2000 workers, or nearly a quarter of the town's occupied population, were employed at the Mills, and large numbers of suppliers and tradesmen were directly dependent upon its prosperity. The major public buildings – the Town Hall, the Mechanics' Institute, the Art Gallery, the Boys' Grammar School, as well as a substantial proportion of the city's housing stock (48 per cent in 1960) – all date from the Victorian and Edwardian eras, a testimony to the town's rapid growth during that period.

Since 1850 population trends within the area have largely reflected the labour requirements of the floor-coverings industry, especially the Mills. The industry's expansion in the late nineteenth century and subsequent stabilisation were indicated by demographic changes within the city. Population growth was most rapid during the second half of the nineteenth century, the population doubling between 1851 and 1891: Casterton grew from 14,000 people in 1851 to 33,000 in 1891, and to 40,000 by the turn of the century, although boundary changes make precise calculations impossible. Since 1900 the population has remained relatively stable: 41,000 in 1911, 43,000 in 1931, 51,000 in 1951 (mainly because of the establishment of munitions factories in the area during the Second World War), and 48,000 in 1961. The population growth which might have been expected in recent years on the basis of national demographic trends has not occurred because of continuous emigration: for the decade

1951–61 the net excess of emigrants over immigrants was 0·63 per cent, an excess likely to increase in future years since the emigrants were younger than the immigrants, and thus future children have been lost.

This picture of geographical isolation and demographic stagnation was confirmed by an analysis of the birthplaces of the men employed at Casterton Mills whom we interviewed: Casterton Mills workers were predominantly 'locals', however that term is defined. A majority of both manual and non-manual workers had been born in the community or nearby, and only a very small number outside the North of England; a substantial majority of both manual and non-manual workers had parents and parents-in-law living in the area; a small majority had siblings living in the area. The following table shows the birthplace of the sample as one index of this localism:

Place of Birth of Casterton Mills Ex-Employees (Q. 251)

	Manual %[4]	Non-Manual %
Casterton and district	54	61
Casterton county	17	16
North of England	14	14
Elsewhere Britain	10	6
Abroad	5	5
	N = 116	N = 88

More workers were employed in the floor-coverings industry than in any other industry throughout the period between 1850 and 1967 the year of the redundancy which forms the subject of this study. For example, in 1931, one of the few years for which complete data are available, 26·6 per cent (3362) of the male economically active population were working in 'other manufacturing industries', primarily floor-coverings. Retail distribution was the second largest 'industry', employing 12·9 per cent (1626) of the male and 16·1 per cent (910) of the

---

[4] Percentages here, and elsewhere, rounded to nearest whole number. Where the number of respondents does not total 207 this is because of non-response or the omission of the relevant question from the postal questionnaire.

female economically active population, and local government the third largest, employing 7·4 per cent (930) of male and 10·4 per cent of female workers. Three and a half per cent of male workers, and 23·9 per cent of women workers were employed in personal service jobs. The only large manufacturing industry, apart from floor-coverings, was silk manufacture, employing 5·9 per cent of the male and 9·5 per cent of female workers. Casterton's economic structure has been changing in the last fifteen years, with former floor-coverings firms diversifying into plastic sheeting and artificial fibres, with the establishment of large chemical and petroleum plants nearby, and with the creation of major new educational institutions in the area discussed in detail below, pp. 148; yet, until the redundancy, Casterton Mills and the floor-coverings industry were mainly responsible for prosperity or depression in the area as a whole.

There was in Casterton a large but fragmented working class, employed mainly in the Mills, other floor-coverings firms, and a large number of primarily small workshops.[5] The Census Reports do not contain separate occupational data for towns with a population below 50,000, and it is therefore impossible to trace the community's occupational development in detail; and in any event Census occupational data provide an inadequate basis for assessing the social class distribution of the population within a community. Nevertheless, the occupational data published in the 1951 Census Report provides a broad indication of the relative sizes of the different social classes within the community: 35·9 per cent of the occupied male population were members of the semi- and unskilled working class (the Registrar General's social classes 4 and 5), compared with 31·9 per cent of the occupied male population in the county as a whole, and 29 per cent in England and Wales; only 14·7 per cent of the occupied male population were members of social classes 1 and 2, compared with 15·0 per cent for the county as a whole and 18·3 per cent for England and Wales.

---

[5] For the 'status-enhancement' rewards of working in small enterprises see G. K. Ingham, *Size of Industrial Organisation and Worker Behaviour*, Cambridge: Cambridge University Press, 1970, p. 101.

The population of Casterton thus included a large semi- and unskilled working class, larger than that of well-publicised working-class towns like Bolton, celebrated by the Mass Observation team, and Huddersfield, studied in depth by Brian Jackson, Dennis Marsden, and the Institute of Community Studies.[6] The importance of retail distribution and local government offices as sources of employment was responsible for the largely petit-bourgeois character of the middle class in the community: there were relatively few members of the professional and higher managerial strata. Although there is no comparable data for other years there is no reason to believe that the occupational structure was significantly different in earlier decades (although there *may* have been a slight increase in the relative size of the working class in the years immediately following the Second World War with the boom conditions which prevailed in local industry). The city's housing stock, with relatively few dwellings of a high rateable value, large numbers of small semi-detached houses, and very large numbers of terraced houses – now being demolished under urban renewal programmes – provides physical confirmation for this picture of a very small upper middle class, a large lower middle class, and a large lower working class.

This occupational structure was partly the cause, and partly the consequence, of a generally low level of education in the area. In 1951 79 per cent of the male occupied population had completed their full-time education aged 14 or younger, and under 1 per cent aged 20 or more, compared with figures for England and Wales as a whole for the same year of 75·4 and 2·3 per cent. The relatively low level of education for the community as a whole was also characteristic of the labour force at Casterton Mills: 84 per cent of manual workers and 56 per cent of non-manual workers had left school at the first opportunity, at either 14 (for those who completed their education before 1947) or 15. There were, of course, a number of white-collar workers who had attended selective secondary

[6] T. Harrison, *Britain Revisited*, Victor Gollancz, 1961; B. Jackson, *Working Class Community*, Routledge and Kegan Paul, 1968; B. Jackson and D. Marsden, *Education and the Working Class*, Routledge and Kegan Paul, 1963.

schools, 27 per cent, and a small minority, 5·5 per cent, who had attended university.

Physical isolation from other major industrial centres, close ties with surrounding rural areas, economic dependence upon a very small number of large firms, especially the Mills, and a large number of small ones, demographic stagnation, and a large semi- and unskilled working class, with a correspondingly low level of education, provided the ideal environment for the development of paternalist capitalism. But the Casterton family was responsible for transforming potential into reality, and for establishing political and social hegemony in the area comparable with that possessed by the Hornby family in Blackburn and the Guest family in Merthyr Tydfil during the late nineteenth century, and by the Pilkington family in St Helens until the present.[7] The family adopted a patriarchal role within the community, a role endorsed by many but not all other members of the community; a quasi-feudal dependence relationship evolved, compounded of domination, generosity, and deference. The family's successful claim to represent the borough at Westminster, or to have a decisive say in the selection of the Liberal candidate, in the last decades of the nineteenth century showed clearly the family's dominance of local political life; whilst the donation of two parks, two impressive memorials, and a number of small items to the city and to local charities indicated considerable generosity. Deference towards the family was shown clearly by the respectful attitude of the local press, and by the comments of many older workers at Casterton Mills, both manual and non-manual. 'Lord Casterton always had a feeling, what could he do best for his work people. I've always found him a very human man – I'm fortunate to be able to quote him' (51-year-old supervisor). The attitude expressed by the Consett and District Friendly Society to the General Manager of the Consett Iron Works found repeated echoes in the Casterton press and in the conversation of Casterton

[7] For Blackburn see P. F. Clarke, 'British Politics and Blackburn Politics', *Historical Journal*, 1969; for Merthyr Tydfil see H. J. Hanham, *Elections and Party Management: Politics in the Time of Disraeli and Gladstone*, Longmans, 1959, pp. 72–3; for St Helens see A. Lane and K. Roberts, *op. cit.*

workers: 'We . . . beg to return to you our sincere thanks for the many favours we have received at your hand. . . . We feel assured that it is to a sincere desire on your part to forward the welfare of our members and their families that we owe the generous aid that you have given us. . . . It is a matter for congratulation with us that . . . we should have the countenance and support of a gentleman possessing the influence which your position amongst us naturally gives us.'[8]

II

Political life within the community, whether with reference to national or local issues, was directly influenced by the quasi-feudal relationship between the Casterton family and the community. Two members of the Casterton family represented the borough at Westminster, and the family's support was essential for any late nineteenth-century candidate hoping to win a substantial proportion of the local artisan vote. The borough returned either an entrepreneurial Liberal, or their intellectual descendants the Conservatives, in every election between the Reform Act of 1884 and the 1960s; comparison with earlier years is impossible because of changes in the franchise and in the boundaries of the constituency. The Conservatives retained the seat with a substantial majority even in 1945, and the first Labour member was not returned until the 1960s. Members of the family, as well as leading members of the firm's management, also played a prominent part in local politics, serving as city councillors and, on several occasions, as mayor. P. F. Clarke, in his work on Blackburn politics at the end of the nineteenth century, provides an interesting account of this form of political hegemony: 'the Hornby family had represented the borough at Westminster for most of the nine-teenth century and, so Philip Snowden put it, "Toryism had become Hornbyism". Sir Harry Hornby, like his father before him, was popularly known as the "owd gam' cock" and the cries of "Hornby for ever" and "Vote for t'owd gam' cock" were enough to carry him to victory in every election in which

[8] Quoted in J. E. T. Eldridge, *Industrial Disputes*, Routledge and Kegan Paul, 1968, pp. 212–13.

he stood, including that of 1906. Hornby was no politician. . . .
He was a good employer, a strong Churchman. . . . In 1900 he
claimed to have subscribed to over nine hundred causes within
the town within the previous twelve months.'[9] The Casterton
family drew upon similar sentiments, if with less panache.

This pattern of political influence, and the political culture
which helped to sustain it, survived at least until the Second
World War, and in some respects still survives. It is hardly
surprising that the constituency has had one of the largest
deviations in Britain from the usual pattern of social class voting.
In the 1955 General Election the predicted left-wing vote in the
constituency, computed on the basis of the national average
standardised for the age, sex, and social class composition of
the electorate, was $60 \cdot 0$ per cent, but the actual left-wing vote
recorded was only $49 \cdot 0$ per cent, an 11 per cent deviation
exceeded only in Tynemouth, Gosport, Bootle, Liverpool,
Middlesbrough, and Solihull. Although the gap had narrowed
by the 1960s, the deviation between the expected left-wing vote
and that realised was still 6 per cent in 1964.[10]

Yet it is easy to exaggerate the extent and depth of deferential
conservatism in Casterton politics; there were oppositional
elements within the community, and it would be a mistake to
paint a completely one-sided picture. Even before the First
World War the borough rejected one Parliamentary candidate
supported by Lord Casterton, partly because he was a Liberal
standing against the 'patriotic' candidate in the Khaki election
of 1900, and partly because he was not a local man: the borough
suffered a marked drop in local patronage in consequence.
More recently, the balance between Conservatives, Independ-
ents, and Labour on the City Council has been narrowly
poised since the Second World War, and Labour has, occasionally, won control; and the constituency did, eventually,
return a Labour M.P. Since the redundancy the acquiescent
conservatism has diminished further; there were widespread
protests and demonstrations against the firm's redundancy

[9] P. F. Clarke, *Lancashire and the New Liberalism*, Cambridge:
Cambridge University Press, 1971, p. 224.

[10] A. Piepe, R. Prior, and A. Box, 'The Location of the Proletarian and
Deferential Worker', *Sociology*, 1969, pp. 241–3.

policy, and many workers whom we interviewed, especially young workers, believed that management was itself responsible for the redundancy through inadequate planning. It is therefore important to examine the political views of the Casterton workers in more detail, to show the complex nature of the conservatism which characterised the labour force.

The political affiliations of the Casterton Mills workers mirrored those revealed by an analysis of recent General Election results: there was a marked bias towards the Conservative party, especially amongst manual workers. Only 40 per cent of manual workers described themselves as consistent Labour supporters, whilst 27 per cent described themselves as consistent Conservative supporters, and 20 per cent said that they switched their votes according to circumstances, the remainder voting Liberal or never voting. The proportion of manual workers supporting the Labour party was thus below the customary two-thirds, even if the assumption – for which there is no evidence – is made that all switchers were in reality Labour supporters who were unwilling to commit themselves to a party experiencing considerable unpopularity at the time of the interviews (1968–9). Interestingly, the political affiliations of non-manual workers were less 'deviant' from those reported in national surveys: 51 per cent described themselves as consistent supporters of the Conservative party, 4 per cent as consistent Liberals, 23 per cent as switchers, and 23 per cent as consistent supporters of the Labour party.[11] The significance of this contrasting pattern becomes clearer on closer investigation of political commitment, especially of political commitment and trade unionism.

There was little hostility towards the trade unions amongst workers at Casterton Mills: workers did not accept the traditional view of paternalist management, that trade unions were intruders disrupting an integrated hierarchy. Although there are no comprehensive figures available, for neither the firm nor the local union officials concerned had full, reliable statistics, 63 per cent of the manual workers and 36 per cent of the non-

[11] For comparison see D. E. Butler and D. Stokes, *Political Change in Britain: Forces Shaping Electoral Choice*, Macmillan, 1969, Chapter 4.

manual workers whom we interviewed had been trade union members at the Mills. The unions drew most of their support from manual workers in skilled trades and in the power station – the A.E.F., the E.T.U., the Amalgamated Society of Wood-cutting Machinists, and the Power Section of the T. & G.W.U. were especially important – and from works and craft management amongst non-manual workers: 73 per cent of non-manual trade unionists were managers and supervisors, although they comprised under a fifth of non-manual respondents. Very few workers were indifferent towards trade unions: only 11 per cent of manual workers, and 12 per cent of non-manual workers, believed that it did not matter whether one belonged to a trade union or not. A large majority of both manual and non-manual workers thought that non-manual workers ought to belong to trade unions: 89 per cent of manual workers, and 82 per cent of non-manual workers – although the latter figure is inflated by some respondents who had been worried by the redundancy. Support for trade unions at the local level was accompanied by surprisingly favourable attitudes towards trade unions nationally: 75 per cent of manual workers, and 69 per cent of non-manual workers disagreed with the view that trade unions caused trouble between management and workers. 'I think trade unions have done quite a lot of good. If you go back fifty years the trade unions have done a tremendous amount of good.' (49-year-old works manager.) However, the support for trade unions was less than complete, and many workers, including many who thought that trade unions played a positive role in management-labour relations, believed that the trade unions had too much power. Hence, 36 per cent of manual workers, including 25 per cent of manual workers who believed that trade unions played a positive role, and 54 per cent of non-manual workers, including 42 per cent of the 'pro-unionists', believed that the trade unions had too much power. Non-manual workers were especially worried about their attitudes towards trade unions, believing that they were a necessary form of self-defence, but feeling that they were at best a necessary evil. As one 60-year-old clerical worker, who experienced considerable difficulty in getting a job after he was declared redundant, commented: 'I've never been in a union, so I cannot say what the advantages would be. I think it's growing to what it used to be: I daresay it has advantages. But I don't agree with all these strikes . . . the shop stewards are protecting the workers . . . if there were a union [for my present job] I'd be in two minds.'

The political significance of union membership was different for manual and non-manual workers: union membership had little political significance for manual workers, but had some political significance for white collar workers. Union membership did not appear to be an expression of socio-political commitment for manual workers. As the following table shows, manual trade unionists were less likely than non-trade unionists to be consistent supporters of the Labour Party, although the correlation is not statistically significant because of the small numbers involved:

Trade Union Membership and Political Affiliation; Manual Workers Only

	Trade Union %	Non-T.U. %	Total %
Conservative	30	27	29
Labour	45	53	48
Switcher/other	25	20	23
	—	—	—
	N = 60	N = 30	N = 90

Trade union membership, like support for the Conservative Party, was concentrated amongst the skilled men and amongst workers in the power station: 42 per cent of skilled workers and their mates, nearly all of whom were trade union members, and 38 per cent of power station workers, all of whom were trade unionists, were consistent supporters of the Labour Party, compared with 53 per cent of semi- and unskilled process workers and warehousemen. Union membership for manual workers was, in short, a function of the job, not of political or social commitment. For non-manual workers, on the other hand, union membership was more significant as an indication of political viewpoint: trade union members were more likely than non-trade union members to be consistent supporters of the Labour Party:

Trade Union Membership and Political Affiliation;
Non-Manual

	Trade Union %	Non-T.U. %	Total %
Conservative	46	58	53
Labour	31	18	24
Other/switcher	23	24	23
	N = 26	N = 33	N = 59

The numbers involved are too small to permit a definite conclusion, but the figures are suggestive. For non-manual workers Labour voting and union membership were parts of a general socio-political standpoint, running counter to the official ideology fostered by management: trade unionism, and Labour voting, involved a repudiation of the whole value system represented by the firm's culture (see below, pp. 71–2), and did not derive any support from general social norms. Labour voting and union membership represented a greater commitment for non-manual workers than Conservative voting did for manual workers in paternalist capitalism: it is hardly surprising that the leading Labour Party member employed in the clerical section of the firm was reluctant to play a prominent role in the demonstrations against the redundancy.

There were thus elements of an oppositional outlook in the attitudes of the Casterton Mills workers: they were not completely tied to the dominant values of paternalist capitalism. Yet it is easy to exaggerate the extent of the opposition. Trade union membership, and favourable orientations towards trade unions, were more related to occupational requirements than to hostility to the bourgeoisie: trade union members were more likely to be supporters of the Conservative party than non-trade-union members. The Conservative party had considerable support amongst manual workers, especially amongst skilled manual workers, whilst the Labour party had little support amongst non-manual workers, except amongst managerial and supervisory workers, many of whom were former manual workers who had been promoted from the shop floor. Moreover, for manual workers, support for the Labour party was more an expression of subcultural identification than of political aspiration. More Labour supporters than Conservatives believed that it made very little difference who won elections, for 'politicians are all the same' (39 per cent compared with 25 per cent); and the majority of Labour supporters who believed that election results mattered explained their beliefs either in terms of Labour being the workers' party or the Conservatives being the party against the working class. The 'conservative' nature of working-class political views becomes even clearer when they are examined in the light of attitudes towards social class, examined below, and towards the firm, examined later.

III

Political attitudes and behaviour in Casterton were clearly influenced by the mutually dependent relationship between the Mills and the community which had evolved over a century: business leaders became public figures, exercising political influence and social responsibility appropriate to their economic power and social status.[12] Correspondingly, the 'political culture' of Casterton was, in Almond and Verba's terms,[13] 'subject' rather than 'participant', reflecting the historical experience of the inhabitants both in politics and, as we will show later, in work. It is more difficult to illustrate the effect of the economic and social development of the community upon conceptions of the class structure and attitudes towards social class for – except in the most general sense – social structure does not *determine* intellectual concepts or psychological attitudes.[14] However, there must be at least a minimal congruence between individual beliefs and social structure, between interpretations of social reality and that reality itself: too obvious a

[12] J. M. Lee, *Social Leaders and Public Persons*, Oxford: Oxford University Press, 1963 for a parallel analysis of politics in Cheshire.

[13] G. A. Almond and S. Verba, *The Civic Culture*, Princeton: Princeton University Press.

[14] S. Ossowski has shown clearly the very general relationships between dichotomous conceptions of social class and political subjection, and between a multi-layered conception of social stratification and political dominance; the conceptions of the Casterton workers must, in these terms, be a product of 'false consciousness': S. Ossowski, *Class Structure in the Social Consciousness*, Routledge and Kegan Paul, 1963.

contradiction leads to 'cognitive dissonance' and hence to psychological tension for the individual and, in extreme situations, revolution in society.[15] In less dramatic circumstances changes in the social structure can outpace changes in social attitudes, causing social actors to make *ad hoc* and piecemeal adjustments to new situations: the result is often apparently inconsistent sets of beliefs, which only find their rationale in personal biography. The structure of paternalist capitalism was hierarchical, individualist, and restrictive, and these characteristics were mirrored in conceptions of the class structure, and attitudes towards that structure, of Casterton Mills workers.

The majority of Casterton Mills workers, both manual and non-manual, saw society in hierarchical terms, believing that there were several social classes in Britain. As the following table shows: 65 per cent of manual workers, and 74 per cent of non-manual workers, believed that there were several social classes in Britain; only 23 per cent of manual workers believed in the classic two-class model; and only a tenth of manual workers and 9 per cent of non-manual workers accepted the capitalist revisionist view that Britain was virtually a classless society, all belonging to the same social class.

Number of Social Classes (Q. 220)

	Manual %	Non-Manual %
One class	10	9
Two classes	23	13
Several classes	65	74
Other/missing	2	4
	N = 116	N = 91

However, it is easy to exaggerate the significance of these replies, for they may represent only an unformulated response to unfamiliarly general propositions. Moreover, few Casterton workers believed in the absence of social antagonism, an implication sometimes drawn from the multiple class view.

[15] For 'cognitive dissonance' see L. Festinger, *A Theory of Cognitive Dissonance*, Tavistock Publications, 1962.

Lack of space prevents a full analysis of the extended explanations given for answers to our questions on social class imagery.[16] However, Casterton Mills workers generally distinguished between three social classes: an upper class, variously described as 'upper class', 'nobility', 'idle rich', 'playboys'; a middle class, sometimes 'professional people', more frequently 'little bosses', 'supervisors', 'those with a little bit of education who think that they are better than workers', 'people that can have the pleasures in life and a good living'; and a third class, often comprising the working class as a whole, but sometimes being referred to as 'the poor', 'the rough', 'real labouring types'. Numerous inter-related criteria of differentiation were used, as the variety of terms indicates: differences in income, power, status, culture, consumption patterns, were all mingled together, reflecting the confused reality of the class structure, as well as our perceptions of it. Moreover, the same perceptions could be interpreted in conflicting ways. One clerical worker explained why he believed that there were several social classes in Britain: 'Different earnings create different classes: (1) above average level – executives; (2) in-between level – ordinary type; (3) those who cannot get enough to manage on and must put themselves out to get more.' A second clerical worker explained why he believed that there was only one social class in Britain: 'It's only the money that's different and what they do with their money is their own business.' Both believed in the existence of economic inequality: one believed that this comprised the class structure, the other that it did not.

The major conclusion to be drawn from the analysis is a negative one: only a small minority talked the language of direct class antagonism – bosses and workers, or, as one 55-year-old foreman put it, 'like a colony of bees, drones and

---

[16] Images of social class can only be explained fully in the context of the individual's *Gestalt*, an exercise that would be impossible here. For a more detailed, perceptive, but still inconclusive discussion of social class imagery amongst ship-building workers see R. K. Brown and P. Brannen, 'Social Relations Amongst Ship-building Workers', *Sociology*, 1970, pp. 79–81. See also W. G. Runciman, *Relative Deprivation and Social Justice*, Routledge and Kegan Paul, 1966, especially Chapter 17. It is intended to present a more extended analysis separately later.

workers'. This negative conclusion is reinforced by consideration of the views of Casterton workers upon the relative
importance of solidarity and individualism.

Respondents were asked to express their preference for one
of two alternative statements: (1) 'Working-class people have
got to stick together and stand up for each other'; (2) 'Working-
class people should strike out on their own, it is no good being
held back by the rest'. The former was envisaged as a representative expression of the traditional proletarian emphasis
upon solidarity, the latter as a classic expression of the bourgeois
ethic of individual self-help. As the following table shows, a
substantial majority of all respondents were individualists, a
large majority of non-manual workers, and just under a half
of manual workers.

Preference for Solidarity/Individualism (Q. 221)

	Manual %	Non-Manual %	Total %
Solidaristic	45	11	30
Individualistic	47	77	60
None/missing	9	12	10
	N = 116	N = 91	N = 207

'Strike out on own: if you stick together you get nowhere fast'
(60-year-old power-station worker). 'Can't get on a lot in a
crowd – on your own a better chance' (35-year-old process
worker). 'According to attitude either selfish or normal. I
believe in raising the standard of the masses' (55-year-old
foreman). 'Very difficult. Process unskilled got to stick together
but skilled man got to be an individualist' (57-year-old
craftsman).

This emphasis upon the importance of striking out on one's
own was also reflected in replies to a similar question directed
at middle- rather than working-class experience. Respondents
were asked whether they believed that 'if middle class people
are successful it is because they help each other with their
wealth and position', or that 'if middle class people are successful it is because they have individual ability and put individual
effort into things', or neither. As the following table shows, the
majority of both manual and non-manual workers believed that

individual initiative was responsible for middle-class success: 59 per cent of manual, and 64 per cent of non-manual.

Explanations for Middle Class Success (Q. 222)

	Manual %	Non-Manual %
Mutual assistance	27	17
Individual initiative	59	64
Neither	12	13
Both	1	5
N/A	2	1
	N = 116	N = 90

Thus, only a minority of manual workers, and only a very small minority of non-manual workers believed in the importance of sticking together. But not even this minority showed evidence of class consciousness. According to conventional interpretations of traditional working-class attitudes, workers who stress the importance of solidarity should also see the class structure in dichotomous terms: the solidarity of Us against Them.[17] However, there was no such tendency amongst the workers at Casterton Mills: believers in the importance of sticking together were just as likely as individualists to say that they believed that Britain was divided into one, two, or several classes.

Believers in Solidarity and Conceptions of the Class Structure

	Manual Workers Only*	
	Solidarist %	Individualist %
One class	10	11
Two classes	23	26
Several classes	67	62
	N = 52	N = 53

* There were not enough non-manual believers in solidarity to justify further analysis.

[17] As in the classic account of the 'traditional' working class, R. Hoggart, *The Uses of Literacy*, Chatto and Windus, 1957; also J. H. Goldthorpe, D. Lockwood, F. Bechhofer, and J. Platt, *The Affluent Worker in the Class Structure*, Cambridge: Cambridge University Press, 1969.

Belief in the importance of solidarity was associated with limited aspirations and with a defensive concern for security, see below p. 57, instead of with a particular conception of the class structure.

In short, the popularity of the multi-layered view of the class structure and the belief in individualism is consistent with our interpretation of the evolution of Casterton, and the dominant role of the Mills in that community. Manual workers did not see society as comprising a pair of mutually antagonistic corporate blocs: there is little evidence for the existence of traditional proletarian views of society – although of course we have not analysed conceptions of the class structure in great detail. Within paternalist capitalism economic difficulties led to a defensive adjustment of expectations, rather than to a belief in collective solidarity.

However, we do not wish to claim too much for this analysis: the ambiguities and confusions amongst sociologists about conceptions of social class are, not surprisingly, paralleled in more popular beliefs. Casterton workers readily recognised the validity of the concept of social class, and used it as a method of categorisation without difficulty. Yet there was no generally agreed and articulated uni- or multi-dimensional view of the class structure: conceptions of the class structure were the blurred and insubstantial reflections of social reality, viewed from divergent perspectives and expressed in unfamiliarly general terms. As such we do not attribute independent causal significance to them: rather, they were part of the complex of attitudes which reflected and sustained the structure of paternalist capitalism.

IV

In this chapter we have traced the outlines of the social and economic development of Casterton over the last hundred years, relating it to political events and attitudes, interpreted widely, and to conceptions of the class structure. Casterton is an isolated, largely self-contained community, a medium-sized industrial town situated in a rural area in the North of England. The town grew rapidly during the late nineteenth century, changing from a large village to a substantial city in two generations: Casterton Mills and other floor-coverings firms proved a powerful drawing force for workers from surrounding rural areas, and to a lesser extent from Ireland. Population grew to 40,000 in 1900, and since then it has fluctuated between 40,000 and 51,000. Since 1900 there has been little immigration into the area, apart from a small number of evacuees during the Second World War, and virtually none from outside the North of England; emigration has kept down the population growth which might have been expected in recent years on the basis of national trends. Apart from Casterton Mills, and another floor-coverings firm which formed an oligopoly within the city, the major source of employment has long been retail distribution – in 1931, for example, 13 per cent of economically active males, and 16 per cent of economically active females were employed in retail distribution – and other service industries. Reflecting the importance of the Mills, and the service sector, the town included a large number of semi-skilled and unskilled manual workers, and large numbers of sales and clerical workers.

The community's geographical isolation and social and economic development were largely responsible for the development of a particular form of business dominated community, paternalist capitalism. Casterton Mills, as the largest employer in the area, was able to act as the leader of local business, and to exercise considerable influence upon the political life of the community. This influence was exercised both directly, through active participation in leading political roles, and indirectly, through moulding the work experiences of a large section of the population, and thus influencing their attitudes towards authority, including political authority. The resulting form of society showed many of the characteristics of feudal society, especially the well-developed consciousness of hierarchy. One respondent, an outsider ('offcomer' in local terms), commented on the similarity between Casterton and the Indian village in which he had spent a large part of his working life, with its coherence and its elaborate caste system.[18] Both provided

[18] Cf. L. Dumont, *Homo Hierarchicus*, Weidenfeld and Nicolson, 1970.

security, psychologically and, at least to a minimal extent, economically, both fostered respect for authority, suspicion of outsiders, and acceptance of the world.

The consequence of this structure was the development of a distinctive type of working class: Casterton's working class was large, but individualist as much as collectivist, petit-bourgeois as much as proletarian. There was only fragmentary evidence of political and industrial class consciousness, which was never transformed into a coherent viewpoint, or used as a basis for collective action. The majority of manual workers saw society in multi-class terms, and believed that the middle class owed its success to individual initiative, and more believed that working-class people should strike out on their own than believed that the working class should stick together. Although there was substantial support for trade unionism, this was a function of job requirements rather than socio-political commitment; and although there was considerable support for the Labour party (40 per cent of manual workers described themselves as consistent supporters of the Labour party), this was associated with considerable scepticism about the effectiveness of political activity.

The general social and economic development of Casterton was thus largely responsible for the development of paternalist capitalism: the community's evolving social structure and the attitudes towards politics and social class 'fitted' each other. Yet it is impossible to assess the significance of this 'fit' without examining the major link between them in more detail – work, and experience of work. Recent work by Turner and Lawrence in the United States, by Touraine and Ragazzi, and Karpik in France, as well as by John Goldthorpe and his colleagues in Britain, has shown how non-work factors influence work behaviour, demonstrating that work is only a partially autonomous area of social life.[19] But the interaction between work and

[19] A. N. Turner and P. R. Lawrence, *Industrial Jobs and the Worker*, Boston: Division of Research, Harvard Business School, 1965; A. Touraine and O. Ragazzi, *Ouvriers d'Origine Agricole*, Paris: Editions du Seuil, 1961; L. Karpik, 'Urbanization et satisfactions au travail', *Sociologie du Travail*, 1966; J. H. Goldthorpe, D. Lockwood, F. Bechhofer, and J. Platt, *The Affluent Worker: Industrial Attitudes and Behaviour*,

non-work aspects of life is a two-way process, especially in industrial society: life experiences at work influence attitudes and behaviour outside, whilst experience outside influences attitudes and behaviour at work. We turn to this inter-relation in the next two chapters, focusing firstly upon work in general, and secondly upon the firm, and upon workers' attitudes towards it, and relating these to the structure of paternalist capitalism outlined here. The clear outlines of consistent value systems disappear under the microscope, to be replaced by the blurred images of more or less coherent sets of attitudes; but sufficient clarity remains to conclude that, at the minimum, the attitudes of Casterton Mills workers towards work and towards their firm were not inconsistent with our analysis of paternalist capitalism.

Cambridge: Cambridge University Press, 1968. 'Recent' is perhaps a misnomer, for as long ago as 1908 Weber raised the question of 'to what extent industry . . . is governed by given qualities arising out of the ethnic, social, and cultural background, the traditions and circumstances of the workers'. A research Strategy for the Study of Occupational Careers, in ed. J. E. T. Eldridge, *Max Weber: The Interpretation of Social Reality*, Michael Joseph, 1971, p. 104.

3 PATERNALIST CAPITALISM: ATTITUDES TOWARDS WORK

In the previous chapter we examined briefly the economic and social development of Casterton between the middle of the nineteenth century and the time of the redundancy, and the leading role played in that development by Casterton Mills. The structure which evolved was one of paternalist capitalism. The attitudes of the Casterton Mills employees towards politics, in the widest sense, and towards social class were shown to be, at the very least, congruent with those which might have been expected to develop within paternalist capitalism: deferential, hierarchical, and individualist. Work experiences and attitudes formed a central link between the structure of paternalist capitalism and such attitudes: work was a central concern of Casterton Mills employees, and their interpretations of work experiences, and their attitudes towards work, coloured their attitudes towards other matters. Understanding work attitudes is important for understanding Casterton in general, and the redundancy at Casterton Mills in particular; for it is impossible to understand the redundancy without understanding the significance of what has been lost, a particular job with a particular firm. In this chapter we examine attitudes towards work; in the following chapter we turn to attitudes towards the firm.

I

There are two major views of the meaning of work in contemporary industrial society. According to the first view man has certain basic psychological needs, which can only be fully satisfied by work: above all the need for self-realisation or psychological growth. Sayles and Strauss represent this school when they write: ' . . . in this book we shall speak of three forms of need satisfaction: (1) *Physical and security needs.* These relate to the satisfaction of bodily functions . . . as well as to the need to be secure in the enjoyment of these. (2) *Social needs.* Since human beings are dependent on each other, there are some needs which can be satisfied only when the individual is helped or recognised by other people. (3) *Egoistic needs.* These relate to man's desire to be independent, to do things on his own and to sense accomplishment . . . egoistic needs are chiefly satisfied through the job.'[1] (Italics in original.) Marx, as well as modern social psychologists like Frederick Herzberg, both stress that what differentiates man from animals is the need for psychological growth – although of course they derive different political conclusions from that view. These needs are seen as being unsatisfied, or only partially satisfied, under capitalism, whether because of the expropriation of the ownership of the product, as in Marx's analysis, or because of the inadequate organisation of the methods of production, as in neo-Marxist analyses like those of Georges Friedmann, or in social psychological analyses like those of Argyris and Herzberg, or – at a rather different level – because of moral backsliding, as in the propaganda of the secularised Calvinist apologists for the American dream.[2]

According to the second view, work itself is meaningless, is necessarily a means to an end: work is constrained activity, to be minimized by mechanical invention – personal fulfilment can only be achieved through leisure, unconstrained activity. This view, derived directly from Aristotle, is basic to W. Neff's psychological analysis of the meaning of work; work is defined

---

[1] L. R. Sayles and G. Strauss, *Human Behaviour in Organisations*, Englewood Cliffs, New Jersey: Prentice-Hall, Inc., 1966, pp. 7–8.

[2] This is obviously a very simplified view of a complex debate, and both Marxists and Herzberg and his followers would probably reject this classification. However, there are clear echoes of Marx's famous passage on alienation. 'In what does this alienation consist . . .', reptd. in T. B. Bottomore and M. Reubel, *Selections from Marx: Sociology and Social Philosophy*, Harmondsworth: Penguin Books Ltd., 1963, p. 177, in Herzberg's discussion of the stunting of psychological growth by contemporary society, F. Herzberg, *Work and the Nature of Man*, Staples Press, 1968, Chapters 4 and 5.

as 'an instrumental activity carried out by human beings, the object of which is to preserve and maintain life, which is directed at a planful alteration of certain features of man's environment'.[3] Work is a means to an end, not a satisfying end in itself. As a sixty-year-old Casterton woodcutting machinist explained succinctly, 'It is only work when it is something you dislike.'

In these terms both views share a common fallacious assumption: that there is a single answer to the question 'What is the meaning of work?'[4] As C. Wright Mills argued with customary force: 'Work may be a mere source of livelihood, or the most significant part of one's inner life; it may be experienced as expiation, or as an exuberant expression of self; as a bounden duty, or as the development of man's universal nature. Neither love nor hatred of work is inherent in man, or inherent in any given line of work.'[5] At a psychological level there *may* be universal needs and desires which can only be satisfied by work, as Maslow, Argyris, and others have argued; but, 'from a sociological standpoint what is in fact of major interest *is* the variation in which groups differently located in the social structure actually experience and attempt to meet the needs which, at a different level of analysis, may be attributed to them all'.[6] The meaning of work varies between societies, between groups and between individuals. For each it represents a more or less acceptable compromise between the desirable, the available, and the possible, a compromise whose terms are constantly changing with changes in moral beliefs, patterns of socialisation, and the structure of available opportunities. The sociologist's task is to delineate the compromises, and to

[3] W. S. Neff, *Work and Human Behaviour*, New York: The Atherton Press, 1968, p. 75. For Aristotle and the Greek view of 'labour' see H. Arendt, *The Human Condition*, Chicago: University of Chicago Press, 1958.

[4] For a very clear general account of orientations to work see A. Fox, *A Sociology of Work in Industry*, Collier Macmillan and Co., 1971, Chapter 1.

[5] C. Wright Mills, *White Collar: The American Middle Classes*, New York: Oxford University Press, 1956, p. 215.

[6] J. H. Goldthorpe *et al.*, *The Affluent Worker: Industrial Attitudes and Behaviour*, p. 178. See also A. H. Maslow, *Motivation and Personality*, New York: Harper and Row, 1954; C. Argyris, *Integrating the Individual and the Organisation*, New York: John Wiley and Son, Inc., 1964.

disentangle the cultural, structural, and psychological factors which govern their formulation.

Four different elements, encapsulated in the conventional meaning of the term 'work', need to be distinguished from each other when assessing its significance for members of industrial society: work as the possession of any occupational role; work as a specific job or type of job; work as a term for filling a specific occupational role with a specific employer; and work as the actual task performed in fulfilment of an occupational role. The term 'work' is conventionally used in the first sense in contrast to unemployment: it involves possession of a contract of employment, but little more. Work in the second sense refers to the character of the rights and obligations associated with a particular occupational role, as in 'working as a teacher.' Thirdly, work can refer to a combination of occupational and employee roles, as in 'working at Jones''. Finally, work refers to the task itself, as in 'the work of a piano tuner involves adjusting wires'. In the following discussion we will refer to work in the first sense as 'employment', in the second and third senses as 'job', and in the fourth sense as 'task': the term 'work' will be used when all four elements are considered together. Individuals may or may not possess similar attitudes towards all four elements. Some may value employment, dislike the job, and enjoy the task, as in a low status but interesting manual occupation, e.g. lorry driving.[7] Others may value their employment and their job, but not the task, as in prestigious but boring non-manual jobs. Any full discussion of attitudes towards work should include a discussion of all four elements, and the relationship between them. However, since we are primarily concerned with redundancy, the loss of jobs, and unemployment, rather than with behaviour within the plant, we have not discussed work as 'task' in detail.

II

The majority of Casterton workers, both manual and non-manual, said that they would continue to work even if they had enough money to retire.

[7] P. G. Hollowell, *The Lorry Driver*, Routledge and Kegan Paul, 1968.

If You Have Enough Money Without Working There Is No Reason For Having a Job (Q. 201)

	Manual %	Non-Manual %
Agree	33	20
Disagree	65	73
Other	2	7
	—	—
	N = 116	N = 91

This commitment to employment was fairly evenly distributed throughout all age groups, with a slight tendency for older workers, especially older non-manual workers, to be more committed than younger workers. The following table shows the distribution of replies by occupational status and age:

	Manual					Non-Manual				
Age	–25	25–44	45–59	60–	T	–25	25–44	45–59	60–	T
	%	%	%	%	%	%	%	%	%	%
Agree	—	38	21	54	33	33	21	14	13	20
Disagree	100	60	76	46	65	56	76	69	87	73
Other	—	2	3	—	2	11	3	17	—	7
N =	11	48	33	24	116	18	29	29	18	91

Manual workers over 60 were thus the most likely to believe that one should cease working if one had enough money to do so, whilst non-manual workers in the same age group were the least likely to do so.[8] Manual workers over 60 were well over the peak of their earning power, and in many cases found work physically tiring; non-manual workers, on the other hand, were not subject to the same physical strain. The age group 45–59 was more homogeneous, a large majority of both manual and non-manual workers saying that one should continue working even if one had enough money to stop: there is no evidence, for this group, of a beginning of the process of adjustment to retirement; rather, there is some evidence that ageing increases

[8] Compare N. C. Morse and R. S. Weiss, 'The Function and Meaning of Work and the Job', reprinted in ed. S. Nosow and W. H. Form, *Man, Work, and Society: A Reader in the Sociology of Occupations*, New York: Basic Books, Inc., 1962, pp. 29–31. Morse and Weiss found that commitment declined with age, and interpreted this as an indication of anticipatory socialisation into the culture of retirement.

commitment to present identities, and reduces the ability to embrace alternative ones, or even to envisage alternative ways of spending time, as research into the hardening of political attitudes with age would suggest.[9] This became poignantly clear in the discussions with respondents aged between 50 and 60 on the impact of the redundancy: they felt 'lost' without employment, and suffered the most serious difficulties in finding a job following their dismissal.

Employment was regarded as more than simply a way of passing time; it was invested with positive moral overtones. Manual and non-manual workers alike were nearly unanimous in agreeing that 'those who work extremely hard in order to get ahead in their job' were worthy of admiration: 85 per cent of manual workers, and 79 per cent of non-manual workers accepted this view, although a minority expressed their distaste for those who 'creep hard' in order to get ahead. Such admiration was evenly distributed throughout all age groups. This puritanical view survived even when hard work was explicitly contrasted with leisure. Respondents were asked whether they agreed with the view that 'although leisure is a good thing it is hard work that makes life worthwhile'.

Although Leisure Is a Good Thing It Is Hard Work That Makes Life Worthwhile (Q. 218)

	Manual %	Non-Manual %
Agree	62	55
Indifferent	3	7
Disagree	30	29
Other/missing	7	7
	N = 116	N = 91

The increase in hedonism was due to the greater prominence of leisure for young workers, especially for workers aged under 25. As the following table shows, only a minority of manual workers, and only a small minority of non-manual workers belonging to that age group believed that hard work made life worthwhile.

---

[9] For example, D. E. Butler and D. Stokes, *op. cit.*

Age	Manual				Non-Manual			
	-25	25–44	45–59	60$^+$	-25	25–44	45–59	60$^+$
	%	%	%	%	%	%	%	%
Agree	45	63	61	71	23	69	52	73
Disagree	27	35	24	25	50	21	31	20
Other	27	2	15	4	27	10	17	7
N =	11	48	33	24	18	29	29	15

Nonetheless, a substantial majority of all workers, both manual and non-manual, attached primary importance to hard work.

This moral commitment to employment *may* be discounted as merely an expression of belief in goodness, reflecting perception of social norms. Even if such scepticism were justified, such responses would still represent a significant recognition of social norms (if not a compelling social psychological pressure). However, there is no more reason to doubt the validity of such responses than to doubt other responses to survey questionnaires. We believe, like Morse and Weiss, that respondents regarded the hypothetical questions as meaningful: after all, what to do when the football pools finally come up is a major focus of working class (and other) day dreams. For most workers possession of an occupational role was a necessary basis for self-respect. 'Work gives a man self-respect. Myself, I would feel like a parasite if I did not work' (34-year-old engineer). 'I wouldn't be able to do nothing . . . no purpose in life' (46-year-old process worker). At a less moralistic level, work provided a structure for time, making it pass more quickly, and a way of giving point to non-work activities (and of keeping out of the way of the wife). 'If you haven't a job, you have too much leisure, and thus no purpose in life, leisure palls. You tend to lose your confidence: you haven't any motivation – you vegetate' (41-year-old works study engineer). 'Work is the main thing. You soon get bored with leisure. . . . A week or two off you appreciate and look forward to, but if off a lot you don't' (60-year-old woodcutting machinist). 'I wouldn't finish work. I've been off sick a fortnight and I'm browned off – I'm lost' (30-year-old warehouseman). There was some feeling that employment was desirable even amongst the minority who said that they would stop working if they could. One or two said that those who had enough money should stop

54

working to give others a chance: 'people with money should make way for people who are out of work', explained a 49-year-old process worker. There was an element of self-conscious defiance of convention in the attitude of a 59-year-old power-station worker: 'It's a fool who likes work. If people were honest they would not say that they liked work. . . . I'm better on holiday than working. I don't look forward to going to work in the morning, I look forward to coming home.' Nevertheless, he took a job bringing in £3 a week less than he was getting on earnings-related unemployment benefit because he got bored with life at home.

Employment, for Casterton workers, was a central life interest: it was not merely a marginal aspect of social life.[10] Nor was it simply a means of obtaining money to satisfy non-work needs and fulfil non-work goals. 'Having a job' (possession of an employment contract) was a necessary basis of self-respect for the majority of Casterton workers, as well as, at the minimum, a way of structuring time. *Pace* Marx, there is some suggestion that work gave meaning to non-work activity, rather than the reverse.

Such was the attitude of the majority of Casterton workers towards employment: attitudes towards jobs were more complex, and require more extensive discussion.

III

As we have shown, the majority of Casterton workers, manual as well as non-manual, believed in the need for employment and in the virtues of hard work. This was associated with limited aspirations and considerable scepticism about the rewards to be derived from hard work. Manual workers especially regarded jobs fatalistically, without great expectations. Like the pre-destinarian Calvinists of the sixteenth century, they believed in

[10] In apparent contrast to the conclusions reached by R. Dubin, 'Industrial Workers' Worlds: A Study of the Central Life Interests of Industrial Workers', *Social Problems*, Vol. 3, n.l., 1955, pp. 131–42. Dubin found that work was not a central life interest for the majority of industrial workers. However, he showed that workers did not base their informal social life on the plant, not that work was not important.

strenuously attempting to work for salvation, whilst at the same time believing that the decisions that really mattered to them would be taken by others. There was little extravagance in the aspirations shown by Casterton workers: 'reasonable' wages, security, and 'steadiness' were the attributes sought for in jobs. As a 55-year-old foreman commented, unconsciously echoing Durkheim on the follies of limitless aspirations: 'If a person fully realises what ambition does for him he will settle. Otherwise he doesn't survive – ambition knows no horizon. Once you've climbed this hill there is another ahead.' Moreover, although the majority of both manual and non-manual workers showed a clear preference for interesting jobs, sometimes explicitly at the cost of sacrificing earnings, there was little evidence of strenuous efforts to achieve such desires through moving between jobs. The social world was accepted and justified, not manipulated and criticised.

The majority of manual workers, and a substantial minority of non-manual workers, agreed with the view that 'if a man has a steady job and a reasonable wage then he should be content': 71 per cent of manual workers, and 44 per cent of non-manual workers. The criterion of reasonableness used by most workers in assessing wages was a minimal one, as the level of earnings sought, or regarded as acceptable, following the redundancy showed clearly (see below p. 140). Aspirations narrowed with age, especially for manual workers: 73 per cent of manual workers aged 35 or more, compared with 42 per cent of younger manual workers, limited their aspirations to a steady job and a reasonable wage. Like the older American automobile workers interviewed by Eli Chinoy, older Casterton Mills workers adjusted their aspirations to reality; as Chinoy argues, 'workers' aspirations emerge from a process in which hope and desire come to terms with the realities of working class life'.[11] Casterton workers came to realise that there was little hope of achieving promotion and, as the following table shows, concern with promotion becomes rare amongst older workers, whether manual or non-manual. Respondents were asked which of the two following statements they agreed with:

[11] E. Chinoy, *Automobile Workers and the American Dream*, New York: Doubleday and Co. Inc., 1955, p. 111.

(1) 'I would rather have a safe job with limited prospects of promotion'; or (2) 'I would rather have a job with plenty of opportunity for promotion, even if the job was rather insecure'. The following table shows the distribution of replies according to age:

Preference for Security or Promotion (Q. 229)

	Security	Promotion	Other*
–25	40	56	4
25–34	39	37	24
35–44	63	29	9
45–49	71	29	0
50–54	54	31	16
55–59	62	15	23
60–	63	27	10

* Other = indifferent, don't know.

There was very little interest in promotion amongst the over 35s whether manual or non-manual. A preference for security rather than promotion opportunities was particularly noticeable amongst workers who had earlier said that one should be content with a steady job and a reasonable wage: only 22 per cent of manual workers, and 25 per cent of non-manual workers who had expressed their satisfaction with a steady job said that they would prefer a job with promotion prospects over one which provided security.

Almost half the Casterton workers who did not possess authority would have liked to have done so: 46 per cent of manual workers and 50 per cent of non-manual workers, including a substantial majority of younger workers (76 per cent of those aged under 25). Yet Casterton workers, especially manual workers, did not rate their chances of becoming bosses very highly, believing that connections, capital, and a good opportunity were as important as hard work and ability in getting ahead: 'If you've no backing you've no chance to go high' (46-year-old process worker). A majority of manual workers (55 per cent), including 45 per cent of those who said that they greatly admired those who worked hard to get ahead, believed that ordinary people had no hope of becoming bosses;

such scepticism was shared by 37 per cent of all non-manual workers. Casterton Mills workers, especially young workers, would have liked to get ahead within the firm, but had little expectation of doing so. Accordingly, like the American automobile workers studied by Chinoy, many hoped to escape into the autonomous world of small business.[12] For 49 per cent of manual workers had considered seriously the possibility of starting up their own business, and 14 per cent had actually done so. The results of such attempts were not, however, very successful: as one unsuccessful fish-and-chip-shop owner commented, 'All I got was a load of debt'.

Casterton workers had little hope of fulfilling extravagant aspirations, and accordingly limited their hopes to the opportunities that the community offered; they shared with the pottery workers of Arnold Bennett's *Clayhanger* 'the resigned fatalism of the governed'. There were few opportunities within the community for the achievement of high occupational aspirations, and once workers had committed themselves to the local labour market they were extremely reluctant to move (see below, Chapter 8). The labour force had evolved the attitudes and aspirations appropriate to the reality of the employment which the community offered, and in so doing helped to perpetuate the system of paternalist capitalism which largely created that reality. This accommodation was evidenced in the attitudes shown towards their jobs.

The attitudes towards jobs shown by Casterton workers were diverse, ambiguous, and not always clearly articulated, the changing reflection of the imperfect moulding of personal preferences by socialisation, occupational experience, and differential exposure to cultural and subcultural norms. 'Jobs are rather peculiar, seemingly insignificant things about a job make a great deal of difference to people' (34 year-old-engineer). Nevertheless, it is possible to analyse the factors which Casterton workers liked and disliked about different jobs, the reasons why they took, and left jobs, and to relate these to the economic system of paternalist capitalism. The following table shows the overall distribution of reasons given by Casterton workers for liking the jobs they liked most:

[12] *Ibid.*, Chapter 7.

Reasons for Liking Jobs (Q. 46)

	Manual %	Non-Manual %
Intrinsic	63	54
Pay	14	23
Other extrinsic	8	18
Expressive	10	4
Residual	3	2

N = 207   N = 155

% = % of all reasons mentioned: respondents were permitted two choices.

This classification is based upon a more elaborate one derived largely from the responses themselves. 'Intrinsic' factors include the work itself, the responsibility, authority, and initiative associated with it, the amount of variety or monotony, the degree of 'meaningfulness', and the opportunities provided for advancement. 'Other extrinsic' factors include ease of access, physical conditions, hours or work, especially shifts, security of employment, and other terms and conditions of employment. The classic human relations elements of supervisory style, company atmosphere, and relations with mates, are included within the category of 'expressive' factors. Finally, the residual category includes incidental factors, like the opportunity the job provided for the fulfilment of non-work projects.

As the table shows, the most popular type of reason given for liking the most liked job related to the characteristics associated with the task itself, and the independence and autonomy it permitted: 63 per cent of all reasons given by manual workers, and 54 per cent of all reasons given by non-manual workers, belonged to this category. 'Interesting – variation on everything – servicing, installation, the lot' (46-year-old electrician's mate). 'I was my own boss, as far as my work was concerned. While I was doing something, preparing things, I worked to my own schedule. It was fulfilling, a hell of a lot fulfilling . . . actually achieving something' (41-year-old work-study engineer) 'I was on my own. I'd rather work on my own. More or less your own boss if you did your job: you had a paper in the morning with what to do, and you did it' (36-year-old warehouseman). There is ample confirmation here for the importance attached to the need for intrinsically interesting tasks if workers are to be satisfied stressed by Georges Friedmann, Argyris,

Herzberg, and by many others.[13] Casterton workers plainly preferred to be fully involved in their work, to have responsibility, variety, and autonomy. However, it would be a mistake to attach overwhelming weight to these expressed preferences, for three reasons. Firstly, workers *may* have automatically assumed that our question ignored money, and answered simply in terms of other factors: the primary importance of economic reward may be so ingrained in attitudes towards jobs that it is ignored when answering the question 'Why did you like that job best?' However, this is not a significant objection for, even if true, it would not invalidate the scale of preferences: it would indicate that the level of economic reward was a constant factor, not decisive in determining variations in preferences. If this were so preferences would not, of course, necessarily be a good predictor of behaviour. Secondly, the concept of intrinsic interest was often a minimal one, for many workers representing only marginal variations in job content: one operative found his job interesting although it involved only a small number of manual operations upon a simple machine which he had been doing for twenty years. And thirdly, preferences were not mutually exclusive, and social behaviour is the result of the weighting of often marginal differences in costs and benefits: preferences, as well as choices, are governed by a number of factors which cannot be generally, and *a priori*, weighted. As a foreman electrician succinctly pointed out: 'Everyone works (*a*) for money, and (*b*) for interest'. 'It all depends on your circumstances. Take a young person – he'll want money and would tolerate boredom. I'd have interest now as I am – routine job gets boring, and affects health and attendance' (60-year-old assistant foreman). It would be difficult to classify this response as either intrinsic or extrinisic.

As a way of assessing directly the relative importance of intrinsic and financial factors in job preferences respondents were asked whether they would prefer a routine job paying £20 per week or a more interesting job paying £15. We felt

[13] G. Friedmann, *Industrial Society: The Emergence of the Human Problems of Automation*, Glencoe, Illinois: The Free Press, 1955; Argyris, *op. cit.*; Herzberg, *op. cit.*

that this posed a real issue for most respondents, and would give some indication of the value attached to 'interest', despite the apparent arbitrariness of the figures chosen; as the limited range of variation in earnings aspirations indicated, relatively small amounts of money had considerable significance for Casterton Mills workers (cf. below, pp. 140–1). A narrow majority of manual workers, and a substantial majority of non-manual workers, said that they would prefer an interesting job with less money.

Attitudes towards 'Interest' vs 'Money' in Jobs. (Q. 228)

	Manual %	Non-Manual %	Total %
Money	43	20	33
Interest	51	63	56
None	3	7	5
Missing	3	12	7
	N = 116	N = 91	N = 207

There was no clear correlation between age and primary concern with money, the most instrumental age group being the 45–49 group, 46 per cent of whom preferred a routine job to an interest ng one with less money. The age group 60 plus were more concerned with interest than any other group, 71 per cent saying that they would prefer an interesting job to a routine job paying more money, presumably reflecting the reduced commitments of that age group. However, such a choice represents *preferences*, not necessarily what Casterton workers would actually do. 'I would *prefer* an interesting job: everyone wants a job that they like. But everyone wants as much money as possible. I would always change from an interesting job that I could not manage on' (25-year-old crafts-man). As we show later, preferences proved poor predictors of behaviour, below pp. 63–5.

The reasons given for disliking the least liked job were not the obverse of the reasons given for preferring jobs: they belonged to a different dimension, not simply to a different location on the same d mension. As Herzberg has argued, 'the factors [that] lead to satisfaction (achievement, recognition, work itself, responsibility, and advancement) . . . contribute very little to job dissatisfaction. Conversely, the dissatisfiers

61

contribute very little to job satisfaction.'[14] As the following table shows, intrinsic factors were less important, extrinsic factors more important, in determining dislikes than in determining preferences, especially for manual workers:

Reasons for Disliking Jobs (Q. 48)

	Manual %	Non-Manual %
Intrinsic	21	40
Pay	2	6
Other extrinsic	33	22
Expressive	25	15
Domestic/personal	3	4
Residual	14	12
	N = 166	N = 149

% is % of reasons given: respondents permitted two choices

Whereas 63 per cent of the reasons given by manual workers for liking their most liked jobs related to intrinsic factors, only 21 per cent of the reasons given for disliking the least liked job did so; similarly, whereas 54 per cent of reasons mentioned by non-manual workers for liking most liked jobs related to intrinsic factors, only 40 per cent of reasons given for disliking least liked jobs did so. This decline is compensated for by a substantial rise in the importance of a wide variety of extrinsic factors, especially hours of work, job security, and relations with management for manual workers, and conditions and terms of employment for non-manual workers.

In short, Casterton Mills workers liked interesting jobs, but were prepared to put up with uninteresting ones: 'interest' was the most popular type of reason given for liking most liked jobs. A wide range of factors, of which interest was the third most popular for manual workers and the most popular for non-manual workers, were mentioned as sources of dissatisfaction.

Such preferences and dislikes should provide a basis for predicting the behaviour of the Casterton Mills labour force, or at least for predicting the explanations that would be given for behaviour. As Julienne Ford and Steven Box argue, largely on the basis of George Homans' version of the felicific calculus:

[14] F. Herzberg, *Work and the Nature of Man*, p. 77.

'In choosing between alternative occupations a person will rank the occupations in terms of the relation between his values and the perceived characteristics of the occupation, the higher the coincidence between the characteristics and his values the higher the rank. The higher the person perceives the probability that he will obtain employment in the higher ranked occupation, the more likely he is to choose that occupation.'[15] These propositions may form the basis for a theory of occupational choice amongst adolescents (although the relationship between the two propositions is likely to be highly problematic in any situation); but they do not form an adequate basis for analysing labour mobility in Casterton. The assumptions of rationality, knowledge, and a tractable environment were not justified. There was little correspondence between the reasons given for preferring jobs and the reasons given for taking jobs, and only slightly more correspondence between the reasons given for disliking jobs and for leaving them amongst manual workers. Non-manual workers revealed a greater, but far from perfect, consistency. This disjunction between preferences and choices is clear both at the aggregate and at the individual level.

The emphasis upon the intrinsic basis of the satisfaction derived from best liked or ideal jobs was not reflected in actual behaviour. Hence, although 63 per cent of the reasons given by Casterton Mills manual workers for liking their most liked jobs related to intrinsic factors, only 9 per cent of the reasons given for taking jobs at the Mills were related to intrinsic factors; comparable figures for non-manual workers were 54 and 16 per cent. Similarly, 'other extrinsic' factors accounted for only 8 per cent of the reasons given for preferring jobs, but for 21 per cent of the reasons given by manual workers for taking jobs at Casterton Mills. Moreover very few individuals mentioned intrinsic reasons for preferring jobs and intrinsic reasons for taking jobs at the Mills: only 12 per cent of manual workers and 22 per cent of non-manual workers. The coefficient of association between mentioning an intrinsic factor as a reason for liking a job and mentioning one for taking a job at the Mills was $-0 \cdot 01$, virtually nil, for manual workers, and a more

[15] J. Ford and S. Box, Sociological Theory and Occupational Choice, *Sociological Review*, Vol. 16, 1968, p. 289.

respectable but still small $+0 \cdot 43$ for non-manual workers. In short, neither manual nor non-manual workers showed a high level of consistency between their preferences and choices, between their likes and the reasons given for behaviour: but the level of consistency was appreciably higher for non-manual workers than for manual workers.

There is thus little justification for explaining the job choices of the Casterton workers by reference to their preferences as revealed by the reasons given for liking the jobs they liked best. However, this failure to achieve occupational goals, or apparent lack of rationalism, is less surprising than the lack of correlation between patterns of dislike and avoidance, for there is some evidence that patterns of dislike and avoidance are more clearly defined than patterns of preference and choice. Rosenberg, for example, found in his classic study of occupational choice amongst college students that 97 per cent of students selecting 'people-oriented' values avoided 'self-interested' occupations (e.g. business), although only 50 per cent actually chose a 'helping' occupation (e.g. social work, education), despite seeing these occupations as the major way of realising 'people-oriented' values. Similarly, 92 per cent of the 'misanthropes' avoided 'helpful' occupations, although only 23 per cent actually chose a 'self-interested' occupation.[16] There was a marked contrast between manual workers and non-manual workers in the extent to which reasons given for disliking jobs and reasons given for leaving jobs were related to each other: non-manual workers showed considerably greater consistency. Thus, 21 per cent of the reasons given by manual workers for disliking their least liked job related to intrinsic factors, whilst only 11 per cent of the reasons given for leaving the jobs they had before working at Casterton Mills related to intrinsic factors; 35 per cent of the reasons given for disliking jobs related to pay and other extrinsic factors, compared with 45 per cent of the reasons mentioned for leaving the jobs held immediately prior to working at Casterton Mills. Moreover, the coefficient of association between giving an extrinsic reason for disliking jobs and giving such a reason for leaving pre-Casterton Mills jobs, the largest

[16] M. Rosenberg, *Occupations and Values*, Glencoe: Illinois: The Free Press, 1957, p. 30. The examples are Rosenberg's.

class of reasons in both categories, was only +0·37. Dislike was more closely related to leaving for non-manual workers: 40 per cent of the reasons given for disliking jobs related to the intrinsic characteristics of the job, compared with 41 per cent of the reasons given for leaving jobs held immediately prior to working at Casterton Mills. Similarly, 28 per cent of the reasons mentioned for disliking jobs related to extrinsic factors, compared with 28 per cent of the reasons given for leaving pre-Casterton Mills jobs. For non-manual workers the coefficient of association between giving an intrinsic reason for disliking a job and giving such a reason for leaving the job held immediately before working at Casterton Mills was +0·5.

The correspondence between expressed attitude, whether of preference or of dislike, and expressed reason for behaviour is thus far from close, especially for manual workers. However, it might be objected that no one would expect a close association between preferences and attributed reasons for past behaviour, or between present dislikes and past avoidances, particularly in a sample of honest respondents: preferences change, and factors now regarded as important may previously have been neglected, and the converse. If so, one would expect a correspondence between the kind of reason given for leaving pre-Casterton Mills jobs and the kind of reason given for taking a job at Casterton Mills, but not between other explanations. However, this is not the case. The coefficient of association between giving an extrinsic reason for leaving pre-Casterton Mills job and giving an extrinsic reason for taking a job at Casterton Mills is 0·16 for manual workers and a minimal 0·01 for non-manual workers. There is, however, a strong correlation between giving an intrinsic reason for leaving pre-Casterton Mills job and giving such a reason for working at Casterton Mills amongst non-manual workers, +0·69, by far the highest correlation between any two categories. There is thus one, relatively small group, for whom the intrinsic characteristics of the work probably form the basis for mobility between jobs.

This lack of fit between preferences and explanations for behaviour, and between dislikes and avoidances, was largely due to the constraints of the labour market; the environment

E

was far from tractable. As we have seen, Casterton Mills largely dominated the local labour market, and there were relatively few alternative employment opportunities, particularly in the years before the Second World War. '[Why did you go to work at Casterton Mills in the first place?] There was hardly anything else. Either that or Smith's. . . . I hadn't much choice in Casterton. . . . You used to have to queue up then for a job, an old chap in the office would point to men in a crowd of 60' (61-year-old security officer). 'Couldn't get a job anywhere else. Influenced by a friend who knew the group secretary, in the same cricket club, he got me an interview. Had to have matriculation certificate even before they looked at you, not like today' (49-year-old clerical worker). 'There was only the Mill in Casterton' (61-year-old redundant line manager).

Unfortunately, it is impossible to construct an index of job opportunities available to the sample when they went to work at Casterton Mills for two reasons. Firstly, official job vacancy statistics correlate imperfectly with the real level of demand for labour, because of the failure of employers to notify the Employment Exchanges of vacancies available or of vacancies filled: job vacancy statistics may exaggerate, or may under-estimate, the number of employment opportunities available locally.[17] Some respondents believed that local management did not inform the Employment Exchange of available vacancies: 'I think a lot of managements didn't give the Labour Exchange the information they should do. If I go to the Labour Exchange "Oh, no, no jobs at Casterton Mills". If I go down to Casterton Mills "Oh, yes, we'll take you on".' (58-year-old warehouse-man). Other evidence suggests that employers over-estimate their requirements to the Exchange, particularly during periods

[17] Cf., K. Cowling, M. Dean, G. Pyatt, and S. Wabe, *An Investigation into the Demand for Manpower and its Supply in the Engineering Industries: A Pilot Study*, Coventry: University of Warwick Papers in Social and Economic Research, n.d.: '. . . nobody has attempted to check vacancies registered with employment exchanges against vacancies from surveys of firms. Some people suggest firms do not bother to register vacancies in periods of high excess demand, others say that they notify more vacancies than they actually need to fill at these times (p. 2.14).' This is obviously an area where further research is needed.

of labour shortage. Secondly, our respondents were recruited by Casterton Mills over a long period of time, and it would be impossible to examine the official data on vacancies for the time of the recruitment of each respondent. However, job choice and labour mobility, like other forms of risk-taking behaviour, are determined by perceived opportunity structure, not by the actual structure: geographical, industrial, and occupational background, degree of involvement in contact networks, personal preferences, and other factors all help to 'distort' the individual's perceptions of available jobs. And 44 per cent of Casterton Mills workers said that jobs had been difficult to get when they went to work at the Mills, especially of course older workers. Although Casterton did not experience the tragically spectacular levels of unemployment suffered by ship-building towns in the North-East, or by mining towns in South Wales in the 1930s, memories of the economic difficulties of the inter-war years, with crowds gathering outside the Mills early in the morning and hoping to be called in for work, were still vivid. 'I went down to the Mills and queued. A chap in the window nodded his head if he wanted to accept you, and if he shook his head he did not want you. After 14 days he nodded his head' (64-year-old process worker). Moreover, a fifth of manual workers said that they had to leave their pre-Casterton Mills jobs involuntarily, occasionally for indiscipline but more frequently because of redundancy.

The greater explanatory consistency of non-manual workers compared with manual workers may have been due to their higher educational level, or to their greater commitment to achieving self-realisation through an occupational career. Non-manual workers had, of course, a higher level of education than manual workers: only 27 per cent had left school at 14, compared with 51 per cent of manual workers, and 27 per cent had left school at 18 or more, compared with only 13 per cent of manual workers. Consequently non-manual workers were better able to maintain, or impose, internal consistency in their responses to related questions placed at widely spaced intervals in a long questionnaire. However, differences in consistency were more than an artefact of sophistication in dealing with questionnaires: they reflected differences in attitudes, and differences in behaviour. Non-manual workers as a group were more committed to individual self-advancement through labour mobility than manual workers, as we will show in the following chapter in the discussion of attitudes towards the firm. However, this commitment was less than complete, for many non-manual workers shared with manual workers a fatalistic acceptance of occupational limitations, until they reached an intolerable level. Accordingly, there is more evidence of leaving jobs which were disliked, or disliking jobs which were left, than of consciously planned occupational careers, involving active job seeking and self-conscious choice – until the stimulus provided by the redundancy.

IV

The majority of Casterton Mills workers believed in the virtues enshrined in the classic Protestant ethic: hard work, individual effort, and a fatalistic acceptance of the tribulations caused by a largely intractable and hostile environment. Possession of a job was regarded as a necessary basis of self-respect, and considerable hostility was shown towards 'malingerers' who did not work when they could; 36 per cent of manual workers, and 37 per cent of non-manual workers spontaneously distinguished between the deserving and the undeserving recipients of unemployment benefit. '[If a man is out of work do you think he should get an income equivalent to what he would get in a full time job?] Very difficult question. Opposite me there is a man fit, maybe fitter than me, not working and getting National Assistance, and we have to work for what we've got . . . should get benefit in cases of illness or unemployment when they cannot get a job. But when there is a job and they don't *want* to work then no, they shouldn't get it . . . a lot don't want to work' (49-year-old process worker). 'Not the lazy types, the ones that won't have work . . . at the moment seem to get as much out of work as in work, especially those with families' (44-year-old process worker). Moreover, a large majority of both manual and non-manual workers admired those who worked hard in order to get ahead in their jobs. However, there was considerable scepticism about the results that effort would bring, about the rewards granted to the virtuous. A substantial number of workers who admired hard work, especially manual workers who admired hard work, did not believe that effort and ability were enough to get ahead; opportunity, luck, and connections were also regarded as necessary. Promotion was desired, especially by younger workers, but not expected, especially by older workers.

Such fatalism was also evident in attitudes towards jobs. The majority of Casterton Mills workers, manual and non-manual, preferred jobs which were intrinsically interesting to jobs which carried high earnings. This was apparent in the responses to questions asking for their explanations of why they liked the jobs they liked best, and in replies to a fixed choice question asking for a choice between a routine job paying £20 per week and an interesting job paying £15 per week. However, very few workers, especially manual workers, changed jobs because of the interest provided by the prospective job, or the lack of interest provided by their present job, and many said that their preferences would have to be sacrificed to their responsibilities when faced with a concrete choice between interest and earnings. There was little correlation between preferences and the reasons given for choosing jobs, or between dislikes and the reasons given for leaving jobs, especially for manual workers. There is some evidence that non-manual workers were more successful in achieving their occupational aims, or at least more successful in making their answers sufficiently consistent to seem so: a substantial minority left their pre-Casterton Mills jobs because they did not find them interesting, and worked at the Mills because it seemed to provide an interesting job. But the evidence is not very substantial.

This fatalistic acceptance of the limitations of the labour market, and adjustment of expectations to reality, was accompanied by, and was perhaps responsible for, the heavy dependence of Casterton Mills employees upon their firm, and their acceptance of its distinctive company culture. It was also apparent in the reactions of many workers to the redundancy, in their belief in its inevitability and in the uselessness of protest.

4 PATERNALIST CAPITALISM: CASTERTON MILLS AND ITS WORKERS

Industrial enterprises, like other social institutions, possess their own more or less distinctive cultures, based upon customary patterns of thought and behaviour. As A. K. Rice said in his study of Indian textile and chemical companies: 'The culture of an enterprise is the customary and traditional way of thinking and behaving within it. It is shared to a greater or lesser extent by all members, and new members must learn it, and at least partially accept it, if they are to stay. It includes the way managers customarily behave; their own and their subordinates' attitudes towards authority, responsibility, and discipline; the values placed upon the tasks performed; the ways of performing them; and the less conscious customs and taboos'.[1] Some enterprises, for example Quaker firms like Cadburys and Rowntrees, have developed a distinctive culture centred upon social responsibility and concern for their employees; as Edward Cadbury stated long before human relations had become a popular managerial philosophy, 'The supreme principle has been the belief that business efficiency and the welfare of employees are but different sides of the same problem'.[2] Similarly, the Pilkington Glass Company had developed a distinctive company culture, accepted by managers as the basis for interpreting the managerial role: moral commitment to the firm, and autocratic paternalism towards employees, were the major elements in the Pilkington's culture – the culture of nineteenth-century Nonconformity.[3]

[1] A. K. Rice, *The Organisation and the Environment*, Tavistock Publications, 1963, p. 239.

[2] Quoted in J. Child, *British Management Thought: A Critical Analysis*, George Allen & Unwin, 1969, p. 37. Several members of the Pilkington family are still active members of the Congregational Church.

[3] A. Lane and K. Roberts, *op. cit.*, pp. 37–8.

I

Casterton Mills, like Cadburys, Rowntrees, and Pilkingtons, had developed a distinctive company culture, one of autocratic but often benevolent paternalism. The clearest expression of this autocracy was in management's attitude towards trade unions. In the 1930s attempts to form trade unions amongst both process workers and clerical workers were successfully jumped upon, and some enthusiasts were dismissed. 'Trade unions didn't agree with [the old] Lord Casterton, he didn't recognise them. We asked a demand and he took no notice' (65-year-old clerical worker). 'Years ago . . . anybody who joined a trade union was thrown out on his neck' (60-year-old clerical worker). Since the Second World War trade unions have become accepted, and the A.E.U., the E.T.U., the A.S.W., the N.U.G.M.W., D.A.T.A., and a number of other smaller unions all recruited within the plant; there were even members of A.S.S.E.T. amongst lower supervisory grades in the plant. As we have shown, 63 per cent of manual workers and 36 per cent of non-manual workers were members of trade unions. However, despite changes in company policy, and relatively smooth working relationships between the personnel function and the unions, management remained unenthusiastic and occasionally hostile towards trade unions. 'Trade unions weren't a thing that the firm went in for.' There was no plant level bargaining before the redundancy, and no preliminary discussion with the unions about the redundancy. Similarly, the representative Works Council played only a marginal role in the plant, and seems to have played scarcely any role at all in the redundancy.

Autocracy was accompanied with benevolence: the corporate concern allegedly characteristic of the most modern enterprises had existed for many years. As a 60-year-old woodcutting machinist explained: 'When we joined the firm we had a booklet saying they were happy to employ us, and if we had any complaints to go to the Personnel Officer: they didn't like upsets. They would even help with domestic problems. You could buy clothing there, the canteen was good. They were ideal employers from that point of view.' Good canteen facilities were provided,

71

even if they were elaborately graded according to rank (rank being also a preoccupation of medieval feudalism): the chairman's, the directors', the management's, staff, and works.[4] Moreover, a job at Casterton Mills was a job for life, and hardly anyone, whether management, staff, or works, was ever dismissed – at least not until the redundancy. '[It] was a very old fashioned place. When people got a job there they tended to stick for ever – not necessarily through any deep loyalty, although they were quite a loyal crew. Just a "for ever" job if you kept your nose clean: people tended to give in to it and remain there for ever. A civil servantish attitude' (41-year-old works study engineer). The firm showed a generous attitude towards the sick, the disabled, and the mentally ill, employing more than its quota of disabled personnel – 7 per cent instead of 3 per cent, according to the firm – and providing a number of quasi-retirement jobs for elderly workers: 'if you could stagger down there you were kept on' commented one warehouseman. The Mills provided employment for many who 'were a bit eightpence in the shilling' (slightly subnormal), and who proved to be unable to find work again once they had been declared redundant.

Management at Casterton Mills thus continued to operate within the framework of paternalist capitalism until the 1960s, with only marginal adaptations to meet new circumstances. Workers at Casterton Mills did the same; their attitudes were, to a large extent, complementary to those of management. Casterton Mills workers believed in loyalty, obedience, and the need to accept managerial authority; they respected the virtues which helped to sustain paternalist captalism.

II

Despite the experience of the redundancy there was widespread agreement amongst both manual and non-manual workers on the importance of loyalty and willingness to put oneself out for the firm. Hence 72 per cent of manual workers, and 82 per cent

---

[4] Status differences were, of course, regarded as a spur to effort by management, not simply – as in feudalism – as an expression of natural order.

of non-manual workers who answered the question believed that 'the good employee is loyal to his firm even if it means putting himself out'. A 61-year-old supervisor summarised the views of many when he said: 'He should be able to give that little bit extra into the job he's doing.' Such feelings were widespread amongst all age groups, but older manual workers were more likely to value loyalty than younger manual workers: there was no difference between the non-manual workers of different ages.

The Good Employee Is Loyal to His Firm Even If It Means Putting Himself Out (Q. 205)

| | Manual | | | | Non-Manual | | | |
| | −25 | 25–44 | 45–59 | 60– | −25 | 25–44 | 45–59 | 60– |
	%	%	%	%	%	%	%	%
Yes	40	71	85	79	78	100	85	87
No	60	29	15	21	22	—	15	13
N =	5	31	27	19	9	17	20	8

The overwhelming support for loyalty, and the small number of respondents in the extreme age categories, makes it impossible to form any firm conclusions about the significance of age for beliefs in the value of loyalty; but it is suggestive that younger manual workers were different from older manual workers, whether because of the different problems faced by workers at different stages of the life-cycle, or the different labour market conditions which operated in Casterton before the Second World War, or because of the longer exposure of older workers to the subculture of paternalist capitalism (see also below, p. 90). It is also significant that there was very little difference between young and old non-manual workers in the extent of their belief in loyalty, suggesting that such beliefs had a different significance for non-manual workers compared with their significance for manual workers.

Such evidence is interesting, if in itself limited, for it implies, at the very least, a particular conception of virtue; good workers are loyal to management, rather than rebellious – even if the precept is not always honoured. But the commitment was

73

often more than that, more than the recognition of a general, or local, social value. 'I've put myself out all my life. You just keep on working. You do your extra. I'd never dream of walking out of my department at night without every piece of paper being seen to. I'd go in on Saturday and Sunday for nothing' (49-year-old clerical worker). Although this explicitness and dedication was unusual, many workers, manual and non-manual, emphasised that the employer was the 'master', and that if employees were unwilling to accept that authority they should change their jobs. However, the picture is more complex than this portrayal of submissive deference suggests.

The belief in the importance of loyalty to the firm was widespread amongst both manual and non-manual workers, but it meant different things to the two groups. For manual workers, especially older manual workers, it was one aspect of the subcultural value system which had evolved within paternalist capitalism: it was accompanied by a belief in the virtue of obedience and respect and acceptance of managerial authority, and by a preference for security rather than risky opportunity. For non-manual workers the belief in the value of loyalty and putting oneself out for the firm was an aspect of their belief in occupational achievement as a method of personal fulfilment. Further examination of this contrast reveals much of the complex basis of employee commitment to Casterton Mills.

Respondents were asked whether they agreed or disagreed with the view that 'the best way to win respect is to stick with one firm'. As the following table shows, substantial numbers of manual workers, but very few non-manual workers, agreed with this view:

The Best Way to Win Respect Is to Stick with One Firm (Q. 202)

	Manual %	Non-Manual %
Agree	50	21
Disagree	42	71
Other	9	8
	N = 116	N = 91

Whereas half of manual workers believed that the best way to win respect was to stick with one firm, only slightly over a fifth of non-manual workers took the same view. There was only a slight tendency for all manual workers who believed in the importance of putting oneself out to believe that loyalty would bring respect: 60 per cent compared with 54 per cent. But there was a strong tendency for older manual workers to be more likely than younger manual workers to believe both; 64 per cent of manual workers aged 45 or more, compared with 52 per cent of manual workers aged below 45, who believed in the importance of putting oneself out also believed that loyalty would bring respect. In short, older workers were more likely than younger workers to believe in loyalty, respect, and putting oneself out, although there was evidence of such beliefs amongst all age groups.

Some manual workers may have regarded loyalty to the firm as an instrumental value, a way of achieving promotion, realising that the acquisition of specific expertise, a reputation for 'integrity', and formal and informal rights of tenure constituted substantial claims for recognition, especially in a firm like Casterton Mills. Those who believed that loyalty would bring respect were more likely than those who did not to believe that loyalty would also bring promotion, although the numbers involved are small: 47 per cent of those who believed that loyalty would bring respect also believed that loyalty would bring promotion, compared with only 31 per cent of those who did not believe that loyalty would bring respect. However, there were many manual workers who believed that loyalty would bring respect, but who did not believe that loyalty would also bring promotion, and for whom no such instrumental explanation is even possible: instead, the explanation must be sought in the distinctive subculture of the manual worker under paternalist capitalism.

Belief in the value of loyalty as a means of acquiring respect was part of a subcultural value system whose other elements included an emphasis upon the virtues of obedience and respect, upon the acceptance of managerial authority, and upon the value of security. A substantial majority of manual workers (69 per cent) believed that 'obedience and respect for authority are the most important characteristics of the good worker', compared with only 56 per cent of non-manual workers. Belief in the importance of commitment to the firm and in the virtues of obedience and respect for authority were correlated with each other: 86 per cent of manual workers stressing the importance of loyalty as a basis for respect also believed in the virtue of obedience, compared with only 61 per cent of manual workers attaching less importance to loyalty. Loyalty and obedience were, in turn, correlated with favourable attitudes towards managerial authority. Respondents were asked two related questions, at different points in the interview: whether they agreed or disagreed with the view that 'managers are there to give orders and those workers that are under them should obey'; and whether they accepted or rejected the view that 'managers make the major decisions in industry and other employees should accept them'. The majority of respondents agreed with both propositions, some with one, and some with neither. The following table shows the relationship between commitment to the firm and replies to these questions:

Attitudes towards Loyalty, Obedience, and Authority

	Manual Workers	(N)	
	2	1	0
Loyalty	26	10	5
Nt. loyalty	12	7	15
Indifferent	4	2	2
	Non-Manual Workers	(N)	
Loyalty	8	2	3
Nt. loyalty	24	8	7
Indifferent	0	1	1

2: agrees with both statements
1: agrees with one statement
0: agrees with neither statement

Hence, those who believed that loyalty would bring respect were more likely than those who did not to accept managerial authority; and the more favourable the attitude towards management the more likely the manual worker was to empha-sise the importance of loyalty as a basis for respect. There was no such tendency for non-manual workers; non-manual workers were likely to adopt a favourable attitude towards management regardless of their attitude towards loyalty. Similar results were obtained by examining the relationship between attitudes towards management and belief in the importance of obedience; the more favourable the former the more likely the latter for manual workers, no relationship for non-manual workers. Finally, manual workers stressing loyalty, obedience, and the acceptance of managerial authority were noticeably cautious in their job aspirations; hence 77 per cent stressing the value of obedience preferred jobs which offered security over jobs which offered promotion prospects, compared with only 48 per cent of those who did not stress the virtues of obedience.

Non-manual workers shared some beliefs with manual workers, but not all. As we have seen, a large majority of non-manual workers believed that good employees should be willing to put themselves out in the interests of their firm. Similarly, and not surprisingly, a large majority (79 per cent of those who expressed a view) believed that 'managers are there to give orders and those workers who are under them should obey'. Finally, a majority of non-manual workers, especially older ones, believed that obedience and respect for authority were the most important attributes of a good worker. However, whereas these beliefs were combined with a belief in the importance of sticking with a firm amongst manual workers, they were not amongst non-manual workers: non-manual workers were not 'committed' to their employers in the same sense as manual workers. A willingness to put oneself out was in part a matter of self-respect: 'As a matter of self-respect, if you feel you sold yourself short you feel bad' (42-year-old senior clerical worker). But it was also one aspect of the middle class ambition to 'get ahead' in terms of an occupational career. Non-manual workers were more likely than manual workers to believe that the only way to achieve promotion was by 'moving around from job to job, on the look out to improve your own position' (60 per cent, compared with 47 per cent). 'You need to give the impression that you have ambition to gain respect from your bosses' (21-year-old clerical worker). This belief in the relationship between mobility and promotion was particularly common amongst non-manual workers who played down the importance of loyalty: 66 per cent of non-manual workers who did not believe that loyalty would bring respect believed that the only way to get ahead was by changing employers, compared with only 40 per cent of non-manual workers who believed that loyalty would bring respect. The association between limited commitment and the belief that promotion would only be achieved by changing jobs was particularly marked for non-manual workers who had lived outside Casterton; indeed, only 6·5 per cent of non-manual workers who had lived outside Casterton believed that promotion would come through sticking with one firm, although 27 per cent of non-manual workers who had always lived in the community did so. In short, non-manual workers believed that the best way to get ahead was by changing employers, rather than sticking with one firm, and in doing so played down the importance of loyalty as the basis for respect; this tendency was particularly strong amongst non-manual workers who had lived outside Casterton.

Casterton Mills workers, especially manual workers, thus revealed a high degree of commitment to the firm both in their attitudes and, as we will show, in their behaviour. Loyalty, obedience, and acceptance of managerial authority were highly regarded values. However, this was not associated with a general *identification* with management and acceptance of a unitary conception of the firm. Although more manual workers accepted a unitary conception of the firm than in other studies, this was far from universal, and was not closely related to belief in the virtues of loyalty, obedience and security.[5] Respondents were asked: 'Some people say that the interests of management and workers are opposed, others that they are the same. What do you think?' The following table shows the distribution of replies by occupational status:

[5] It is unclear whether we should have expected them to be associated or not. On the one hand, acceptance of managerial authority, etc., may have been expected to lead to a unitary conception of the firm, such identification involving a unity of interest. On the other hand, the essence of feudalism is the recognition of the complementarity, not the identity, of interests; but that would not, of course, explain the incidence of opposition. It is probably only coincidental, but interesting, that manual workers were almost equally divided on the issue!

Attitudes towards Management/Worker Interests (Q. 316)

	Manual %	Non-Manual %
Opposed	50	49
Same	41	46
Depends	9	5
	N = 96	N = 61

There was thus a surprising similarity in the distribution of opinion in the different occupational statuses: 50 per cent of manual workers and 49 per cent of non-manual workers believed that the interests of workers and management were opposed, 41 per cent and 46 per cent respectively thought that the interests were the same. This pattern of responses differs from that found by others, for example by A. J. Sykes in his study of clerical and manual workers in a firm in Glasgow.[6] After expressing some well-justified reservations about the significance of data on conceptions of the firm, Sykes concluded: 'Clerks and industrial workers see the work situation very differently, and, accordingly, react to it very differently. In brief, each has a different industrial ethos. . . . It would appear that in each case a distinctive industrial ethos [has] grown out of having, or not having, opportunities for promotion.' The manual workers at Casterton Mills were more harmonious, non-manual workers more antagonistic, than their Glasgow counterparts.

Conceptions of the firm and political affiliation were related to each other, but the interpretation of the evidence for that relationship is difficult and inconclusive. However, it is possible to show that the 'deviant' conceptions were not the direct consequence (or cause) of political beliefs. Amongst manual workers there was no tendency for those who believed that the interests of management and workers were opposed to consider themselves Labour supporters: 40 per cent were consistent Labour supporters, 27·5 per cent switched their votes according to circumstances, and 25 per cent considered themselves consistent Conservatives, proportions similar to the overall distribution of political affiliation amongst manual workers.

[6] A. J. M. Sykes, 'Some Differences in the Attitudes of Clerical and Manual Workers', *Sociological Review, 1965*, pp. 307–8.

However, there was a tendency for manual workers who believed that the interests of management and workers were the same to support the Conservatives: the 'harmonists' divided 33 per cent Labour, 18 per cent switchers, and 33 per cent Conservative. Although those who believed in industrial unity were disproportionately Conservatives, Conservatives were not disproportionately believers in unity, suggesting that political affiliation may be a consequence of a syndrome of attitudes of which a unitary conception of the firm is a part rather than the reverse, if it is possible to make any estimate at all on the direction of causality. Amongst the middle class there was a tendency for Labour supporters to believe that the interests of management and workers were opposed, but not for Conservative supporters to believe that they were identical; Labour supporters split 27 per cent unitary, 73 per cent dichotomous, Conservative 50/50. The closer correlation between political beliefs and conceptions of the firm amongst non-manual workers perhaps indicates, as we have suggested in a previous chapter (p. 38), the greater deviance of Labour voting for non-manual workers than of Conservative voting for manual workers. The figures suggest such an interpretation but no conclusions can be more than suggestive in view of the small numbers involved and the general fuzziness of conceptions of the firm.

The relationship between conceptions of the firm and trade union membership is more straightforward.

	Manual		Non-Manual	
	Trade Union %	Non-T.U. %	Trade Union %	Non-T.U. %
Opposed	46	61	67	39
Same	42	29	33	50
Depends	12	10	0	11
	N = 57	N = 31	N = 24	N = 36

There was a tendency for manual workers who were members of trade unions to believe in a unitary conception of the firm, reflecting the fact that union membership was more a consequence of job requirements than political commitment: union members were the more stable and committed members of the Casterton Mills labour force. Conversely, there was a tendency for non-manual trade unionists to be more antagonistic than

80

non-manual non-trade unionists; non-manual workers, particularly in a firm like Casterton Mills, which had historically discouraged trade unionism, were required to make a considerable ideological commitment to trade unionism if they wished to become members, for it involved a repudiation of the whole value system represented by the firm's paternalist policies, and did not derive any support from general social norms.

Unitary conceptions of the firm were embedded in the ideology of capitalist paternalism, the industrial equivalent of the 'One Nation' ideas of traditional Toryism, and were accepted as such by many, especially older, manual workers. Old manual workers were more likely than young manual workers to believe that the interests of management and workers were the same: 49 per cent of manual workers aged 50 or more, compared with only 32 per cent of manual workers under 35, believed that the interests of management and workers were the same. Similarly, 48·5 per cent of the unitary manual workers, but only 40 per cent of antagonistic manual workers, were aged 50 or more. Moreover, many of the manual workers who believed that the interests of management and workers were opposed believed that they *should be* one and the same: 'I think they should be the same, but they aren't the same, I don't know why' (65-year-old electricians' mate) – but since respondents were not asked explicitly about what they thought relations between management and workers ought to be it is impossible to provide any figures on the extent of this sentiment. There was no tendency for the redundant to be more antagonistic than those who left voluntarily; instead, the redundant were more likely than the voluntary leavers to believe that the interests of management and workers were the same, probably because of their greater age: 47 per cent of redundant manual workers, compared with 28 per cent of those who left of their own accord, believed that the interests of management and workers were the same. This acceptance of a unitary conception of the firm is all the more surprising in view of the difficulties experienced by older manual workers during the redundancy.[7]

[7] An additional factor which may have contributed to the difference between the results found in Casterton and elsewhere in Britain is the difference in the wording of the question. Sykes, Goldthorpe *et al.*, and

Two groups were largely responsible for the incidence of antagonistic views amongst non-manual workers, redundant works managers, a relatively old group, and voluntary leaving clerical workers, a relatively junior group. The redundant works managers were primarily 'locals' who had worked their way up within the firm (and, incidentally, showed considerable resentment against young trainees recruited on the basis of educational qualifications and given accelerated promotion) and were acutely aware that they had changed sides: as managers who had been workers they were conscious of the different pressures they were under, the different interests they were serving. The voluntary leaving clerks were less committed to the enterprise than the works managers, and did not regard their white collar jobs with the gratitude and deference shown towards them by older clerical workers: both objectively and subjectively they had more in common with manual workers of their own age group than with older clerks. However, the numbers involved are too small to justify statistical analysis or to permit any definite conclusion on the roots of non-manual antagonism.

others all asked variants of the football team question: 'Here are two opposing views about industry generally: I'd like you to tell me which you agree with more. Some people say that a firm is like a football side – because good teamwork means success and is to everyone's advantage. Others say that teamwork in industry is impossible – because employers and men are really on opposite sides. Which view do you agree with more?' (Goldthorpe *et al.*, Vol. 1, pp. 73–4). We omitted any reference to football teams, and returned to a literal translation of the question asked by Willner in his original celebrated study of French iron miners: *'Ce que veulent les patrons et ce que veulent les travailleurs, pensez-vous que cela s'oppose ou pas?'* (A. Willner, 'L'Ouvrier et L'Organisation', *Sociologie du Travail*, 1962, p. 343). Although the concept of interest is a difficult one to interpret – one respondent commenting that the interests of managment and workers are the same, they are both interested in money – it is less confusing than the ambiguously picturesque concept of the football team. Interestingly, Willner's findings on manual workers were more comparable to ours than to those of Sykes: 37 per cent said that the interests of management and workers were not opposed or opposed only in part, compared with 61 per cent who said that they were mainly or completely opposed (*ibid.*, p. 343).

III

As many respondents pointed out, Casterton Mills was a 'family' firm. Until the redundancy management had always maintained a traditionally paternalistic attitude towards employees, and Casterton Mills employees, especially manual workers, had responded. Management had followed a policy of autocratic benevolence, opposing the development of trade unions, but recognising the importance of 'looking after' employees, for example by providing quasi-retirement jobs for long service workers who were 'past it'. Workers' attitudes to the firm were complementary to this interpretation of the managerial role. The majority of workers, manual and non-manual, believed in the virtues of loyalty, obedience, and the acceptance of managerial authority. For manual workers especially this was part of the sub-culture of paternalist capitalism, a more or less coherent set of beliefs centred upon the firm; for non-manual workers it was partly this, and partly a recognition of the attitudes that were necessary to 'get on'. Substantial numbers of both manual and non-manual workers believed that the interests of management and workers were the same, and some of those who did not think that they were the same thought that they ought to be. Although there was considerable support for trade union membership as a form of 'crisis insurance' – if not for trade unionism in general – this was not associated with hostility towards management; manual trade union members were more likely than non-members to believe that the interests of management and workers were the same.

Why did this system survive? As we showed in Chapter 2, Casterton's geographical position made the development of paternalist capitalism possible, by minimising the 'contaminating' influences of the outside world and by increasing local dependence upon the Mills; Casterton's social and economic development in the period after 1850 confirmed this. The policies of the Casterton family translated potential into reality, and once that reality had been established it was likely to continue; inertia and tradition are powerful forces for ensuring the persistence of patterns of behaviour, like institutions, beyond the conditions that were responsible for their creation. However, the persistence of paternalist capitalism in Casterton until the 1960s cannot be explained by inertia and tradition alone, for the historical conditions of the post-war period were so different from those of the inter-war period that one might have expected a new pattern to develop. Instead, the continuing lack of alternative employment in the city, accompanied by the firm's prosperity during the post-war consumer boom, provided the ideal economic environment for the continuation of the pre-existing structure; the autocracy was possible because of the continued dependence of the labour force upon the Mills (and, of course, by the fact that many of the workers had been with the firm since before the war); the benevolence was made possible by the profits. New recruits to the firm were socialised into this culture, and thereby helped to perpetuate it. A combination of favourable economic circumstances, in-plant sociali- sation – facilitated by the presence of a large core of long service workers and by recruitment through family connections, and in the last resort managerial power, were responsible for the survival of paternalist capitalism.

The first condition for the survival of paternalist capitalism was the continued dependence of the labour force upon the Mills; as we showed in the previous chapter, 44 per cent of respondents reported that jobs had been difficult to find when they went to work at the Mills. Even more reported that they had expected that jobs would be difficult to get when the redundancy was announced: 80 per cent of manual workers and 79 per cent of non-manual workers. Although unemploy- ment was not a serious problem in Casterton in the post-war period until the late 1960s (the highest level before the announce- ment of the redundancy was $1 \cdot 6$ per cent in 1963), there were never many vacancies, and many school leavers left the area because of the limited job opportunities available locally. In 1965, for example, the level of unemployment in the area was only $1 \cdot 5$ per cent but there were only 108 vacancies listed at the local Employment Exchange (see below, pp. 147–9, for details on the opportunity structure of the area).

The second economic precondition for the continued survival of paternalist capitalism was the firm's continued prosperity until the early 1960s. The period between the end of the Second World War and the early 1960s was of course one of high consumer demand for domestic consumer goods, including floor-coverings. Casterton Mills shared in the general prosperity, being able to sell almost as much as it could produce: turnover reached a peak in 1959. Although the firm's earnings record was erratic, and the return on capital invested never generous, management was able to invest £1½ million in new plant in Casterton, and to diversify into new fields through the purchase of ailing companies. This high level of production, combined with the willingness of major shareholders, especially the Casterton family, to accept a lower return on capital than they could obtain elsewhere, permitted the loose control over expenditure which sustained the 'indulgency pattern' (to use Gouldner's expressive phrase) of the 'old' Casterton Mills.[8] Substantial feather-bedding in fulfilment of informal social obligations was common in all departments – clerical and professional, production, and especially maintenance; extensive empire building occurred; and, as professional employees commented gratefully, it was possible to purchase and use the best equipment available regardless of cost, because management accepted any expenditure that was necessary to do a 'proper job'.

Economic circumstances permitted the continuance of traditional beliefs long after they had been repudiated elsewhere; but these circumstances were not in themselves decisive. An additional reason for their persistence lay in the strength of the process of socialisation. Beliefs, once established, persist unless specific pressures emerge to change them, for existing beliefs provide the paradigms for future explanations, and thus tend to generate their own confirmation; and belief in the value of loyalty, commitment to the firm, obedience, and the acceptance of managerial authority had not been significantly challenged by a class-conscious industrial or political movement. Hence the inevitability of the process of socialisation, the unquestioned acceptance of beliefs handed down from generation to generation: 'It's the way you've been brought up' said one 65-year-old process worker when explaining the reasons

[8] A. W. Gouldner, *Patterns of Industrial Bureaucracy*, Glencoe: Illinois: The Free Press, 1954, Chapter 2.

for his belief in the importance of loyalty. This process of socialisation was all the stronger because it was reinforced by a substantial overlap between family and work roles: Casterton Mills was a family firm in the strict sense of the term, as well as in corporate image – there were a number of extensive kinship networks within the firm. The majority of workers interviewed, manual and non-manual, had relatives either working at the plant at the time of the redundancy, or with previous experience of the plant: 51 per cent of manual workers and 58 per cent of non-manual workers. In addition, the wives of 36 per cent of manual workers and of 31 per cent of non-manual workers had relatives with experience of working at the Mills. Many employees had more than one relative with such experience, the largest 'Mills family' we discovered totalling 13 – husband, wife, father, two brothers, two uncles, two cousins, nephew, father-in-law, brother-in-law, and sister-in-law (nearly all manual workers) – and many respondents had more than half a dozen. Nor was there any tendency for younger workers to have fewer relatives: although older workers were more eloquent about the importance of relatives, especially in recruitment, younger workers were more likely to have relatives with experience of the firm: 63 per cent of those aged under 25, 51 per cent aged 25–34, 63 per cent aged 35–44, 50 per cent aged 45–49, 62 per cent aged 50–54, 36 per cent aged 55–59, and 56 per cent of those aged 60 or more. During the 1930s the best way to obtain a decent job at the Mills was to have a relative already working there. 'My Dad worked there, so his son did: Dad knew the boss' (65-year-old craftsman). 'In them days you had to have a relation in the know to get into the Mills . . . my grandfather was a foreman and he put in a word for me' (54-year-old craftsman). Family tradition and 'speaking for' continued into the post-war period: as a 36-year old process worker explained: 'I started [at Casterton Mills] from school – uncle spoke for me and father too: more or less the whole family worked there and I was just following them.'[9] (For further discussion of contemporary job seeking see below, pp. 141–7.)

[9] For similar practices in nineteenth-century Lancashire see M. Anderson, *Family Structure in Nineteenth Century Lancashire*, Cambridge:

The limited alternative employment opportunities available, and the existence of extended kinship groups within the Mills, the 'Mills families' referred to by many respondents, helped to create a relatively stable labour force. The majority of Casterton Mills workers were long service workers, as the following table shows:

Length of Service

	Manual %	Non-Manual %
Under 6 months	7	2
6 months – 1·11 months	10	9
2 years – 4·11 months	12	14
5 years – 9·11 months	25	15
10 years – 19·11 months	22	27
20 years – 29·11 months	13	9
30+ years	12	23
	N = 116	N = 91

Thus 47 per cent of manual workers, and 59 per cent of non-manual workers, had been with the firm for 10 years or longer: 72 per cent of all those declared redundant had been with the firm for 10 years or longer. Length of service was, of course, associated with age: old workers had a record of longer service than young workers, and long service workers tended to be old. For example, 68 per cent of workers aged 55–59 had been with the firm for 10 years or longer, whilst as many as 20 per cent of workers aged 25–34 had been with the firm for less than two years, the largest proportion of any age group with such short service. Moreover, few employees had considered leaving the firm before the announcement of the redundancy – a mere 23 per cent, compared with the 47 per cent who actually left of

Cambridge University Press, 1971, pp. 118–20. 'Many employers consciously set out to recruit whole families, or all the younger members of families as they reached working age, or at least welcomed especially relatives of their employees. . . . Even where employers did not follow a deliberate policy of recruiting family members, workers, particularly if they were reliable, could often obtain places for children and other kin in the firm of a preferential basis. Thus, in cotton, . . . it was "customary upon the part of a father that you employ to make application to you, when a child is of the age of eight or nine years, to take him into a factory" ' (pp. 118–19).

their own accord following the announcement of the redundancy. In short, the majority of employees had been with the firm for a considerable proportion of their working lives, and a substantial majority regarded their commitment as a long term one.

Favourable economic conditions were a precondition for the continuance of paternalist capitalism, whilst the existence of kinship networks and a large core of long service workers within the firm facilititated the process of socialisation. Yet, in the last resort, paternalist capitalism rested upon power, derived partly from the firm's central role in the local labour market, and partly from the multitude of ties, economic and attitudinal, which bound Casterton Mills workers to their firm. This power was not usually exercised, needing to be used only when authority was challenged. But its importance is clear from management reactions to the protests which were organised following the announcement of the redundancy.

Two weeks after the announcement of the redundancy a protest march, followed by a public meeting in the Town Hall, was organised. Local MPs, trade union officials, council leaders, and other notables concerned with the effect of the redundancy upon the community, and with attempts to attract industrial investment to the area, spoke to the meeting. There were varying guesses about the size of the march and the meeting, estimates of the former ranging upward from 300. The major groups behind the march were the skilled craftsmen (electricians, engineers, printers), the focus of trade union activity within the plant; there were relatively few process workers (although some white collar workers said that the majority of marchers were from 'the process end', indicating clearly the existence of physical and social distance between the groups), and very few white collar workers: 40 per cent of the manual workers, and 10 per cent of the non-manual workers whom we interviewed went to the meeting in the Town Hall. Fatalism, status consciousness, and fear were the major reasons for the reluctance to go on the march. 'Just a waste of time – it was a *fait accompli* – it had been done. Waste of time even if had arranged a dozen meetings' (49-year-old manager). 'I felt as a staff man that I shouldn't go' (49-year-old manager). Management regarded the protest as at best a waste of time and at worst a betrayal, and actively discouraged employees from taking part. Foremen warned manual workers that they would be 'seen to' if they went on the march, an effective disincentive during the confusion of the redundancy, even if the warning was not acted upon. In one department overtime notices for the following weekend were held back until the march was over and the meeting had begun. One of the few white collar workers who went on the march explained: 'I nearly got the sack for it. The management said that anyone who went on the march would be sacked. I have always been a union man, and I thought that every union ought to be there. With management saying that, others were a bit frightened in our department, but I went with another chap. Up before management we made excuses. Me that I had gone to the dentists – I'd made an appointment and I called his bluff. If he had found out that I had been at the meeting I would have been out.'

The protest march, and the reactions to it of both management and workers, crystallised inchoate attitudes, providing a substantiated focus for the preceding discussion of general, and therefore in many respects speculative data. It reveals dramatically the complex of attitudes and resources which sustained the social structure: the mixture of dependent fatalism, of status consciousness, and in the last resort of power which sustained the structure of paternalist capitalism in the late 1960s. Normatively based authority becomes power once that authority is questioned or defied: but such questioning or defiance only occurs during a crisis. The redundancy at Casterton Mills was such a crisis for Casterton, and the events which surrounded it revealed much of the taken-for-granted world that had gone before.

IV

As the attitudes and behaviour of both management and workers showed, paternalist capitalism survived until the late 1960s. Yet there were indications that the system was disintegrating even before the official announcement of the redundancy early in 1967. As some respondents commented, younger men were unwilling to accept what their fathers had taken for granted, and many older respondents had children who had left the community in search of better opportunities elsewhere. Although a majority of young workers, especially young manual workers, still revealed 'traditional' attitudes, more young than old workers questioned the values of loyalty, obedience, and the acceptance of managerial authority. For example, only 66 per cent of manual workers aged under 45 believed that obedience and respect for authority were the most important characteristics of the good worker, compared with 88 per cent of those aged 45 or more; similar figures for non-manual workers were 48 and 66 per cent. Similar differences were revealed in the responses to other questions (Questions 205, 207, 213, 202), as the following table shows:

Manual Workers

% agreeing with:	-25	25-44	45-59	60-
putting self out	40*	71	85	79
managers give orders	67	75	68	80
obedience	45	71	81	78
loyalty leads to respect	83**	52	58	59

* only 5 respondents
** only 6 respondents

Non-Manual Workers

putting self out	75	100	85	88
managers give orders	50	80	94	71
obedience	39	52	54	92
loyalty leads to respect	15	19	29	36

It is unfortunately impossible to say whether or not the present older workers would have revealed a similar pattern of responses when younger to that revealed by present younger workers: even if it had been possible to obtain retrospective data from the sample it would not have been very useful, for obvious reasons. However, there is some indication that the difference between the age groups represented a difference between generations as much as a difference in life-cycle position, not least the informal comments made by many respondents. 'I think people of my generation are subservient, you know, a serf, they are tied, like to a farm. They are easily pushed around, cornered . . . not like my son . . . work isn't plentiful here, and beggars can't be choosers . . . lack of adventure built up over the years . . .' (55-year-old manager). The higher level of education of present younger workers, their greater exposure to different life styles through the mass media, the breakdown in the isolation of the community through improvements in road transport, the feedback into the community of information about ways of life elsewhere by emigrants, have all increased awareness of events and attitudes outside the community, and contributed to the slow change of traditional attitudes.

Such changes would probably have destroyed paternalist capitalism in the long run; support for managerial authority of the old kind would have slowly dribbled away, and management would have had either to resort to power more often, or to adopt a new style. However, the structure was initially threatened, and then destroyed, by another factor, the collapse of the floorcoverings market. As we have shown, the floorcoverings industry expanded and prospered during the post-war consumer boom. However, the market began to change in the early 1960s, and demand for Casterton Mills' products dropped sharply. This slump led to a defensive merger with a former rival, and consequently to considerable reorganisation, rationalisation, and eventually redundancy, examined in detail in subsequent chapters. But management began to adopt a more cost-conscious policy well before the announcement of the redundancy, and many workers complained of a change in the 'atmosphere' of the plant. The 'indulgency pattern' which had characterised the old family firm gave way to a more rigid and cost-conscious policy; the 'happy' atmosphere which had existed prior to the merger which preceded the redundancy changed to one of uncertainty and distrust. 'I was happy at Casterton Mills early on. It seemed to change completely after the merger: everything seemed to go "dead". At one time you could have a laugh and a joke – it was queer. . . . It changed the whole atmosphere' (37-year-old craftsman). The redundancy finally destroyed paternalist capitalism in Casterton, leading to an unfreezing of attitudes revealed in many of the interviews, just as the 1970 strike at Pilkington's Glass Company destroyed a similar structure, with similar attitudes, in a similar community, St Helens. It is to the redundancy, and to management's handling of it, that we turn now.

5 MANAGEMENT AND REDUNDANCY: THE PROCESS OF REDUNDANCY

In previous chapters we have attempted to depict the broad outlines of the recent social and economic development of Casterton and Casterton Mills, showing how the histories of the community and the Mills were bound up with each other, and how paternalist capitalism developed. Simultaneously, and partly in response to this community situation, Casterton Mills evolved its own distinctive enterprise culture, composed of an autocratic but often benevolent managerial style, and a deferential acceptance of managerial authority by subordinates. However, this culture was disrupted by the collapse of the economic conditions which had enabled it to persist, by a merger with a former competitor, by rationalisation, and eventually by the redundancy which forms the focus of this study. The problems this process of redundancy posed for management, the pressures to which management were subjected, form the subject matter of this chapter. Two related questions are answered. How did management cope with the redundancy? Why did management decide that certain workers were to be made redundant?

Answering these questions is complicated and difficult, partly for general theoretical reasons, partly for reasons specific to the study of redundancy, and partly for reasons specific to our research in Casterton. The general problems of inadequate self-awareness, of inaccurate memory, of 'bias' are difficult to resolve in any research, but are even more difficult where there are only a small number of respondents and each respondent is required to discuss critical events extensively. Moreover, research into redundancy is invariably *post hoc*. Like previous students of redundancy we arrived on the scene too late to observe directly the process of managerial decision making which preceded the redundancy, even if the firm had been willing to allow access to the angry and often bitter discussions which took place. Few sociologists have the close working relationship with a firm which would entitle them to advance information regarding controversial commercial decisions like a redundancy, and the few who have the necessary contacts are inhibited from publishing the results of their investigations by considerations of commercial confidentiality, as well as by justifiable doubts about the possibility of objectivity. Finally, there was considerable confusion at Casterton Mills, and many people, including senior managers, were uncertain about what was going on: managers were offering transfers to junior staff one day, only to find themselves redundant a short time later. One middle manager, who was responsible for choosing some of the redundant, did not know how he himself came to be made redundant – 'I would like to know that myself'. A redundant foreman commented: 'I asked Personnel how the redundant were chosen. They told me that they were dismayed that certain people were going and others staying. Immediate supervisors made recommendations I imagine. It seemed ridiculous that the company still in charge of our destiny didn't know what was going on.' Decisions regarding the detailed implementation of the redundancy were made by individual departmental managers, within guidelines drawn up centrally: confusion, uncertainty, and ignorance were therefore inevitable.

Despite these difficulties, especially those posed by partiality and distortion, the material we obtained from *post hoc* interviews with some of the managers involved and with the redundant themselves provides useful indications of some of the considerations likely to be important for those attempting to cope with redundancies or with other unpredictable processes. And even a partial study is useful in view of the dearth of published empirical studies of managers in action; despite the rapid expansion of industrial sociology in Britain, France, and the United States during the last fifteen years, and the emergence of large departments of 'management science', there is little empirical sociological data on managerial behaviour.[1] We have attempted to assess what managers were trying to do at Casterton Mills, and to elucidate the constraints that were operating upon them and preventing them from fulfilling their goals. This involves discussing managerial goals, both under normal operating conditions and during redundancy, and the constraints deriving from the managerial political system, as well as from the environment within which managers were attempting to operate – especially the economic, socio-technical, and labour relations environments.

I

Managers are concerned with a multitude of changing, often conflicting, individual, group and organisational goals, attempting to maintain some semblance of balance between them in a changing environment: the platitude that the only permanence is change is well justified. As Leonard Sayles has stressed, 'The one enduring objective of management is to build and maintain a predictable, reciprocating system of relationships, the behaviour patterns of which stay within reasonable physical limits. But this is seeking a moving equilibrium, since the parameters of the system . . . are evolving and changing.'[2] This moving equilibrium comprises the balance of exchanges necessary and sufficient for the maintenance of the relationship; its location, and survival, depend upon the coincidence of the goals of different actors (not, as some writers have alleged, upon the automatic process of organisational homeostasis).[3] In this fluid situation the relation between the goals of different managers is more comparable to the relation between the moving triangles of kinetic art, with their occasional symmetry,

[1] According to a survey sponsored by the British Sociological Association there were more research projects under way in 1968 in industrial sociology and the sociology of work than in any other specialism (M. P. Carter, Report on a Survey of Sociological Research in Britain, mimeo., n.d., p. 7a). Despite this there is no British work comparable to that of Melville Dalton on managerial behaviour, and the most influential study of managerial behaviour in Britain was published in 1961.

[2] L. Sayles, *Managerial Behaviour*, New York: McGraw-Hill, 1964, pp. 358–9.

[3] For example, A. K. Rice, *op. cit.*; cf. below p. 182.

95

than to the relation between the static lines of the production engineer's planning chart.

Managers possess three occupational identities, three sets of interests, and three sets of goals – personal, departmental, and organisational. The primary motivation for assuming an occupational role is personal, for income, security, sociability, esteem, autonomy, self-actualisation, or whatever. Consequently, the most important occupational identity, interests, and goals will be personal, and acceptance of departmental and organisational goals will be primarily as a means of achieving personal goals. However, personal goals can only be achieved by satisfying departmental, and, especially, organisational goals, i.e. satisfying the minimal conditions necessary for the maintenance of the relationship. Since the basic condition for the continuance of the organisation is the maintenance of the supply of capital, and the primary determinant of the maintenance of the supply of capital is the comparative rate of return on capital invested, maximisation of the rate of return upon capital invested might be expected to constitute the primary instrumental goal for management. However, this is not so; profit maximisation is not the major focus of managerial concern for three reasons: firstly, the internal provision of capital is extremely important, especially for large international companies for whom the intra-company transfer of capital is a useful means of spreading tax liabilities: secondly, because of the fragmentation of share-holding when capital is raised on the open market, and the consequent difficulty in exercising shareholders' rights; and thirdly, because of the readiness of shareholders to be satisfied with a customary, 'reasonable', rate or return on capital invested. This last was of particular importance at Casterton Mills.

Instead of profit maximisation, managers are normally primarily concerned with growth.[4] Individual, group and organisational goals may be satisfied simultaneously by a

[4] There is of course an extensive literature of managerial goals. For two important works, representing opposite points of view, see: R. Marris, *The Economic Theory of Managerial Capitalism*, Macmillan, 1966; and T. Nichols, *Ownership, Control, and Ideology*, George Allen & Unwin, 1970.

policy of growth. For the individual, growth provides greater opportunities for responsibility and thus self-actualisation, as well as increased income. For the department, overall growth increases the total amount of resources available for use, demonstrates success to the outside world, and reduces the intensity of inter-departmental conflict. For the organisation, growth may be justified as a demonstration of corporate prestige, an obvious indication of success, and as a way of maximising the (long run) rate of return on capital invested. In short, in game theory terms, managers are involved in a positive sum game during periods of growth; all interests can be successfully reconciled.

During periods of economic stability the primary managerial goal is thus growth, of the firm in general and of the department in particular. However, during redundancies different circumstances obviously obtain, for growth is patently impossible; the happy congruence between individual, group, and organisational goals disintegrates. The primary individual goal is withdrawal from the firm in the most favourable circumstances, and with as little discomfort, as possible. At Casterton Mills some younger managers, with transferable skills, left as soon as possible; the much larger group of older managers either stayed with the firm and accepted transfer to headquarters, or attempted to negotiate favourable terms and conditions for redundancy and left. This group of redundant line managers were to experience the most acute problems in finding further employment, as we will show later (below, pp. 133–4). Pressing personal preoccupations thus limited managerial involvement in the organisational and departmental systems.

Management's major official goal during the redundancy was the reduction of labour costs by the planned release of manpower and the retention of control over a labour force whose inducements to contribute to the enterprise were declining. The redundancy exacerbated problems of work discipline, undermining managerial authority over young workers who were looking out for the best opportunity to leave the firm, and exaggerating managerial authority over older workers who were fearful of being declared redundant: the result was inevitably acrimony, 'stabbing each other in the back', demoralisation, confusion, and reduced productivity. As one clerical worker who left of his own accord explained: 'When they started making people redundant they had us all in the office, and told us that we would be made redundant in 3, 6, 12 or 18 months, or that our jobs were secure. I was selected to stay on. I didn't think we were being treated fairly. We were not getting anything extra, financially, for the extra work we were doing. With people being made redundant we were getting extra work thrown on to us. They amalgamated two departments, and we were promised that we would be financially better off, but nothing came of that that we would not have got by the normal processes of increases. Then I was promoted, if you can call it that . . . got nothing for it.' At the same time, the redundancy allowed managers to repay obligations, or to pay off old scores, amongst the committed workers. Managers could reward favoured long-service employees by arranging a mutually convenient date for redundancy, providing workers with a substantial lump sum cash payment whilst minimising the risk of unemployment. They could also pay off old scores by arranging for the transfer of known trouble-makers from department to department, under cover of reorganisation, until the worker's demoralisation became acute and caused him to leave of his own accord, with consequent loss of redundancy pay.

Managerial goals, and the relations between them, are thus completely different during redundancies from those obtaining under more stable operating conditions. Normally, managers can satisfy individual goals, reach satisfactory arrangements with other managers, and fulfil organisational goals at the same time, through seeking growth. This is impossible during redundancies; individuals cannot satisfy their personal goals through satisfying organisational and departmental ones. Individual goals cease to be consistent with departmental and organisational ones, which cease to be consistent with themselves and with each other; the usual system of alliances and joint preference rankings collapses. The general tightness of resources, the need to struggle to retain 'essential' workers in the face of external pressure to achieve labour economies, and attempts to limit burgeoning interference by the personnel function, exaggerate competition between departments. Mutually convenient arrangements between departments, like the 'indulgency pattern' established between some production departments and the personnel office at Casterton Mills, are thrown into disarray. Departmental goals conflict with organisational goals, as well as with the goals of other departments; departments wish to maintain pre-existing patterns of behaviour, and thus costs, whilst the organisation wishes to reduce costs, and thus disrupt pre-existing patterns of behaviour. Hence individual, group, and organisational goals can only be satisfied at the expense of each other; individual goals at the expense of those of other individuals, departments and the organisation; departmental goals at the expense of individual, other departmental, and organisational goals, and organisational goals at the expense of those of individuals and departments. In short, a positive sum game has become a zero-sum game – with the sum continually diminishing.

Such a transformation highlights the managerial political system.

II

Organisations are political, as well as administrative, systems; individuals group themselves into coalitions on the basis of statuses, individual, group, and organisational goals, and divergent role conceptions, and maintain these coalitions through formal and informal interactions. Individual and group differences lead to conflicting preferences, resolved only by the formulation of conditional, compromise, joint preference orderings, the outcome of competition and reconciliation within a partially integrated culture. The respective power of the different coalitions, the extent of their control over relevant desired resources, determines the outcome of such competition. Amongst managers, the most important desired resources are the control over men and materials necessary for the fulfilment of departmental and organisational goals, and knowledge. Although there are normally bureaucratic rules governing the allocation of resources for managerial use, efficient operations involve obtaining the required resources at a specific time, often in competition with others with an equally legitimate claim upon them; informal understandings, like those between some line managers and stores managers at the Milo plant analysed by Melville Dalton, are often necessary.[5] Similarly, although there are recognised channels for communicating relevant information to managers, advance information about impending changes is often helpful. Alliances, and antagonisms, develop out of such operationally required informal understandings. Bureaucracy, in the Weberian ideal-type, is characterised by formality, rationality, authority, and hierarchy; industrial organisations, if they are to be effective in a changing environment, require informality, non-rationality, power, and lateral communication.

Political alliances and coalitions become of primary importance during periods of uncertainty and rapid change, like redundancies, as managers attempt to control a problematic environment. Change and uncertainty lead managers to activate their informal alliances, to cash their 'obligations cheques', at best as a means of obtaining advance notice about their own fate, at worst as a means of assuaging their own feelings of vulnerability. Consequently, the manager responsible for administering redundancies is likely to be subject to intense formal and, especially, informal pressure from managers eager to preserve their own empires or, where authoritative policy decisions make this impossible, to secure their own future in the general disorder. Hence the political strength of the personnel function becomes of primary importance during redundancy. This strength is likely to be greatest where the relevant official has not already built up a network of contacts and obligations, which others will attempt to use to their own advantage, and which he will be unable to disregard unless he is prepared to face social isolation. Management consultants, or specially recruited personnel officers, are popular with firms worried by excessive costs and considering rationalisation and redundancy, because of their isolation from the firm's political

[5] M. Dalton, *Men Who Manage*, New York: John Wiley & Son, 1959, esp. Chapter 3. See also M. Crozier, *The Bureaucratic Phenomenon*, Tavistock Publications, 1964, for management as a political system.

system, their lack of political obligations, as much as for their professional expertise.

The policy adopted for the reorganisation of Casterton Mills was the result of an investigation by management consultants, the management consultant responsible for the report being brought into the firm specifically to carry the reconstruction and rationalisation through; a new personnel officer was appointed with responsibility for the Casterton Mills plant, again to carry through the changes. Both were outsiders, isolated from the firm's political system. Both proved capable of resisting pressures from other managers who wished to maintain the pre-existing structure, resulting in some cases in the resignation of opponents during the early stages of the argument over reorganisation. Production managers, worried about their own futures, doubtful of their ability to maintain output quotas with a changing and demoralised labour force, and jealous of any reduction in the size of their departments and thus in their company status, attempted to maintain their labour force, without success. At the same time, they were reluctant to accept the transfer of long service or other particularly valuable workers from other departments due to be closed or run down, because of the anticipated disruption of established work groups and known procedures. A latent function of the decentralisation of the selection of personnel to be declared redundant was the reassurance it provided line managers that they were still in control of at least one aspect of their formal responsibilities.

In short, managerial goals, personal, departmental and organisational, and managerial role conceptions, form the basis for coalitions and political alignments, and through the medium of formal and informal preference rankings help to determine the process of the redundancy. The central organisational objective of the planned release of manpower is rendered problematic. However, such factors are tractable, capable of manipulation by a determined senior management pushed by compelling economic difficulties. Less tractable are the external constraints, especially where redundancy is the result of uncontrollable changing patterns in consumer demand rather than technical change. Amongst the most important 'external' constraints are the firm's market situation, the plant socio-technical system, the power of the labour force, and the overarching network of norms and values which regulate redundancy procedure, whether enshrined in statute or merely in informal understandings. The remainder of this chapter discusses these external constraints, and their variable salience.

III

The significance of the firm's market situation for the process of redundancy obviously depends upon whether the reason for redundancy is technological change or changes in the level of demand for the good produced. Where changes in the demand for labour are due to technological change manpower planning can be integrated into an overall development plan, and to some extent insulated from uncertainties, especially where closure is sectional rather than unit: wastage, early retirement, stoppage of recruitment, and other practices can be used to avoid redundancy, as in the chemical, printing, and steel plants investigated by L. C. Hunter and G. L. Reid in their research on the impact of technological change upon the labour force.[6] Where changes in the need for labour are the result of changing market preferences there is less room for management to manoeuvre, and market constraints are the most salient and pressing.

The redundancy at Casterton Mills was the result of changes in consumer preferences. The market for floor-coverings began to decline sharply in the early 1960s, and Casterton Mills, like other floor-coverings firms, experienced a sharp fall in earnings. The company failed to make the necessary swift adjustment to changes in consumer preferences, and attempts to buy smaller companies in related fields as a means of diversification and expansion were not completely successful. Consequently, in the early 1960s Casterton Mills was forced to merge with a former rival. The domestic market collapsed completely in the mid-1960s, and profits slumped, eventually disappearing completely in 1966 and 1967. The effects of the reorganisation which

[6] L. C. Hunter, G. L. Reid, and D. Boddy, *Labour Problems of Technological Change*, George Allen & Unwin, 1970.

followed the merger were slow to work through, and commercial difficulties continued beyond the announcement of the redundancy: between 1967 and 1968 the financial situation scarcely improved; a trading loss of £478,000 in 1967 was followed by a profit of £174,000 in 1968, a derisory return on turnover of over £15 million. This continuing poor performance was due to three major reasons, purely financial considerations, for example the need to buy out minority interests, the costs of rationalisation and reorganisation which would pay off in the long run, and the continuing problems of the floor-coverings industry. The declining demand and intense competition which had led to the need for reorganisation continued throughout the redundancy; in 1968 the floor-coverings division of the company produced a profit of under £100,000 on a turnover of over £15 million. As if to compound confusion, new lines began to catch on whilst the traditional products continued to face acute difficulties; the demand for some new patterns and for recently introduced lines soared, as the demand for conventionally made floor-coverings dropped. Unfortunately, the firm had difficulty in predicting patterns of demand in this confusing situation.

This unpredictable situation obviously exerted considerable pressure upon management, attempting to rationalise production, realise surplus assets, and run down the labour force as quickly as possible, yet eager to take advantage of any upsurge in consumer demand, however temporary it may prove to be. Some managers were seeing their departments, and their jobs, disappear whilst others were taking on more labour; competition and confusion were inevitable. Decline and uncertainty effected the labour force directly, as well as indirectly through management behaviour: 'I would have stayed, except that towards the end I got fed up, you didn't know if you would be there next week, plus the fact that was no new work coming in [to our department]. The atmosphere was shocking . . . the people who stayed would give anything to get out' (35-year-old craftsman). Even before the redundancy the decline in demand had resulted in reduced production bonuses (an important component in earnings in an industry with a low basic wage), and less overtime. There had been an increase in turnover, especially among young process workers for whom bonus payments and overtime were an important element in earnings. The announcement of the redundancy, and the increased publicity this attracted to the firm's marketing difficulties, exaggerated this concern, and led to a change in the character of labour turnover (see below, pp. 110–1). The result was to distort the age structure of the labour force in the direction opposite to that desired by management, who could only retain control over older, committed workers who feared the prospect of having to look for another job, and who wished to retain their redundancy pay entitlement.

IV

During the redundancy at Casterton Mills the major constraints upon managers were economic, the need to reduce labour costs because of declining profitability. However, decisions about laying off labour cannot be made solely on the basis of economic considerations, for there are obvious technological limitations to the extent to which certain sections of a plant can be closed, certain work roles dispensed with. This is obviously so where operations are to be continued at a reduced level, where closure is 'sectional' rather than 'unit', but it is equally so where production is to be phased out.

There are four major strategies for reducing labour requirements, in addition to simply closing particular sections: reducing the speed of running machinery, and consequently reducing handling staff; watering down manning levels; reducing the number of shifts; and reducing the number of machines performing similar tasks. The technological requirements of the production system are the major determinants of the relevance of each strategy. Reductions in the speed of running machinery are only possible where materials used in manufacture do not degenerate, as chemicals do, and only likely where the ratio of capital to labour costs is low. The degree of flexibility possible in manning levels is obviously limited by the nature of the work roles, and by the requirements of safety regulations; in any case, attempts to reduce manning levels are likely to cause industrial relations problems at a time when industrial relations are likely to be strained. The number of shifts can obviously only be reduced where shift working has been introduced because of the level of demand for output, not where it is a technical necessity; in industries with continuous process technologies, for example chemicals in general and artificial fibres in particular, continuous running is required to prevent machinery from clogging up.

In short, the extent of the interdependence between different parts of the production process is obviously a major determinant of management's room for manoeuvre.

For these purposes socio-technical systems can be classified into three categories: long-linked, in turn sub-divided into large batch and process, mediating and intensive, each of which has a distinctive pattern of interdependence and therefore poses different problems for management.[7] Long linked technologies, for example motor car assembly plants and chemical plants, have a basically sequential type of interdependence, completion of one operation being a necessary precondition for starting on the next. Mediating technologies (for example banking) have a basically pooled type of interdependence, individual operatives drawing materials from a common pool but not depending directly upon any other single operation. Intensive technologies (for example dentistry) are characterised by a minimal level of interdependence, work tasks comprising a complete cycle of operations on a single object. Long linked technologies, especially large batch, impose the tightest restrictions on managerial initiative, intensive technologies the least, with mediating technologies in the middle. The interconnectedness of the production process, and the interdependence between work roles, makes the reduction in the number of operatives difficult, although it is sometimes possible to reduce the speed of the line, increase the scope of operations at particular 'conversion stations', and thus thin out the line. On the other hand, intensive technologies pose no comparable problems: if the

[7] J. D. Thompson, *Organisation in Action*, New York: McGraw-Hill' 1967, pp. 16–17, where the terms are defined only slightly differently from here. For a useful survey of the literature on technology and worker behaviour see M. Meissner, *Technology and the Worker*, San Francisco: Chandler Publishing Co., 1969.

105

demand for dental treatment declines the dismissal of one dentist has few implications for the work of those remaining. Redundancy increases unit costs in mediating technologies, but does not produce the additional difficulties cited in long linked technologies.

This threefold classification of technologies provides a framework for the analysis of the implications of socio-technical systems for managerial decision-making during redundancy, but cannot be applied automatically to particular plants, for plants cannot be easily categorised in unitary terms. The apparent chaos of the Casterton Mills plant, the result of over a century of piece-meal expansion, diversification, and technological change on a large site, comprised five major sections: production departments of various kinds, maintenance departments, warehouse and despatch departments, the power station, together with their supporting handling staffs, and scientific and administrative offices. Each section possessed a different socio-technical system, and thus imposed different constraints. The production departments, especially the floor-coverings departments, possessed a long linked technology, with small groups manning machinery in a sequentially inter-dependent production system: manning levels were determined by the demands of the machinery, custom and practice, and work group power – during the period of the redundancy primarily the first. The major strategies followed for losing labour were a reduction in the number of shifts, and a reduction in the number of machines performing similar work. It was impossible to reduce the speed of running the line, for some processes involving the use of paint and oil possessed invariable time spans; the only way to save staff was by the introduction of expensive mechanised or automated monitoring and control systems, clearly impossible in the circumstances. The warehouse and despatch and maintenance departments possessed 'intensive' technologies, and posed few problems for management. In the warehouse, individual workers, or very small groups of workers, were engaged in packing and despatching the finished product in variable but usually small batches; work loads were determined directly by the level of sales and the availability of transport, and indirectly by the output of the plant. As sales and output fell the warehouse could be run down as management wished. The major tasks of the maintenance departments were the regular upkeep of plant and buildings, the occasional repair of plant during production, and the production of one-off prototypes or special jobs. Since such tasks involved only a simple division of labour and little interdependence between work roles, there was little technical difficulty in achieving the planned run-down of manpower. Finally, the power station possessed a long linked technology of the process kind; the generation of electricity involved continuous operation. Manpower levels could be somewhat reduced to meet the smaller work load required by the diminishing demand for power from the rest of the plant, but below a fairly high critical point continuing operations became unsafe, as well as uneconomical. The power station could therefore only be closed as a unit, all the staff, except for a small group retained for maintenance work, being declared redundant at the same time.

In short, the socio-technical system, and especially the degree of interdependence between work roles, sets variable limits to management's ability to implement redundancies according to its own wishes. Except where feather-bedding is the rule, labour can only be released where it is substitutable; the extent to which substitution is possible is determined by the socio-technical system. Where individuals or departments are superfluous, or substitutable, other considerations determine the process of redundancy.

V

The power of the work group may be organised, through trade union representation and less formalised institutions, or unorganised, expressing itself in group activities of varying degrees of formality or in individual initiatives. Both formal and informal expressions of work group power constitute significant constraints upon managerial behaviour. Trade unions exert pressure for work sharing, or where this is impossible for the cessation of hiring and allowing 'natural wastage' to take its course and for transfers within the company, or where external factors make some dismissals inevitable for strict adherence to agreed procedures. However, trade unions exert less influence upon managerial behaviour during redundancies, especially redundancies caused by changes in the demand for a firm's product, than might be expected, partly because managers are already subject to pressing economic exigencies, and partly because redundancies pose acute moral problems for trade unions who fear that readiness to discuss redundancy procedures could be interpreted as acceptance of redundancy itself: unions surrender their claim to the joint regulation of redundancy by opposing redundancies completely. The absence of standard procedures and payments in the printing industry, where the trade unions are of course extremely strong, is largely due to union reluctance to countenance redundancy. Similarly, the National Union of Railwaymen refused to discuss with British Railways which railways workshops should be closed in 1962 on the grounds that 'they could not be a party to condemning any of their members to unemployment and that the choice for closure must be a managerial decision'.[8] It is thus not surprising that the trade union movement initially opposed the Redundancy Payments Act, preferring to concentrate attention upon wage-related unemployment benefits instead; nor that the Redundancy Payments Act makes no provision for trade union participation; nor that only 91 per cent of the managements interviewed by the Government Social Survey in their survey on *Effects of the Redundancy Payments Act* reported that they had redundancy agreements with trade unions.[9] Union interest in the joint regulation of redundancy has been limited, and union attempts to influence redundancies generally ineffective: in the Government Social Survey report 61 per cent of redundant union members who received redundancy pay, and 69 per cent of redundant union members who did not receive redundancy pay reported that their union had not taken any action at all, and 26 per cent and 17 per cent respectively reported that the union or the shop stewards had offered advice but not action.[10]

[8] D. Wedderburn, *Redundancy and the Railwaymen*, Cambridge: Cambridge University Press, 1965, p. 37.

[9] S. R. Parker, C. G. Thomas, N. D. Ellis, W. E. J. McCarthy, *Effects of the Redundancy Payments Act*, H.M.S.O., 1971, p. 49.

[10] S. R. Parker *et al.*, *op. cit.*, p. 80. Of course some workers have taken the matter into their own hands, as recent events at Clydebank and Alexandria show.

Organised work group power exerted only a limited influence upon redundancy procedure at Casterton Mills, and virtually no influence at all upon the number of men who were declared redundant. The seriousness of the firm's economic problems, and the only limited flexibility permitted by the socio-technical system of large sections of the plant, as well as the generally low level of unionisation, limited the significance of organised work group power. The level of unionisation was highest amongst the maintenance workers, especially the electricians, where the constraints imposed by the socio-technical system upon management were least, and among workers in the power station (the Power Workers Section of the T.G.W.U.). Accordingly, although the unions were unable to resist the redundancy, they had relatively little difficulty in securing adherence to the principle of last in first out amongst electricians and engineers, despite the general rule of dismissal at the discretion of the departmental manager. Elsewhere the level of unionisation was too low to make much impact upon management. Unfortunately the only department with a high level of unionisation and a high degree of interdependence between work roles was the power station, where technological considerations dictated redundancy procedure: management had no alternative but to close the power station as a unit, and there was no room for bargaining or manoeuvre. There was no other department where examination of the contrasting demands of the socio-technical system and organised work groups would permit an assessment of the relative importance of the two sets of constraints.

The relative ineffectiveness of trade unions in influencing management during the redundancy at Casterton Mills did not mean that workers were completely powerless; even an atomised work force can exert pressure upon management, by voting with its feet, especially where management wishes to keep the plant operating at a lower level of output. Unexpected changes in the character of labour turnover, and the unpredictability of consumer choice, disrupted the redundancy schedule at Casterton Mills, placed difficulties in the way of management attempting to continue operating part of the plant, and eventually forced management to halt the redundancy completely. From the beginning of the reorganisation management had intended to continue operating part of the plant at Casterton Mills, and to introduce new processes; this original intention was reinforced by a sudden improvement in the level of demand, and by unexpected difficulties in transferring work and labour to the newly consolidated plant. However, employees acted upon their own evaluation of the firm's prospects and of their own prospects in a potentially tight local labour market, and exaggerated the rate of decline in the firm's manpower requirements; the redundancy, which should have been spread over three years, lasted for less than two. Young workers particularly, untrammelled by the prospect of forfeiting substantial redundancy payments, tended to leave within the first few months of the announcement of the redundancy, and before there had been any substantial dismissals: the accuracy of their assessment of the labour market was revealed by their success in obtaining better earnings than redundant leavers (see below, p. 150). Comparisons between the level of turnover for the period of redundancy and earlier years are difficult to make, for the firm suspended recruitment and, by so doing, probably reduced its level of turnover compared with 'normal' years, when a substantial drifting population of semi- and unskilled workers were taken on to cope with seasonal peaks in demand. However, although there was little change in the overall level of turnover, there was a marked change in its character; the usual floating population of unskilled workers who made up the bulk of labour turnover was supplemented by a number of more stable workers, who had been with the firm for a number of years, and had gained useful firm-related skills. As the following table shows, the proportion of voluntary leavers who had been with the firm for more than two years but less than ten, who were marked out as forming the nucleus of the reconstructed labour force, rose from 13 per cent in 1964–5 to 36 per cent in 1967–8, the period of the redundancy (the figures have been calculated from February to February, to maintain comparability with the period of the redundancy). Some of these workers would perhaps have been made redundant anyway, but many would have been retained as the core of the reduced labour force.

110

Manual Workers: Length of Service of Voluntary Leavers 1967–8 and of All Turnover in Three Previous Years

Length of service	1967–8	1966–7	1965–6	1964–5
	%	%	%	%
Under 2 years	55	68	61	75
2–5 years	19	11	13	9
6–10 years	17	9	11	4
11–20 years	7	8	10	5
21–30 years	1	2	1	3
over 30 years	—	3	4	3
Not known	1	—	—	—

The significance of increased, or more costly, labour turnover obviously depends upon the importance management attaches to keeping the plant open, or to maintaining control of the redundancy. Where the plant is to be closed completely an increase in labour turnover may simply facilitate the process, or modify the schedule; where management intends to continue operations it is obviously a serious blow, which management must attempt to avert.

VI

In the widest sense cultural values seep into managers through the process of socialisation, moulding characteristic responses; cultural environment in this sense is beyond the scope of our study. Here we are primarily concerned with narrower and more direct influences, with the formal prescriptions and the informal norms regarding redundancy which have been embodied in legislation and in authoritative public pronouncements. The Contracts of Employment Act contains minimum rules for dismissals in general, and the Redundancy Payments Act specifies required periods of notice and other procedures for dismissals involving claims upon the Redundancy Payments Fund. Similarly, conceptions of equity and job property rights influence managerial attitudes, and prevent a completely instrumental attitude towards redundancy.

Political attitudes towards redundancy are reflected in legislation, and in the amount of pressure exerted to secure implementation of legislation; they may be favourable, unfavourable, or ambivalent. The attitude of different British governments towards redundancies has been ambivalent, although less ambivalent since 1970 than it was during the period of the Labour government between 1964 and 1970; redundancies are approved of in general, but disapproved of in particular situations. The dominant attitude is one of regretful approval: redundancy is regarded as part of the price that has to be paid for a dynamic economy, or one of the costs of wage inflation and industrial inefficiency. The Labour government of 1964–70 repeatedly stressed that redundancy and involuntary labour mobility were necessary 'to achieve the planned use of resources, especially our resources of manpower'; redundancy, and if necessary temporary unemployment, was an inevitable by-product of modernisation, and it was the government's task to minimise the hardships produced, not to prevent redundancies from occurring.[11]

Redundancy has become accepted by successive governments as inevitable. However, it has also become generally recognised that workers possess some forms of job property rights, that redundancies should be carried out in a legitimated and considerate manner, and that workers should be compensated for the loss of their jobs. Hence the level of redundancy payments is related to the value of the job lost, and the worker's commitment to it, not to the extent of the financial problems involved: length of service, and higher earnings, are regarded as implying a heavier commitment to the job, and therefore should be compensated. Similarly, it has been widely argued that the most equitable procedure for carrying out redundancies is adherence to the 'last in first out' principle. As J. E. T. Eldridge has argued, 'At a very general level there is an evaluative consensus relating to the kind of considerations that, it is felt, should apply. These beliefs may be expressed as follows: (1) The number of employees to be dismissed should be kept to a minimum. (2) Length of service should be taken into account so that, broadly, the rule "last in first out" should operate. (3) But the rule may be modified on certain grounds: (*a*) Some groups or individuals may be held to have less claim

[11] See the debate on the Redundancy Payments Bill, April 1965, *Hansard, 1965*, Vol. 711, p. 33.

on a job regardless of their seniority (e.g. married women, men over 65); (*b*) Some groups or individuals may be held to have more claim to a job regardless of seniority, (i) on the grounds of efficiency, (ii) on the grounds of special need (e.g. handicapped workers, young men finishing apprenticeship).'[12]

However, this consensus is far from complete, and may be changing as a result of the operation of the Redundancy Payments Act.[13] For the existence of age-related redundancy payments may have reduced trade union and worker insistence upon the principle of 'last in first out', and thus allowed management to be more 'flexible' in the criteria used for selecting the redundant. Perhaps more importantly, managers may feel that the existence of the scheme legitimises dismissing older workers: 63 per cent of managers who thought that the Redundancy Payments Act made the discharge of employees easier referred to the easing of conscience.[14] Moreover, the generality of the norm of 'last in first out' allows a generous lee-way for variations in interpretation at enterprise level. Dismissal procedures at Casterton Mills were highly decentralised, individual departmental managers being responsible for the final selection, and there were no generally agreed and recognised principles governing who should be selected. This absence of clear principles was not unusual: the Government Social Survey reported that about a fifth of companies which had experienced redundancies had no criteria for selecting the redundant. Moreover, the general weakness of the norm of last in first out is shown clearly by the distorted age structure of the redundant compared with the age structure of the working population as a whole: according to the Government Social Survey, 44 per cent of workers who received redundancy payments were aged 50 or more, compared with 31 per cent of the non-redundant.[15] (For further details of the significance of age for redundancy

[12] J. E. T. Eldridge, *Industrial Disputes*, pp. 207–8.

[13] Professor Eldridge commented, personal communication 1971, that he thought the Consett redundancy he studied (*Industrial Disputes*, Chapter 6) would have happened very differently if the Redundancy Payments Act had been in force when it occurred. Cf. S. R. Parker *et al.*, *op. cit.*, p. 49.

[14] S. R. Parker *et al.*, *op. cit.*, p. 63.

[15] *Ibid.*, p. 95.

see below, pp. 131-3.) Strict adherence to a policy of last in first out would, of course, have resulted in a negatively skewed distribution of ages, instead of a positively skewed distribution. In short, although there are legal and cultural constraints upon managerial behaviour during redundancy, they are relatively weak; the legal requirements are only skeletal, whilst the cultural proscriptions are both vague and limited. Managers are subject to too great an economic pressure, especially during redundancies resulting from changes in the level of demand rather than technological innovation, to pay much attention to worthy but insubstantial cultural constraints.

VII

Managers attempting to carry out the redundancy at Casterton Mills were thus subject to strong pressures – from other managers, from market uncertainties, from the often intractable socio-technical system, from the labour force, and from the expectations of the community at large. In addition, and cutting across these conflicts, was the basic conflict between the demands of economic rationality, i.e. for behaviour which accorded with top management's desire to reduce labour costs with as little expense and trouble as possible, and the pattern of expectations which had evolved as part of the culture of paternalist capitalism. For the announcement of the redundancy struck directly at the long-standing structure of paternalist capitalism, destroying it dramatically. The result was ambivalence and conflict amongst both management and workers.

Some senior managers who were completely opposed to the run-down at Casterton Mills left when they saw that they had been defeated; others stayed and attempted to see that the redundancy was carried out as far as possible according to traditional norms. The company's manifest financial difficulties, its weak political position as the smaller partner in a recently formed combine, and the introduction of a new personnel officer to implement the redundancy, made an approximation to economically rational behaviour likely. However, both the benevolence and the autocracy of paternalist capitalism were also evident. There was some attempt to fulfil obligations by

114

minimising hardship amongst the redundant, and by providing generous assistance to favoured long-term employees. Financial considerations governed the overall conception of the redundancy, but paternal responsibility survived in the rules of the firm's own redundancy payments scheme, and in the way in which the rules were applied in specific cases. The firm was willing to discuss individual problems with the men concerned, and a large number of partially disabled and sick men, whose productivity was low, were declared redundant, to their own advantage as well as to that of the firm. Wherever possible extended periods of notice were given, extending to 18 months in some cases. As one senior manager claimed, 'I think firms with a family background have more feeling there. If Casterton Mills had been I.C.I. the redundancy would have been much quicker, and more ruthless.'

The autocratic aspect of paternalist capitalism was also evident: there was no prior consultation with representatives of the labour force, and little consultation during the implementation of the redundancy, for example over selection criteria. There was no official announcement of the procedures to be followed, and there was considerable uncertainty amongst workers about how the redundant were selected. As the following table shows, 53 per cent of respondents had no idea how the redundant were chosen, and the remaining 47 per cent did not agree with each other:

How Were the Redundant Chosen? (Q. 101)

	Manual %	Non-Manual %	Total Total %
Seniority	6	3	5
Age	12	—	7
Reduction overstaffing	—	3	1
By department	12	35	22
Lower grade first cut	10	—	6
Other	6	9	7
No idea	55	51	53
	N = 51	N = 37	N = 88

It was characteristic of the Mills that this lack of knowledge was not a cause of serious concern.

The reaction of the labour force to management's handling

of the redundancy was predictably ambivalent. On the one hand, it was recognised that the merger and subsequent events made some redundancies inevitable. On the other hand, it was felt that Casterton Mills was still a viable plant, and that it was unfair, as well as uneconomic, for the firm to concentrate its resources elsewhere. Many respondents stressed that the plant to be expanded was badly organised and old-fashioned compared with Casterton Mills: the desire of the other partner to the amalgamation to look after its own, and the mistaken principles of government development area policy, were seen as the major reasons for consolidation elsewhere. The effect of this was to further complicate workers' attitudes towards management's handling of the redundancy, for many respondents distinguished between Casterton Mills 'local' management and the 'higher-ups' who came from the former rival. Respondents were asked whether they thought that management was seriously worried by having to make large numbers of men redundant. As the following table shows, many respondents spontaneously distinguished between local management and the higher management, saying that the former were concerned but the latter were not.

Management's Concern at the Redundancy (Q. 84)

	Manual %	Non-Manual %
Shop management concerned	36	35
General management concerned	1	0
All management indifferent	52	52
No choice	0	2
	N = 100	N = 88

Thirty-six per cent of manual workers, and 35 per cent of non-manual workers, thus believed that shop management was worried at having to declare men redundant, despite the evident responsibility which local management carried for choosing people to be made redundant, for deciding about redundancy pay entitlement, etc. As one white collar worker explained: 'When you talk of management at Casterton Mills do you mean the [new managers] or [those who have always been there]? Those brought in from outside weren't worried, we

116

were only people. The managers [who had always been there] who were part of the new set up were just as concerned as we were. We were a family at Casterton Mills – they knew us all personally. Not just a relationship of boss and employee – we knew them as people and they knew us . . . they were very upset.' Others had a less altruistic explanation for the concern of local management – fear of losing their own jobs: 'I think they were more worried than us . . . they were sacking bosses as well. In fact the bosses and foremen went first – there were too many of them' (49-year-old process worker). 'The local bosses, local management, department supervisors, thought it was wrong. They were scared they'd lose their jobs, more worried than working men to be honest. They felt if they had no men they would have no jobs either' (43-year-old process worker). Older workers were more inclined to believe that local management was concerned than younger workers, and thus the redundant more than the voluntary leavers.

VIII

Management's handling of the redundancy at Casterton Mills was thus determined by two sets of factors: firstly, customary expectations and patterns of behaviour which had evolved over a century, and become accepted by 'old' management and workers alike; and secondly, short-run pressures deriving from the firm's economic difficulties, socio-technical system, the balance of power both between management and workers and within management itself, and general expectations regarding the conduct of redundancies. Analysis of any redundancy must take account of both sets of factors. The extent to which management is able to act 'rationally', i.e. able to run down its labour force according to its own preferences and timetable, will vary with the extent to which management is subject to these pressures. The situation in which management is most likely to be able to control redundancy is where it is agreed amongst itself, and where the external constraints upon managerial behaviour are minimal. Such a situation is most likely to occur where the following conditions are met: the demand for a firm's products drops precipitously; the plant socio-technical system is intensive (or small batch) with loosely connected work roles; the managerial role is conceived in authoritarian terms, with labour regarded as a commodity; there are no ancillary managerial goals; the labour force is atomised, and where the manager responsible for carrying out the redundancy is politically powerful. At the opposite end of the scale, management is least likely to be able to control the redundancy where the constraints upon managerial action are at a maximum. Such a situation is likely where the demand for a firm's products varies unpredictably, the managerial role is conceived in benevolently paternalist terms, political institutions hedge dismissals around with legal and cultural prescriptions, the socio-technical system is long-linked, with a highly interdependent structure of work roles, the labour force is highly organised, management possesses a number of ancillary goals, for example the preservation of status in comparison with other managers in the same area, and the political power of the manager charged with the redundancy is limited.

The redundancy at Casterton Mills, like most redundancies, fell between the two poles. There, the economic environment was highly unpredictable, the socio-technical system was partly long-linked, partly intensive, the work force was badly organised, and the wider social environment posed few difficulties. At the same time, management possessed a number of ancillary goals, and worked within a firmly based tradition of paternalism. The manager responsible for the redundancy was in a politically powerful position, having been brought in specifically to do the job. In short, some factors facilitated the effective fulfilment of managerial intentions, and others inhibited such fulfilment. The result was that management faced considerable difficulty in carrying out the redundancy, largely because the most salient factor in the situation, the economic environment, was the least predictable.

The policies of the management, and the way in which they were distorted by external pressures, determined the composition of the groups of workers dismissed. We turn now to examine directly the experience of the redundant and the voluntary leavers following their departure from Casterton Mills.

6 THE EFFECTS OF THE REDUNDANCY: REDUNDANCY AND UNEMPLOYMENT

Following the merger Casterton Mills management assured its employees that their futures were secure: that the enlarged firm would be better able to compete with other firms, especially in Europe, and that there would be no need for redundancies. Most employees accepted these assurances, only a minority subsequently claiming that they had seen the writing on the wall from the time of the merger. However, management had misjudged the situation in general, and the extent of the economies which management consultants would consider necessary in particular. Substantial redundancies were therefore announced on the afternoon of 31 January 1967, to a general Works Meeting in the Works Canteen, and to a meeting of staff management in the Board Room: staff departmental heads and supervisors carried the information to their subordinates. The announcement came as a complete shock to most employees – many could recall the precise time they received the news in interviews over eighteen months later. '[When did you hear anything at all about a reduction in the number of workers?] 31 January 1967. [How did you hear?] We were called to the Board Room and read a prepared statement – we knew nothing of the move before. [What was your reaction?] Absolute shock. Best guarded secret of all. The merger had been leaked and denied several times' (42-year-old clerical supervisor). 'I was shocked, shattered, we all were' (49-year-old works supervisor). The community at large was equally shocked: 'The Mills have been one of *the* institutions in Casterton. It was part and parcel of the town . . . they never thought that anything could happen to it' (56-year-old foreman).

It was generally believed that the consequences of the redundancy would be disastrous for the community because of the importance of the Mills as the largest employers in the area: 93 per cent of manual workers and 83 per cent of non-manual workers said that they thought that the community had been shocked, very concerned, or disgusted about the redundancy, the majority because of the traditional dependence of the area upon the Mills, and the lack of alternative employment. Yet such fears proved to be exaggerated, at least in the short run: the redundancy caused individual tragedies, but not collective disaster. The level of unemployment in the area did not immediately rise sharply, and the majority of former employees, especially young ones, succeeded in finding work without an extended period of unemployment. Such evidence provided grounds for surprised optimism within the community, a hope that the economic structure of the region was stronger than anticipated. This optimism proved equally mistaken, based upon an undue concentration upon short-run changes in the level of unemployment as an indicator of economic health and prosperity (a fixation also shared by government regional planners). For the redundancy caused many workers, especially non-manual workers, to move from a low-paying manufacturing industry to low-paying service industries, and the permanent reduction in the size of the plant involved a long-term reduction in the number of employment opportunities available for future school leavers. Within three years of the announcement of the redundancy the male unemployment level within Casterton had risen from marginally beneath the national average to over twice the national average. We examine the redundancy, and its effect upon unemployment within Casterton, in more detail in the remainder of this chapter.

I

During the period between the 1 February 1967 and 30 November 1968, 619 manual workers and 322 non-manual workers left Casterton Mills, representing nearly 40 per cent of the labour force at the beginning of the period. Some data is available upon all of the leavers, redundant and voluntary leavers, based upon information kindly made available by the firm. The following table shows the major reasons given for leaving by all male employees: we have not examined the behaviour of female employees, feeling that the labour market behaviour of female employees was determined by different factors from that of male employees, and constituted a separate subject in its own right.

Reasons Given for Leaving by Male Employees:
1 February 1967–30 November 1968

	Manual %	Non-Manual %
Redundant	38	51
'Prospects'	37	40
Announcement of redundancy	4	4
Dislike of job	0	1
Health/domestic/personal	3	0
Retired/deceased	13	1
Discharged	5	0
No reason given	1	2
	N = 512	N = 170
Joined and left within period N = 107		N = 13

Nearly 40 per cent of the manual workers and over half of the non-manual workers who left during this period were thus declared redundant. It is unfortunately impossible to distinguish adequately between those who left of their own accord because of the redundancy, and those who would have left in any case (apart of course from the sample we interviewed), for the personnel department's category of 'prospects' included both types of leaver. Moreover, there were some respondents for whom the announcement of the redundancy merely marked the culmination of doubts about the company, and who might or might not have left without the announcement: as one future student commented, 'I had been thinking of leaving for some time, but the announcement of the redundancy gave me the final push.' Accordingly, the population from which our sample was drawn comprised, firstly, those who were declared redundant and, secondly, those who left the firm either because of the announcement of the redundancy or because of their 'prospects' (voluntary leavers).

Both the manual and the non-manual groups comprised a number of different occupational categories, some of whom

121

were more heavily represented than others amongst the redundant, as the following table shows:

	Manual	
	Redundant %	Voluntary leaving %
Process workers	26	60
Warehouse	6	12
Craftsmen	34	19
Craftsmens' mates	14	2
Power station	16	2
Misc.	4	4
	N = 196	N = 206

	Non-manual	
	Redundant %	Voluntary leaving %
Clerks	28	34
Clerical/supervisory	14	13
Professional	8	11
Laboratary	6	20
Works Management	40	19
Misc.	4	5
	N = 87	N = 75

Although the process workers were by far the largest occupational group within the plant, they comprised only 26 per cent of the manual workers declared redundant. The redundant were drawn largely from the working class aristocracy within the plant, the craftsmen and their mates, and the power station workers, a self-contained group who were highly conscious of the relatively high wages, good working conditions, and pleasant atmosphere of the power station. There were also marked differences between the redundant and voluntary leaving non-manual groups. The largest single group amongst the white collar redundant were works management, who constituted 40 per cent of the total, followed by routine clerical workers, who of course were the largest white collar group, and their supervisors: very few professional employees or laboratory technicians were declared redundant. Clerical workers and laboratory technicians were the two largest groups of voluntary leaving non-manual workers, between them accounting for over half of the non-manual voluntary leavers.

The occupational composition of the two groups was the

result of two factors, management's plans for the future development of Casterton Mills, and the labour market position of the employees concerned. The major production facilities at Casterton were transferred elsewhere, together with most of the administration (sales, personnel, etc.), and a reduced staff was kept on to run the smaller, consolidated plant which was to continue in operation. Accordingly, management wished to run down all sectors of the labour force, but especially the craftsmen (whose numbers had been inflated over the years in excess of requirements), power station workers (since the power station was to be closed completely), and works management (since the new central plant already had its complement of line management). These groups were composed mainly of older, long-service workers, who had worked themselves up to relatively high status positions within the plant. A fifth of the redundant, compared with only 12 per cent of voluntary leavers, had been upwardly mobile, from manual to non-manual jobs, and the redundant manual workers were, as we have shown, mainly in high-status jobs. Since there were few alternative employment opportunities appropriate to their status and their age within the area there was little chance for them to leave of their own accord; they had little alternative but to maintain their tradition of loyalty to the firm, and in the case of works management to supervise the disappearance of their own jobs.

In short, workers who had pursued an occupational career within the firm, especially older workers (manual and non-manual) were bound to the firm, and incapable of obtaining comparable jobs outside: they were thus at the mercy of the employers, and were declared redundant when management wished.

The two sets of factors operated differently for workers who left the firm of their own accord. Management wished to retain many young 'quality' process workers, and laboratory and professional staff, to provide the nucleus for the reduced labour force in Casterton, and to reinforce the headquarters staff: more of those who left of their own accord than who were declared redundant were offered transfers. However, young workers in general, and young professional workers in particular, were not tied to the firm in the same way as older promotees; they were able to obtain comparable jobs elsewhere in the locality (for manual workers especially) or outside the locality (for non-manual professional workers especially). The contrast between the situations of the two groups is clearly indicated by their age composition:

Age Distribution of Redundant and Voluntary Leavers

| | Redundant | | Voluntary Leaver | |
	Manual %	Non-Manual %	Manual %	Non-Manual %
–25	2	5	36	41
25–34	9	9	29	31
35–44	12	11	14	12
45–49	7	15	9	10
50–54	14	11	3	3
55–60	23	20	4	1
60–	32	20	3	1
N = 164		N = 82	N = 202	N = 71

Over half of the redundant manual workers and nearly half of the redundant non-manual workers were aged 55 or more, compared with only 7 per cent of the voluntary leaving manual workers and only 2 per cent of the voluntary leaving non-manual workers. A similar contrast was evident at the younger end: only 11 per cent of the redundant manual workers, and only 14 per cent of the redundant non-manual workers, were aged under 35, compared with 65 per cent of the voluntary leaving manual workers and 72 per cent of the voluntary leaving non-manual workers.

This contrast between the age of the employees declared redundant and the age of those who left of their own accord is a particularly striking example of a tendency suggested by other research. The following table summarises the findings of a number of other studies on the relationship between age and redundancy.[1]

---

[1] Railway workshops: D. Wedderburn, *Redundancy and the Railwaymen*, p. 71; coal: M. I. A. Bulmer, 'Mining Redundancy: A Case Study of the Workings of the Redundancy Payments Act in the Durham Coalfield', *Industrial Relations Journal*, December 1971, p. 19: engineering, D. I. Mackay, 'After the Shake-out', *Oxford Economic Papers*, 1972; national (paid and unpaid): S. R. Parker *et al.*, *op. cit.*, p. 95.

Age Distribution of Redundant

	(1) Railway Workshops %	(2) Coal %	(3) Engineering %	(4) National (paid) %	(5) National (unpaid) %
–40	18	11	41	30	56
40–49	24	32	24	26	19
50+	58	56	35	44	25
	N = 331	N = 99	N = 1178	N = 1860	N = 181

Similar findings were reported by investigators into redundancy in the Belfast ship-building industry, although the age categories used are not directly comparable: 33 per cent were aged under 35, compared with 39 per cent aged 50 or more.[2] Hence, in all redundancies studied the majority of workers declared redundant were aged over 40; in some instances, especially in redundancies in economically backward parts of the country, the majority of workers declared redundant were over 50. This has obvious implications for an evaluation of the effectiveness of the Redundancy Payments Act; it suggests that the Act has encouraged management to release on to the labour market workers who are most likely to have most difficulty in finding further work, and least likely to be able to move house in search of work. Both questions are discussed further below, pp. 170–2.

Age, length of service, and previous earnings were, of course, the major determinants of the amount of redundancy pay received. As the following table shows, a large majority of manual workers (87 per cent) received less than £600, despite their age and length of service, reflecting the low earnings which had been current at the Mills: 73 per cent of manual workers aged 60 or more received below £600. Non-manual workers received more substantial payments, 42 per cent receiving more than £600; 59 per cent of non-manual workers aged 60 or more received more than £600, compared with only 27 per cent of manual workers.

[2] K. I. Sams and J. V. Simpson, 'A Case Study of Ship-building Redundancy in Northern Ireland', *Scottish Journal of Political Economy*, 1968, p. 275.

Amount of Redundancy Payment Received (Q. 104)

	Manual			Non-Manual		
	25–44	45–59	60+	25–44	45–59	60–
	%	%	%	%	%	%
–£200	60	29	26	42	14	15
£200–399	30	47	17	33	9	15
£400–599	10	12	30	9	32	8
£600–799	—	—	13	9	27	15
£800–999	—	12	9	9	14	15
£1000	—	—	4	—	5	31

N = 20 N = 17 N = 23   N = 12 N = 22 N = 13

Only 1 manual and 1 non-manual worker under 25 received redundancy pay.

The use made of the redundancy pay was determined partly by commitments, partly by length of time out of work, and partly by the amount received. Hence the uses of the payments by relatively young workers were more varied than those of older workers, reflecting the need for expenditure on the house and other domestic goods, and the hope of making a go of buying and running a small shop. Older non-manual workers, with most of their commitments paid, used the money mainly for savings; older manual workers, who had not been able to pay off all their financial commitments, especially the mortgage, found the redundancy payments useful for doing so, when it was not required for supplementing income. As the following

Use Made of Redundancy Payment (Q. 105)

	Manual			Non-Manual		
	25–44	45–59	60+	25–44	45–59	60+
	%	%	%	%	%	
	%	%	%	%	%	%
Income	40	59	59	33	41	31
Invest/save	40	18	36	33	55	77
Domestic	45	35	32	25	18	8
Own business	—	6	—	—	25	—
Other	10	12	—	25	9	9

Respondents were allowed two choices: % base is number of respondents in stated age category.

table shows, older manual workers were more likely to use their redundancy pay for income than members of any other group, whilst older non-manual workers were able to save or invest the money.

Both manual and non-manual workers in Casterton were thus more likely to use their redundancy payments for living expenses than the redundant railwaymen interviewed by Dorothy Wedderburn; only 31 per cent of those who were out of work when interviewed between six months and a year after leaving the railway workshops had used their payments for living expenses (although it is not clear whether respondents gave one or more responses on the use made of the money). Respondents did not elaborate on the problems of using the money for ordinary living expenses, but the special purposes mentioned are illustrative of the problems of everyday social life: 'It just dwindled away. We decided to have a good holiday, as the doctor said that the change would do me good. We had a week in Ireland' (61-year-old process worker); 'Put the lot in the bank, but I have spent some since – we had a holiday, the first in 34 years' (60-year-old power station worker). For the small number who used their money to buy their own businesses the redundancy proved to be the chance of a lifetime: what was made of it we do not know.

The redundancy payments proved to be a lucky windfall for some workers, but only a small minority stayed on at the firm to avoid losing them. The redundant were asked whether they considered leaving the firm after the announcement of the redundancy, and if not why not. Only 22 per cent reported that they had stayed on because they did not wish to lose the redundancy pay to which they were entitled, and over a quarter of those who did so were aged over 60 and thus had little chance of obtaining another job in any circumstances. The majority of workers were too worried about the prospects of not getting another job to let the hope of redundancy pay stand in their way if a suitable opening came along. The dilemma was illustrated clearly by a 49-year-old middle manager (although his assessment of general practice was awry): 'I dropped £600 in redundancy pay. It seemed to stagger a lot of people. I found this among some managers and staff, that the redundancy pay was magic. But to me it was less than 6 months' salary: if I did not get a job and continued to live at the same rate then the golden egg would be soon gone . . . . I thought I would rather have the job, though a lot of people said that they would stay on for redundancy pay. One of my foremen got nearly £800. But he is 50 and his chances of getting another staff post are remote.'

The existence of the redundancy payments scheme thus ensured that workers received compensation for the loss of their job property rights: those who had lost most by the redundancy received the greatest amount of compensation. At best this provided an unexpected windfall, a nest egg to place in the bank or building society; at worst it provided the where-withal to survive unemployment. But the redundancy payments did not significantly modify the workings of the labour market: workers who would probably have stayed with the firm as long as possible anyway were given an additional motive for staying, whilst workers who would probably have left anyway were not persuaded to stay by relatively low redundancy payments. Equity in attempting to achieve the first objective of the redundancy payments legislation, compensation for the loss of job property rights, inevitably meant failure in the second objective, increasing the mobility of the labour force: for those for whom the redundancy payments might have provided the means for mobility were entitled to the lowest redundancy payments (see below, pp. 170–2).

There were thus marked differences between the workers declared redundant at Casterton Mills and those who left of their own accord. Redundant manual workers were mainly craftsmen and their mates, process workers forming the second largest category; works managers were the largest single group of non-manual redundant, followed by routine clerical workers. By contrast, the majority of voluntary leaving manual workers were semi-skilled process workers (60 per cent), craftsmen and their mates only constituting 21 per cent of manual voluntary leavers. There was a similar contrast within the non-manual strata: only 19 per cent of non-manual voluntary leavers were works managers, whilst 34 per cent were clerks. Redundant employees, both manual and non-manual, were considerably older than voluntary leavers: over half of redundant manual workers, and 40 per cent of redundant non-manual workers, were aged 55 or more. This factor of age was to prove crucial for subsequent experience of unemployment.

II

A major determinant of the extent of unemployment following redundancy is, of course, the overall level of demand in the economy. Fortunately for the majority of Casterton workers the general level of demand in 1967–8 was still relatively high: the boom of the 1950s and 1960s was coming to an end, but had not totally collapsed. The level of unemployment in January 1967, the month before the announcement of the redundancy, was 1·7 per cent (1·3 per cent seasonally adjusted) for Great Britain as a whole, 2·4 per cent for Casterton region, and 2·3 per cent for Casterton itself. By Christmas of the following year, when the workers had left Casterton Mills, the level in Casterton had fallen below the national average; the national figure was 3·2 per cent, the regional figure was 2·3 per cent, and the Casterton figure 2·9 per cent. Accordingly, the labour market situation overall compares unfavourably with that examined by Dorothy Wedderburn, whose research took place during the early 1960s, but favourably with the subsequent period.

Casterton opinion believed that the redundancy would seriously inflate these figures, leading to a sharp and substantial rise in local unemployment: the local press carried alarming reports, and the local M.P. asked a question in the House of Commons and helped to organise a deputation to see the Minister then responsible for regional affairs. However, these fears proved to be exaggerated, and there was little immediate increase in the level of unemployment in the area, although the redundancy took only eighteen of the 36 months originally scheduled by the firm. The following table shows the unemployment rate for the Casterton area and for the whole Casterton region, for the months of January 1967 – December 1968, the period during which the majority of workers left Casterton Mills:

129

I

Unemployment Rates Casterton and Casterton Region, 1967–8

| | 1967 | | 1968 | |
	Casterton	Casterton region	Casterton	Casterton region
	%	%	%	%
Jan.	2·3	2·4	2·5	2·6
Feb.	2·1	2·5	2·5	2·7
Mar.	2·2	2·5	2·3	2·5
Apr.	2·1	2·6	2·3	2·5
May	2·1	2·5	2·3	2·4
June	2·0	2·3	2·0	2·3
July	2·0	2·3	2·1	2·2
Aug.	2·2	2·6	2·5	2·4
Sept.	2·3	2·5	2·4	2·4
Oct.	2·3	2·5	2·9	2·4
Nov.	2·3	2·5	3·0	2·4
Dec.	2·3	2·4	2·9	2·3

The absorptive capacity of the local labour market, and the consequently limited impact of the redundancy upon the level of unemployment in the area revealed by the official figures was confirmed by an analysis of the experience of our sample. As the following table shows, the majority of redundant workers, and nearly all of those who left of their own accord, obtained new jobs immediately or after only a short delay:

Length of Unemployment of Casterton Mills Ex-Employees, Compared with Railway Workshops Redundant

| | Manual | | | Non-Manual | |
| | Redundant | Voluntary | Work-shops* | Redundant | Voluntary |
	%	%	%	%	%
Job fixed up before left	22	87	37	29	95
Under 2 weeks	11	4	}15	{ 2	0
2–4 weeks	11	5		4	0
5–12 weeks	21	2	10	18	2
Over 3 months	19	0	17	23	2
Over 3 months: still unemployed	16	0	21	21	0
	N = 62	N = 54	N = 331	N = 49	N = 42

* *Source:* Wedderburn: *Redundancy and the Railwaymen*, p. 71

Whether this is regarded as a good or a bad record depends largely upon one's expectations. It is considerably better than many observers in Casterton thought possible; but it is markedly worse than the experience of workers in other redundancies which have been investigated. For example, as the figures quoted from Dorothy Wedderburn's study show, 37 per cent of all workers declared redundant at the Gorton and Faverdale railway workshops in 1962 found jobs immediately, compared with only 29 per cent of the white collar workers and 22 per cent of blue collar workers at Casterton Mills; 38 per cent of the railway workshops redundant were out of work for more than three months, compared with 36 per cent of the manual workers and 43 per cent of the non-manual workers declared redundant at Casterton Mills.[3] The Casterton Mills redundant were also out of work longer than the national average; Parker and his colleagues found that 25 per cent of those who received redundancy pay found work immediately, 21 per cent were unemployed for under two weeks, 14 per cent for between two and four weeks, 21 per cent for between one and three months, 12 per cent for over three and under 6 months, and 6 per cent for more than six months.

Although the majority of Casterton Mills workers found work either immediately or after only a short delay, there was a substantial minority who were out of work for over three months, or who still had not obtained work at the time of the interview. As the following table shows, workers aged 55 or more experienced considerable difficulty in finding jobs.

Length of Unemployment of 55 Plus Age Group

	Manual (N)	Non-Manual (N)
None	3	4
Under 2 weeks	4	0
2–4 weeks	4	2
5–12 weeks	5	3
Over 3 months	9	9
Still unemployed	7	9

[3] D. Wedderburn, *Redundancy and Railwaymen*, p. 71; S. R. Parker *et al.*, *op. cit.*, p. 108.

Although the numbers involved are small, there is clear evidence of the employment difficulties of older workers: 80 per cent of those who were out of work at the time of their interview (a variable length of time since both the redundancy and the interviews occurred over a period of months), and 82 per cent of those who were out of work for over 3 months, were aged 55 or more. Moreover, older workers were less likely to have been able to fix up a job before they left Casterton Mills than young workers.

This data confirms, on a small scale, the findings of more extensive surveys. For example, D. I. Mackay and his colleagues showed clearly in their survey of redundancy in the West Midlands that age was significantly related to length of time out of work: whereas 56·0 per cent of the redundant aged under 30 were out of work for less than two weeks, only 28·4 per cent of those aged 55+ were so lucky; whereas 23·4 per cent of respondents aged under 30 were out of work for more than two months, 55·8 per cent of those aged 55+ were. Moreover, the regression coefficient between age and length of period out of work was 11·80, significant at the 1 per cent level.[4]

How did the elderly react to this situation? Some of the elderly unemployed were not seriously worried by their plight, especially those approaching their 65th birthday; for them the redundancy payments represented an unexpected windfall which would prove helpful in retirement. As one 64-year-old power station worker, with all his family grown up, commented: 'I was not so much worried, we knew we were all right . . . the majority in our plant didn't bother in the first six months, they were getting such good repayments, what with the income tax rebate.' With over £1000 in redundancy payments, income tax rebate, and earnings-related unemployment benefit, he was one of the few fortunate ones. However, there were very few for whom the redundancy brought an early, welcome, and unexpectedly comfortable retirement. More characteristic was the experience of a 56-year-old foreman. Despite intensive searches in newspapers, visits to the Labour Exchange, calling round on firms with his son, and asking around among his

[4] D. I. Mackay *et al.*, 'After the Shake-out', *Oxford Economic Papers*, 1972.

friends even before being declared redundant, he was out of work for ten months, and the greater part of a substantial redundancy payment was used up. Eventually, through a chance meeting with a friend in a pub, he got a job as a packer and despatcher in a bakery, earning two-thirds of his former wage and getting 'no satisfaction at all'. Another elderly foreman, out of work for several months, had a similar experience: 'I was looking for any job barring navvying. I was prepared to take process work, or sweeping up in a factory. I even applied for a process job at the Mills, but the management said that the government might think that it was collusion . . . I had no particular level of earnings in mind, it was a job I wanted mostly.' Eventually he obtained a job as a car park attendant at £10 per week, well under half his earnings at Casterton Mills.

Supervisors and senior foremen had particular difficulty in finding suitable work; none of the line managers over fifty obtained employment comparable to his position at the Mills. The numbers involved are, of course, very small, but the experiences reveal clearly the problems posed for redundant senior personnel, especially senior personnel who have worked themselves up from the ranks within one firm. One was declared redundant at 64, and thereby gained a substantial and un-expected lump-sum payment; two were registered sick (one aged 61, the other aged 51) and neither expected to work again; two were unemployed, and had been for over a year (both aged 55); and five (aged 62, 61, 56, 55 and 50) were in semi-skilled manual jobs, earning considerably less than they had been getting at the Mills. The men on the sick register may have gained from the redundancy, as it forcibly removed them from stressful work conditions: both believed that the release from work tensions had improved their health. But the unemployed and the semi-skilled workers were of course extremely upset by their experience, and resentful of the way senior management had acted: 'I was really disappointed [when the redundancy was announced]. Shocked. I came home, I was really perturbed about it. At my age I hope I don't get finished. [Senior manage-ment] wasn't concerned at all . . . the higher ups didn't care that much.' One 55-year-old professionally qualified manager chose to stay unemployed rather than take a job as a labourer:

'Round here I have no hope whatever of getting a job without dropping a mile down the scale, and even then there are younger men. The moment you mention your age you sign your death warrant. I'm looking for a job very much less well paid [than my former job] but without moving I cannot get a job. I'm not prepared to throw away the house I've struggled to get.' Those who took semi-skilled jobs recognised that they had taken a step backward, but could see no alternative. 'I knew the limitations [upon the sort of job I could hope to get]. I was 54 and I knew full well that I had no hopes of a similar job, so I thought more or less that I would be in some factory doing a shop floor job' (55-year-old senior foreman).

Older Casterton workers thus experienced considerable difficulty in finding work, because of their age not because of their lack of skills, which, as we have seen, they clearly possessed. Over 80 per cent of workers said that they had thought that jobs would be difficult to get when they left the Mills, including all of those aged 55 or more. '[Do you have any idea why you were not offered the jobs you applied for but failed to get?] The age barrier. When applications asked for age I did not receive an interview; when age was not included I got an interview' (57-year-old craftsman). ['What sort of people have most difficulty in getting new jobs?'] 'Elderly people, those aged 45 and above. Because of the age limit imposed by firms. Firms think people can work harder between 20s and 45' (60-year-old warehouseman). 'I thought it would be difficult getting a job because of my age more than anything. . . . You can't pick and choose at 56' (56-year-old craftsman). Casterton employers, like those at Gorton and Faverdale, were cautious about hiring older workers, doubtful about their sickness records, their adaptability, and the amount of effort that could be obtained. The result was considerable anxiety for many older workers and acute distress for a minority.

The redundancy at Casterton Mills led to economic difficulties for the workers concerned which were not fully compensated for by redundancy payments; older workers, who were out of work for an extended period of time, of course suffered particularly severely. Financial difficulties led, for a minority, to the need to reduce expenditure and alter life-styles. As one skilled manual worker, who had taken a job as a doffer in a textile mill, commented: 'I no longer go to the club like I used to – I can't afford it.' But financial difficulties only affected a minority, and there was surprisingly little evidence of severe financial hardship or substantial changes in life style. Although precise data is not available, earnings had, of course, been relatively low at the Mills, and styles of life had evolved accordingly. More important, for the majority, were the effects of the redundancy upon individual confidence: the redundancy destroyed an occupational identity and status constructed over a work life spanning, in some cases, thirty years; a new identity, consistent with present reality but preserving as far as possible a continuity with a previous identity, had to be constructed. This involved the development of a number of coping techniques, designed to put the best possible face on the situation, and sustained to varying degrees by kin, friends, former work mates at Casterton Mills, present work mates, and the Labour Exchange. It is unfortunately impossible to be exhaustive about the coping techniques used, for they became apparent in informal discussions around the interviews, rather than in the interviews themselves, and could not, of course, be discussed explicitly. The most common techniques, used to a greater or lesser extent by all the elderly redundant, included: retrospective status; status enhancement; outright rejection of present status; shift of the basis for status claim; and withdrawal. These constituted techniques for achieving role distance where present roles were substantially lower in status than those occupied at Casterton Mills, a form of 'management of spoiled identity': retrospective claims – 'I'm not really a messenger, I'm a fitter'; enhancement – 'You don't realise how important messengers are'; rejection – 'I'm not really a bloody messenger but it's a living'; or the shifting of the basis for status claim – 'But the money's bloody good'. Finally, workers who recognise the impossibility of re-employment at a comparable level, and who suffer from vaguely diagnosed complaints like 'back trouble' or 'a heart condition' may, with the support of the doctor, withdraw completely from the labour market. This withdrawal does not, of course, constitute work-shyness; on the contrary, it indicates an excessive involvement in work, with a consequent inability to maintain personal equilibrium in the face of dismissal.

The redundancy at Casterton Mills thus seemed to pass off with surprising ease for the community, the majority of the redundant finding work without suffering from extended periods of unemployment. Yet this appearance of success proved to be deceptive, a merely temporary phenomenon. Whereas unemployment was only 2·9 per cent in December 1968, at the end of the redundancy, by the following December it had risen to 3·8 per cent, and to 6·8 per cent by the time of writing, June 1971. Economic depression harms weaker economies relatively more severely than strong ones and the recession since 1969 has hit the economically underdeveloped parts of Britain particularly severely: the range of inter-regional variation in the level of unemployment has widened from 2·6 per cent in October 1967 to 3·0 per cent in October 1970, the absolute level of course rising at the same time.[5] Casterton has been a victim of this development, further serious redundancies in the area following the run-down at Casterton Mills. At the time, the Casterton Mills run-down proceeded relatively smoothly, from the community's point of view if not from the firm's, with 'natural wastage' and the restriction on recruitment complementing the redundancy dismissals. But the permanent reduction in the firm's labour requirements has proved a serious blow to a region already suffering from serious economic difficulties: the limited employment opportunities available for new entrants to the labour force were further circumscribed, all the more so with the greater cost-consciousness shown by management, and the reduction in prospective 'retirement-vacancies' through the creation of a younger labour force.

Equally important was the increased exposure of the Casterton Mills redundant to future redundancy. For the Casterton Mills

[5] For a discussion of the changing relation between regional and national unemployment levels see P. Hall, *New Society*, 23 March 1972, and letter from D. Gane, *New Society*, 20 April 1972. The evidence indicates a widening gap: in 1966 the region with the highest level of unemployment had a rate 1·3 per cent above the national rate; in 1971 the region with the highest rate had a rate of 2·4 per cent above the national average. See also *National Institute Economic Review*, February 1972, p. 19, for some misleading figures.

redundant could no longer claim special consideration for their length of service, a recognised if often disregarded claim for being kept on during a run-down. Moreover, the redundant often moved into marginal jobs, for example in marginal service industries, and were thus likely to be the first to find their jobs disappear in an economic down-turn. Finally, the informal mutual understandings between employer and employee which form a basis for the mutual recognition of commitments take a long time to develop. It is important that future research into redundancy should follow the subsequent occupational careers of the redundant, to assess the long-term effects of experience of redundancy upon future job prospects; it is possible that redundancy marks the beginnings of a downward occupational career, the effects of each involuntary dismissal being cumulative. It would have been interesting to follow up our sample and to see how many found themselves out of work a second time within three years of the redundancy; a small number of white collar workers had been declared redundant a second time when we interviewed them, within eighteen months of their dismissal from Casterton Mills, and some of the firms to which others went have since folded up. But we have no way of knowing how extensive this experience was.

The long-run effects of the redundancy, both upon the community and upon the redundant themselves, are thus likely to be more serious than their immediate experience of unemployment suggests. But even the short-run effects were more substantial than was generally recognised at the time, for although there was only limited experience of unemployment, many workers moved into jobs that were paying less than Casterton Mills. In the following chapter we turn to job seeking and job finding to justify this view.

7 JOB SEEKING AND JOB FINDING

One view of job-seeking is to regard it as a form of consumer behaviour, determined by the same laws of supply and demand: job choice, like the choice of consumer goods, is determined by preferences (ranked in terms of 'price', the perceived costs and benefits of the designated job) and opportunities. As we have seen, on p. 21, some labour economists view movement between jobs as being 'broadly controlled by supply and demand'. The consumer behaviour model also underlies the analysis of the job mobility of the affluent Luton workers presented, with considerable supporting empirical material, by John Goldthorpe and his colleagues.[1] However, such a model would not provide a very satisfactory basis for analysing the labour market behaviour of the Casterton Mills employees, for two sets of reasons. Firstly, as we have indicated in Chapter 3, there are considerable problems involved in constructing a reliable index of preferences – there is no currency, no recognised set of exchange rates. Secondly, there is little evidence of Casterton Mills workers attempting to maximise their returns on effort through 'working' the local labour market. For Casterton Mills workers, like the steel workers in Buffalo, New York, interviewed by F. F. Foltmann, 'satisficed' rather than 'maximised', i.e. made do with the first job which came along which satisfied minimal criteria of desirability, instead of seeking out the most favourable opening; usually this was the

---

[1] J. H. Goldthorpe *et al.*, *The Affluent Worker: Industrial Attitudes and Behaviour*, *passim*. For a more extensive discussion of theoretical problems in the analysis of labour mobility, see R. Martin, 'The "Rational Maximizing" Model of Labour Mobility,' in ed. R. Loveridge, *Industrial Relations and Manpower Planning*, Heinemann Educational Books, forthcoming.

first job applied for and offered.[2] Hence 79 per cent of manual workers and 77 per cent of non-manual workers accepted the first job offered, and there was no significant difference between the redundant and the voluntary leavers. Moreover, the major techniques of job-seeking used, especially the reliance upon kinship networks and personal contacts by the manual workers, were not likely to favour market rational behaviour. In the first section of this chapter we examine the job aspirations of the Casterton workers, together with their minimum requirements, and the methods used to achieve them; in the following section we turn to their destinations.

I

As we have suggested earlier, two sentiments were paramount within the value system of the Casterton worker, fatalism – an acceptance of the workings of an often hostile environment – and an attachment to hierarchy. These two values pointed in contradictory directions during the period of the redundancy. On the one hand, all recognised that jobs were scarce and would be difficult to find, especially for older workers, and that many would have to suffer some decline in their income, status, or conditions of work. On the other hand, all those with any pretensions wished to maintain the status and income that they already possessed, whether as white collar workers or as members of the skilled working class. 'I want to keep my status as a clerk for the purpose of getting a job, but I am prepared to stretch a point if other things are favourable, like wages and hours. If I cannot get a clerk's job I am willing to compromise' (53-year-old redundant clerical worker). In part this was a terminal value, in part a means to maintaining claims to a differential reward, a direct echo of the importance of traditional differentials stressed by Lady Wootton:[3] 'With being a tradesman, and having a little common sense, I wanted some-

[2] F. F. Foltman, *White and Blue Collars in a Mill Shut-down*, Ithaca: New York School of Industrial and Labour Relations, 1968, pp. 3–4. The term is of course taken from H. A. Simon and J. G. March, *Organisations*, New York; John Wiley and Son, Inc., 1958.

[3] B. Wootton, *The Social Foundations of Wages Policy*, 2nd edn., George Allen and Unwin, 1962.

thing above the process – something better than that . . . a big come-down for a tradesman when you accept a process job, and you automatically become a process worker in the eyes of the Labour Exchange. While a tradesman they couldn't force me to accept process work. Better off on earnings related as a tradesman, and gave me time to think . . . a cut and a half above a process worker' (27-year-old skilled worker, with industry specific skill). Fatalism and status consciousness were reflected in the answers given to questions about the kind of work respondents were not prepared to do: a large majority of non-manual workers, and a substantial minority of manual workers, stressed that they would only consider work relevant to their previous experience:

Work not Prepared to Consider (Q. 138)

	Manual %	Non-Manual %
Done anything	44	9
Occupational experi-ence/status	40	79
Other	15	12
	N = 52	N = 34

The desire to maintain their white collar status was almost universal amongst non-manual workers, whilst the greater catholicity shown by manual workers is not surprising.[4]

The earnings aspirations of Casterton workers were predictably low, as the following table shows:

Earnings Aspirations (Qs 141, 142)

	Manual				Non-Manual			
	Redundant %		Own Accord %		Redundant %		Own Accord %	
	A	B	A	B	A	B	A	B
£1–10	5	22	0	11	0	12	6	31
£11–13	2	27	4	15	3	15	17	14
£14–16	48	32	19	41	23	34	9	11
£17–19	17	7	23	17	15	5	9	17
£20–24	10	5	35	11	15	15	14	6
£25–	7	2	8	0	25	7	29	11
None	5	8	6	7	15	10	9	3
As Ct. M.	2	0	2	0	5	2	14	8
	N = 60		N = 48		N = 40		N = 35	

Column A is the % seeking a given level of earnings
Column B is the % prepared to accept a given level of earnings

[4] The question 'What type of job are you not prepared to consider?' proved more useful than the question: 'What type of job are you looking for?'. Dislikes were more clearly defined than preferences.

The majority of redundant manual workers were thus looking for a job paying £16 or less, whilst the overwhelming majority were prepared to accept that level. The manual workers who left of their own accord regarded a higher level of earnings as desirable but a majority were similarly prepared to settle for £16 or less. These figures compare with national average earnings for manual workers in all industries (including some services) of £22 5s, and for manual workers in 'other manufacturing industry' (the category covering Casterton Mills) of £22 17s in April 1968, in the middle of the redundancy. Non-manual workers, of course, had higher aspirations: 40 per cent of the redundant and 43 per cent of the voluntary leavers were looking for more than £20 per week, and 22 per cent of the redundant and 14 per cent of the voluntary leavers said that they would not consider anything below that level. However, at the bottom end of the scale, 61 per cent of the redundant and 56 per cent of those who left of their own accord were willing to accept £16 or less (the latter percentage including a number of relatively junior office and laboratory staff). In short, the earnings aspirations of Casterton workers were circumscribed, and the minimum requirements extremely so.

The extent to which the job-seeking techniques of the Casterton workers were adapted to the labour *market* varied, there being significant differences between social classes and between the redundant and the voluntary leavers in methods used. Respondents were asked about the methods used to look for work, the method they regarded as the most successful, and the method which actually succeeded in getting them a job. The following table summarises the data on the methods used and the method regarded as the most successful:

Methods of Job-Seeking (Qs 151, 152)

	Manual %		Non-Manual %	
	A	B	A	B
Employment Exchange	26	15	23	15
Advertisements	17	21	37	40
Friends/relations	30	19	24	22
Calling on spec.	23	42	14	12
Other	4	3	3	11
	N = 111		N = 82	

Column A is the % mentioning a given method: two choices permitted.
Column B is the % thinking that a given method is the most successful.

Manual workers thus tended to rely upon chance calls upon firms, upon asking around amongst friends and relatives, and upon the Employment Exchange, and paid little attention to the press. Non-manual workers, on the other hand, relied heavily upon the press, less so upon friends and relations and upon the Employment Exchange, and comparatively little upon calling at firms on chance. The largest number of manual workers believed that the most successful means of looking for work was simply calling at firms on chance, the second largest number that answering press advertisements was the most successful (although only a comparatively small number mentioned using this technique), and the third most popular successful method mentioned was asking relatives and friends. Comparatively few believed that the Employment Exchange was the most successful way to find work. The order of priority of success attributed by non-manual workers paralleled directly the order of popularity of use. The major contrast between the redundant and the voluntary leavers is the greater importance attached to the Employment Exchange by the redundant than the voluntary leavers, and the greater importance of newspaper advertisements for the voluntary leavers. Newspaper advertisements were plainly most useful to workers in a relatively strong labour market position, at whom they were probably directed, leaving the Employment Exchange the more difficult task of helping those who had already failed to obtain work through newspaper advertisements, or who had been unable to secure a job for themselves before being declared redundant at Casterton Mills.

The majority of redundant manual workers actually found jobs through relatives and friends (53 per cent); replying to advertisements, calling on firms on chance, and through the Employment Exchange were all of more or less equal importance: 15, 15 and 13 per cent finding their jobs through those means respectively. Relations and friends were less important for manual workers who had left Casterton Mills of their own accord, only 32 per cent finding jobs through them: calling on firms on spec (42 per cent) and replying to newspaper advertisements were more significant than for the redundant, the Employment Exchanges less (15 per cent). Replying to newspaper advertisements was by far the most common means successfully used by non-manual workers to get work: 49 per cent of the redundant and 71 per cent of the voluntary leavers obtained their jobs in this way. Contacts through relatives and friends were the second in importance, successfully used by 30 per cent of the redundant and 12 per cent of the voluntary leavers. (A very small number of non-manual workers stressed that they asked friends but *not* relatives.) The remaining methods of looking for work were not noticeably successful: only 11 per cent of the redundant and 4 per cent of the voluntary leavers found work through the Employment Exchange, and only 8 per cent of the redundant and 10 per cent of the voluntary leavers found jobs by making chance calls on employers.

These findings confirm the central role of informal methods of job seeking in redundancies, especially 'asking around' amongst relatives and friends. This was the most successful method for manual workers, and the second most successful method for non-manual workers: such techniques were also by far the most successful for the redundant railwaymen interviewed by Dorothy Wedderburn, 46 per cent finding jobs through personal contacts.[5] 'Best way friends or contacts at firms' (45-year-old stoker); 'Personal contact – only way' (50-year-old process foreman); 'Bumped into manager who was personal friend' (49-year-old craftsman); 'The best way *I* know is to know someone already working in a certain factory or type of work' (61-year-old works manager). The working of the local labour market at the micro-level is highly idiosyncratic, and no example could be typical. However, the experience of a 50-year-old process worker was characteristic: 'My car is garaged, and the caretaker there is a fitter at [a local mill], and was one of those who put in some new machines there. The boss there said that he got the machine, but no one to run it – the foreman had one week's training, but was no good. My friend mentioned me to the boss [as I had experience of the same

[5] D. Wedderburn, *Redundancy and the Railwaymen*, p. 148. For similar evidence of the importance of personal contacts in the nineteenth-century labour market see G. Stedman-Jones, *Outcast London: A Study in the Relationships between the Classes in Victorian London*, Oxford: Oxford University Press, 1971, pp. 83–5.

machine at Casterton Mills] and he sent for me to ask my advice, and in the end he asked me to go there.'

Relatives and friends provided knowledge, validation, and often influence. 'I went to this firm to ask for a job. The Personnel Manager said "How old are you?" and I said "62". He said "You're too old". Then a feller came in the office who knew me from when a lad. He said "What are you after?" and I said "A job, but the Personnel Manager says I'm too old". He turned to the Personnel Manager and said "I'll start him on Monday"' (62-year-old process foreman). In the 1930s it had been essential to have a special relationship with someone at Casterton Mills to obtain work there: a relative, a friend, or even simply someone with a common interest. Such factors continue to play a part in a clearly defined local labour market, where 'who you are' is important as well as 'what you could do'. Nor is the practice of 'speaking for' necessarily simply favouritism. Where tasks are unspecified, and being a 'good worker' is thought to depend upon qualities of 'character' as well as upon often only marginal differences in qualifications and experience, acquaintance with a prospective employee's relatives or friends might be the best predictor of reliability available to management; his reliability is vouchsafed by his peers. (The practice is not limited to manual occupations, as the stress upon character by many managers indicates.)[6] Similarly, prior knowledge of the unspoken understandings which underpin the formal contract of employment, and of the informal norms of the plant, is helpful for the future employee, for they will largely determine how he will 'fit in'.[7]

The corollary of this heavy reliance upon personal methods of job seeking is that the formal mechanisms of job-seeking, especially the Employment Exchange service, are reduced in

[6] Cf. T. Nichols, *Ownership, Control, and Ideology*, George Allen and Unwin, 1970, for a discussion of the 'anti-professional' emphasis upon 'character' amongst managers in a Northern city.

[7] M. J. Mann stressed the importance of the 'informal contract' between managers and workers, and the disadvantageous consequences of changing that contract and thus disrupting traditional expectations, in his study of the relocation of the General Foods plant from Birmingham to Banbury, M. J. Mann, *Sociological Aspects of Factory relocation: A Case Study*, unpublished D.Phil. thesis, Oxford, 1970.

significance. They played only a relatively marginal role in the job seeking of Casterton workers. The majority of redundant workers registered with the Exchange (77 per cent) but only 41 per cent were actually sent to jobs by the Exchange, and only 19 per cent of redundant manual workers and 8 per cent of redundant non-manual workers actually obtained jobs through the Exchange. Very few workers who left Casterton Mills of their own accord registered with the Exchange at all. The placement rate for redundant manual workers for the Casterton Exchange compared favourably with that for the Gorton and Faverdale Employment Exchanges reported by Dorothy Wedderburn, 13 per cent of redundant railway workshops employees obtaining their first post-redundancy job through the Employment Exchange service, and quite favourably with the engineering survey placement rate, 17·5 per cent.[8] But the difficulties experienced by the Exchange brought some criticism, especially from older white collar workers: 'Totally useless organisation, going off their general attitude. They didn't seem to care at all. They had a problem, of course, with so many to see – organisation didn't seem geared up to the situation and the number of people being made redundant. Really encouraging people to be layabouts. A man made redundant wants a job, not to be told by the layabouts and regulars how to get more money' (43-year-old foreman). One manual worker expressed more traditional objections: 'Labour as far as I am concerned is too much of a rigmarole and want to know too much of your private business, (30-year-old welder). There undoubtedly were organisational difficulties, deriving mainly from the continuous pressure of benefits payments business which made it impossible to give long, detailed interviews to the redundant (and, incidentally, was responsible for bringing highly status conscious white collar workers into contact with the long term unemployed, the 'regulars', resulting inevitably in friction and in a down-grading of the estimation of the Exchange). However, the major problem stemmed from the limitations and character of the local labour market, and

---

[8] D. Wedderburn, *op. cit.*, p. 137; for a more elaborate discussion see G. L. Reid, 'The Role of the Employment Service in Redeployment', *British Journal of Industrial Relations*, Vol. 9, 1971, pp. 170–2.

K

was outside the control of the Employment Exchange. The potential role of the Employment Exchange is obviously limited where workers are fully aware of the major employers in the area, and believe that making personal calls on employers and answering advertisements are the most effective methods of looking for work. The Exchange becomes a last resort, to be used only when other methods have failed. Moreover, employers have little incentive to notify the Exchange of vacancies, partly because they can rely upon workers looking for a job to call on spec, especially of course those with a little 'initiative', and partly because the concept of 'vacancies' particularly for manual workers, is itself ill-defined, responsive to the availability of labour: vacancies appear when 'suitable' workers turn up. Hence the role of the Employment Exchange was relatively marginal, and the official job vacancy data seriously under-estimated the absorptive capacity of the local labour market.

In such circumstances the major role of the Employment Exchange was to provide information about vacancies elsewhere in the country for the very few workers who were prepared to leave the area (see following chapter), and to bring government retraining facilities to the notice of likely candidates. There was more interest in Government Retraining Centres than we had expected, 17 per cent of manual workers saying that they had seriously considered attending one, and one member of the sample, who subsequently obtained a job on the basis of his training, had actually attended a centre. Most interest was of course shown by the redundant (including one or two redundant non-manual workers): 21 per cent of redundant manual workers had seriously considered attending the government retraining centre, situated about 30 miles away. The major reasons given for not attending were age, and the feeling that they already possessed a skill and that a further one would be superfluous: 'What do I want further training for, I've already served my time' (Electrician).

In short, it is impossible to discuss the process of selling and buying labour, and the distribution of labour which results from interaction between the two, in the conventional market terms appropriate to the buying and selling of consumer goods: the local labour market does not operate according to the more or less mechanical operation of the laws of supply and demand, costs and returns. Behaviour is determined partly by chance, partly by the extent of knowledge, partly by the variable preferences of the workers concerned, and partly by the structure of opportunities available, each imperfectly matched with the other. Very few respondents went as far as one warehouseman, who commented: 'I didn't really think [of any specific level of earnings]. It never entered my head to look for anything. It just happened.' However, more or less idiosyncratic personal experiences, knowledge, and preferences were as important as market considerations, both in bringing labour and hirer together, and in causing that meeting to result in a new job for the worker. Manual workers especially were very dependent upon relatives and personal friends for information about local employers and the availability of openings, and such contacts were even more important in *successful* attempts at job seeking as a whole. The prerequisite for rational, market orientated behaviour, knowledge of the overall situation, was lacking. However it is doubtful whether greater overall knowledge would have led to more successful job seeking, given the nature of the situation.

II

Occupational preferences, methods of search, area of search, and especially the structure of opportunities available determined the jobs found by the Casterton Mills workers following the redundancy. As we have shown, the majority of Casterton workers were looking for jobs similar to the ones they had possessed at the Mills, although a minority were prepared to accept anything: the median level of earnings sought was £14–16. The major methods of search used were calling at firms on chance, asking around amongst relatives and friends, and, for non-manual workers, answering newspaper advertisements. Preference, and method, both limited the area of search to the locality, or at most the region, for few possessed the resources to travel long distances on the mere chance of a job, and contact networks were highly circumscribed. Accordingly, the structure of opportunities available in the locality largely

147

determined future job choice, within the limits outlined earlier. This structure, and the eventual distribution of Casterton Mills workers within it, forms the subject of this section.

The Casterton economy was already under strain before the announcement of the redundancies at the Mills. Like other 'grey areas' it suffered from a sluggish rate of economic growth, low earnings, reliance upon a small number of often declining industries, increasingly under control from outside the community, and a substantial rate of emigration of economically active males, resulting in an ageing population. The major industries in the area were floor-coverings, textiles, plastics, chemicals, construction, and service industries, including public administration: between them they accounted for over 80 per cent of local jobs. Apart from floor-coverings, which declined by 6 per cent p.a. between 1956 and 1966, these industries were expanding, especially plastics and chemicals; however, this growth was slower in Casterton than elsewhere, and the slow growth in output did not lead to any substantial increase in the demand for labour. Whereas the national average rate of expansion in plastics was 10 per cent p.a. between 1956 and 1966, the rate of expansion of output in the major plant in the area was only 6 per cent; whereas the rate of expansion of oil refining, a major sector of the local chemicals industry, was 12 per cent nationally, it was only 2 per cent locally.[9] The area received only 0·1 per cent of new industrial building between 1954 and 1964, although it contributed 0·2 per cent to the gross national product. Moreover, at the time of the redundancy there were no plans for major capital investment projects in the area, except in public utilities, and the prospects of further rationalisation and closure, in addition to those at Casterton Mills, were very real. Since 1968 further redundancies have occurred. These trends were responsible for the 'considerable anxiety' that was expressed by local officials to the members of the Hunt Committee on the 'Grey Areas' when they visited the area.

Industry in Casterton was not expanding, even before the announcement of the run-down at Casterton Mills. Using past

[9] We are grateful to Mr John Rhodes, of the Department of Applied Economics, Cambridge, for information on this point.

experience and the current plans of local employers as a basis, it was predicted that the demand for labour in Casterton would be exactly the same in 1970 as it had been in 1964, *except* for the substantial redundancies at Casterton Mills. Chemicals, and cotton and textiles expected to reduce their labour requirements, man-made fibres and construction expected to expand. Overall, it was expected that the area would lose nearly 1400 jobs, representing the redundancy at Casterton Mills.

Desipte these difficulties the majority of workers who left Casterton Mills during 1967 and 1968 found work without spending long periods unemployed, as we have shown. As the following table shows, the major destinations were plastics and man-made fibres, public administration, retail distribution and other services, and engineering and metal manufacture for manual workers, and retail distribution, public administration, and plastics and man-made fibres for non-manual workers.

	Manual		(N)	Non-Manual		(N)
	R	V	T	R	V	T
Agric./mining	1	2	3	2	1	3
Chemicals	0	2	2	0	1	1
Engin./met. mf.	8	6	14	4	3	7
Plastics, etc.	14	19	33	6	6	12
Other mf.	6	2	8	3	3	6
Construction	2	1	3	1	0	1
Gas, water, elec.	2	1	3	1	1	2
Transport	0	0	0	1	3	4
Distribution	3	5	8	6	3	9
Services	5	4	9	7	3	10
Pub. admin.	10	8	18	4	16	20

Amongst manual workers there was very little difference between the industrial destinations of the redundant and those who left of their own accord: plastics and man-made fibres, distribution and other services, public administration, and engineering were the most popular, in that order, with both groups. However, there was a significant difference between the destinations of redundant and voluntary leaving non-manual workers: more of the redundant than of the voluntary leavers went into retail distribution and other services, whilst more of the voluntary leavers went into public administration, including education. This probably reflects the preference of the voluntary

149

leavers for public administration, with its national wage rates, prospects of advancement, and security, and their stronger labour market position, forcing the redundant to find work in the riskier, more chaotic, and lower-paid service sector.

With this exception, there was little difference between the redundant and the voluntary leavers in the industries entered, but there was a considerable difference between them in their experience once they had found work. The majority of redundant workers, especially redundant non-manual workers, earned less than they had been earning at Casterton Mills, whilst the majority of voluntary leavers, both manual and non-manual, earned more.

Comparison between Earnings at (First) Job after Casterton Mills, and Earnings at Casterton Mills (Q. 117)

	Manual		Non-Manual	
	R %	V %	R %	V %
More	24	58	12	60
Same	16	16	10	13
Less	44	16	53	28
Unemployed	16	0	21	0
Missing		9	4	
	N = 63	N = 45	N = 49	N = 40

Hence 44 per cent of redundant manual workers earned less, and 16 per cent were unemployed at the time of the interview, whilst only 16 per cent of those who left of their own accord were earning less than they had been earning at Casterton Mills; similarly, 53 per cent of the redundant non-manual workers were earning less, and 21 per cent were unemployed, compared with only 28 per cent of those who left of their own accord earning less and none out of work at the time of the interview. There was a tendency for manual workers who were declared redundant and who suffered from unemployment to earn less when they finally got a job than those who went straight into another job, but no similar tendency amongst redundant non-manual workers, very few of whom earned more after the redundancy than before, although the numbers involved are small. Unemployment was thus not an attempt to gain time to look around for a better job (or if it was intended to be it did not work out that way), but a period of enforced idleness. The greater age of the redundant than the voluntary leavers, together with their relatively late appearance upon the labour market, were largely responsible for such subsequent employment problems.

This contrast between the post-redundancy earnings of the redundant compared with the voluntary leavers was largely responsible for their contrasting evaluations of their present financial position compared with five years earlier. As the following table shows, only a minority of redundant workers, 31 per cent of manual workers and 37 per cent of non-manual workers, considered that they were financially better off than five years previously, and in a small number of instances this perceived prosperity was due to relief after serious overworking at the Mills (Q. 174).

	Manual		Non-Manual	
	Redundant %	Voluntary %	Redundant %	Voluntary %
Better off	31	69	37	76
Worse off	49	13	47	12
Same	20	18	16	12
	N = 61	N = 56	N = 49	N = 32

On the other hand, substantial majorities of both manual and non-manual voluntary leavers thought that they were better off than they had been five years previously. This confirms the conclusion of the previous analysis, that the redundancy was a serious blow to the redundant, but proved to be an opportunity for the voluntary leavers.

To summarise, the redundancy at Casterton Mills involved the loss of about 1200 jobs, spread over a period of eighteen months, a reduction achieved partly by restrictions on recruitment, partly by natural wastage, and partly by redundancy. The bulk of the natural wastage comprised young process workers and office staff, whilst the majority of the redundant were elderly workers, skilled manual workers or line managers. The redundancy proved beneficial for many voluntary leavers, stimulating them to move to better paid jobs, and rarely involving any significant period of unemployment. The small number of young workers who were declared redundant experienced similar success. However, it proved to be a different story for the elderly redundant; for them the redundancy proved to be a major calamity, leading to long periods of unemployment, and eventually to jobs with lower status and lower wages. The redundancy payments proved an inadequate compensation, over 48 per cent of those aged 45 or more using their payments for ordinary living expenses during unemployment or whilst holding down a badly paid job, although some were given the wherewithal to take a rare holiday or to redecorate the house.

The effects of the redundancy upon the community were less serious in the short run than had been anticipated; there was no immediate rise in the level of unemployment in the area. The majority of workers were absorbed into plastics and man-made fibres, the largest expanding manufacturing industry in the area, or into tertiary industry, retail distribution and other services or public administration, including education. However, immediate appearances were deceptive, for the redundancy accelerated a process which had already started in the area, the dwindling of manufacturing industry. The lack of new investment, which had shown itself for a decade before the run-down at Casterton Mills, had meant that much of the plant had become out of date. Lacking a large concentration of relevant skills, proximity to markets, or the subsidies attendant upon development area status, and increasingly under the control of absentee ownership, prospects for the continued importance of manufacturing industry in the area have become dim. Casterton Mills had provided the major focus for local hopes, being the larger and more modern plant in a recently formed amalgamation; but these hopes were disappointed, as we have shown in detail. The result, for Casterton, is likely to be a return to its pre-industrial revolution situation, larger, uglier, and richer – a small market town servicing the surrounding rural area, dominated by public authority offices and institutions.

8 REDUNDANCY AND LABOUR MOBILITY: THE IMMOBILE WORKER

Successive governments, Labour and Conservative, have envisaged redundancy payments as part of a wider strategy for fostering economic growth, including also expanded Government Retraining Centres, an improved Employment Exchange service, and wider publicity for grants available for assistance in meeting the travelling, subsistence, and relocation expenses involved in moving to a job in another area. Redundancy payments have been justified historically on the grounds of social justice, as compensation for the loss of job property rights, as a means of securing the co-operation of labour in rationalisation schemes, and as a way of providing assistance for the use of workers willing to move in search of new jobs.[1] Mr Ray Gunter, then Minister of Labour, justified the original Redundancy Payments Act as 'an important step in the government's general programme to push forward the modernisation of British industry as fast as possible, and to enlist the co-operation of workers as well as management in this process'. It was part of an 'active policy to make it easier for workers to change their jobs in accordance with the needs of technological progress . . . to ensure the planned use of resources especially our reserves of manpower . . . an important complement to our efforts to deploy our manpower and other resources where they can make the most effective contribution to the economy'.[2] Firms would be enabled to release workers without the constraints of trade union intransigence or uneasy conscience; other firms, preferably 'export-orientated' and 'science based' would then be able to expand to absorb the labour released. Subsequent Conservative spokesmen have echoed Mr

[1] Cf. S. R. Parker et al., pp. 3, 7–12.
[2] *Hansard, 1965*, Vol. 711, p. 33.

Gunter's sentiments, minus only the exuberant optimism which characterised Labour economic statements during the period of the National Plan.

Declining capital investment and rising unemployment within the last three years have falsified this picture of firms eager to expand but held back by labour shortages or 'bottlenecks': an overall labour 'shortage' has given way to a substantial surplus, especially in Development Areas and in the 'grey areas', including Casterton. No policy designed to encourage labour mobility could be expected to work in the economic conditions obtaining in 1970 and 1971, partly because of the lack of vacancies anywhere in the country, and partly because few workers are willing to take any risks in the current economic climate. However, previous research has shown that British workers are immobile regardless of the economic climate. According to the Government Social Survey Report, *Labour Mobility in Britain, 1953–63*, only 24·1 per cent of the occupied labour force had ever moved house for job reasons, the proportions ranging from 55 per cent of graduates to 22 per cent of skilled but not apprenticed manual workers. Moreover, a large proportion of labour mobility was short range: 39·8 per cent of workers who had moved house for work reasons in the last ten years had moved under 10 miles, 19·1 per cent between 11 and 30 miles, and 17·7 per cent moved between 31 and 100 miles. As many as 57 per cent of the sample said that nothing would ever get them to move.[3] Even in the United States, where the ideology of migration is widely accepted, labour mobility is not seen as the best solution to employment problems: 'Migration can and does make some contribution towards the solution of the depressed area problem, but it cannot bear the brunt of the adjustment. The carrot is more important than the stick'.[4] Research in Casterton confirmed, at the micro-level, the conclusions of the official national survey. The majority of Casterton workers found jobs locally, mainly, as we have seen, in plastics and man-made fibres,

[3] A. I. Harris and C. Clausen, *Labour Mobility in Britain, 1953–63*, H.M.S.O., 1966, pp. 19, 17, 23.

[4] G. Iden, 'Industrial Growth and Areas of Chronic Unemployment', *Monthly Labour Review*, 1966, p. 490.

public services, and various forms of engineering and metal manufacturing. In the short run, the redundancy proved to be a stability-inducing rather than a mobility-inducing event; for mobility depends upon confidence (at least the comfortable side of starvation) and redundancy undermines confidence, especially amongst the redundant.

I

Casterton workers believed that there was a substantial amount of geographical mobility: 80 per cent of manual workers and 85 per cent of non-manual workers believed that there were people who moved house when they changed jobs. The major reasons for these moves were believed to be the better job opportunities which movement provided, as the following table on the attributed reasons for movement shows:

Reasons for Geographical Mobility (Q. 179)

	Manual %	Non-Manual %
Redundancy/unemployment	16	7
Better job/money	71	80
Time for change	11	9
Other	0	4
	N = 70	N = 56

Movement was thus seen as a positive step, a means of achieving occupational goals, whether financial or other, rather than the solution to employment difficulties: over 70 per cent of manual workers and over 80 per cent of non-manual workers saw mobility in these terms. The major groups of people mentioned as moving were the young and the ambitious. This positive conception of mobility was shared by both the redundant and the voluntary leavers: only 13 per cent of the redundant, and 10 per cent of the voluntary leavers, believed that redundancy or unemployment was the major reason for people moving house. Even when respondents were explicitly asked: 'What if there is no alternative work in the area, should people share work, take a less attractive job, with less money, receive unemployment benefit, move house, or do something else?', only 38 per cent of manual workers and 49 per cent of non-

155

manual workers said that one should move house (Q. 195). Over 26 per cent of manual workers, and 29 per cent of non-manual workers said that people should take a less attractive job, with less money, to remain within the area. One elderly power station worker expressed succinctly the general view of the Casterton Mills workers: 'Ordinary people don't move – only those who can better themselves . . . 90 per cent stick and look for work where they belong.'

Casterton Mills workers thus believed that some people moved around the country in search of better jobs, but not 'ordinary people', even following redundancies. This lack of interest was confirmed by the response to the firm's offers of employment at the central plant of the newly amalgamated company. Transfers, with earnings guarantees, housing assistance, and other benefits were offered to a small number of key employees, mainly white collar workers (especially professionally qualified staff) and a few vital process workers: 34 per cent of non-manual workers and 7 per cent of manual workers in our sample were offered transfers, none of whom accepted, although one or two went to the area to look at houses. We asked those who had not been offered a transfer if they would have liked to have been offered one: the overwhelming response was negative, only 12 per cent of manual workers and 7 per cent of non-manual workers saying that they would like to have been offered a job at headquarters. One aspect of this negative reaction may have been the desire to preserve face: 'I would not have gone even if they had asked me.' But there were other explanations for not wishing to go, some relating to the firm, others to the area of destination, and others to Casterton itself. As the following table shows, the most common reason given by manual workers for not wanting to be offered a transfer was attachment to the Casterton area, whilst it was also a reason mentioned frequently by non-manual workers:

Reasons for Not Wishing to be Offered Transfer (Q. 184)

	Manual%	Non-Manual%
Firm related	28	47
Dislike of region	20	14
Like Casterton	42	33

The redundant were particularly committed to Casterton, 45 per cent not wishing to be offered a transfer because they liked the city. Moreover, only 2 per cent had considered taking a job away from Casterton during the redundancy, none considered taking a job which would have involved living away during the week, and very few considered long-distance commuting.

It is thus not surprising that the majority of Casterton Mills workers took jobs within the area after leaving the Mills, as the following table shows:

	Manual		Non-Manual	
	Redundant %	Voluntary %	Redundant %	Voluntary %
Casterton	62	62	49	47
Casterton Dist.	13	20	17	16
Within 25 miles	5	4	9	12
Casterton county	3	10	4	9
Elsewhere	—	4	2	16
Unemployed	15	—	21	—
$N = 61$	$N = 50$	$N = 47$	$N = 43$	

Hence 75 per cent of redundant manual workers, and 76 per cent of voluntary leaving manual workers, found jobs within Casterton or within the immediate vicinity; similarly, 66 per cent of redundant non-manual workers and 63 per cent of voluntary leaving non-manual workers found jobs locally. The only group which contained a significant number of 'spiralists', prepared to leave the area in pursuit of their careers, was that of voluntary leaving non-manual workers. These were the small number of young, professionally qualified staff, committed to their careers and not tied to the locality. 'None of what I would call local people moved out of the area – only people coming from University who wanted to move' (51-year-old redundant 'local' line manager). Although our contact rate with the mobile was almost certainly lower than with those who did not move, despite frequent calls upon neighbours, asking around among friends, and sending postal questionnaires to the last known address, the number who moved, even on the assumption that all non-contacts had moved out of the area, was small. Moreover, our low estimate of the amount of geographical mobility was shared by the respondents themselves, very few being able to think of personal friends who had moved. Like the Durham coalminers interviewed by R. C. Taylor and M. Bulmer, Casterton Mills workers were 'stickers', unpersuaded by official blanishments about the new life offered elsewhere.[5]

Why were the Casterton Mills workers so immobile? The majority of Casterton workers said that they preferred living in Casterton to living elsewhere: 74 per cent of manual workers and 69 per cent of non-manual workers said that they had no wish to live elsewhere. Predictably, the young were more favourably disposed towards moving than the old: 44 per cent of those under 25 said that they would prefer to live elsewhere, largely because of the lack of job opportunities available locally. As the following table shows, the major reasons given for preferring to remain in Casterton were the amenities provided by the area itself:

Reasons for Preferring to Live in Casterton (Q. 247)

	Manual %	Non-Manual %
Kin/friends	6	12
Work	2	0
Custom	26	20
Amenties	66	66
Other	0	2
	N = 65	N = 41

With its rural surroundings Casterton seemed more attractive, especially to the middle-aged and elderly, than a large, grubby metropolitan area: 'I like the countryside. . . . I'd hate to live in Leeds, Birmingham, Manchester or Liverpool. . . . I hate the city jungle and the terraced houses. . . . I like being a member of a small community' explained a 55-year-old redundant line manager, who was obliged to take a lower-status job to stay in the area. However, the emphasis attached to the environment itself may have been partly the result of the focus

[5] R. C. Taylor, 'Migration and Motivation', in ed. J. A. Jackson, *Migration*, Cambridge: Cambridge University Press, 1970; M. I. A. Bulmer, 'Mining Redundancy: A Case Study of the Workings of the Redundancy Payments Act in the Durham Coalfield', *Industrial Relations Journal*, December 1971, pp. 3–21.

of the question asked, 'Why do you like living here?', and
it is necessary to look at the other factors which bound the
Casterton Mills workers to their community, especially relations
with kin and with friends, and leisure activities, to understand
immobility and the attachment to the community whose political
economy was described earlier as paternalist capitalism.

II

As we have seen, the majority of Casterton Mills workers were
locals, whether this is defined in terms of their own birthplace
the birthplace of their parents, or the present residence of
parents. Parents, and parents-in-law, were an especially important tie with the area; the majority of both manual and non-
manual workers with parents still alive had parents living in
the area, and visited them regularly.

Residence of Parents (Q. 255)

	Manual %	Non-Manual %
Casterton and District	71	88
Casterton County	9	7
North of England	5	4
Elsewhere in Britain	9	2
Abroad	7	0
	N = 70	N = 59

Hence 71 per cent of manual workers and 88 per cent of
non-manual workers with parents alive had parents living in
the area. Both manual and non-manual workers visited parents
regularly; 64 per cent of manual workers and 69 per cent of
non-manual workers visited their parents either daily or two
or three times per week. Moreover, 56 per cent of manual
workers with siblings alive, and 58 per cent of non-manual
workers with siblings alive, had siblings resident in Casterton
and the surrounding district, although they were visited much
less frequently than parents: only 24 per cent of manual
workers and 35 per cent of non-manual workers visited siblings
twice a week or more. One manual worker, who had emigrated
to Canada but subsequently returned, was unusually forthcoming about his contacts with his family: 'I would miss the

159

family and the wife's family [if we moved]. I suppose it is hard picking up roots. You know everybody and everybody knows you' (30-year-old warehouse worker). The sentiments he expressed were clearly reflected in the behaviour of the majority of both manual and non-manual workers in Casterton.

Kin played a central role in the concerns of Casterton workers, but not friends. Friends were comparatively insignificant, especially for manual workers: 'I don't have any close friends: I don't have any. Mostly the family like' (65-year-old clerical worker). Only a third of manual workers, and just over a half of non-manual workers gave the occupations and other information about their three closest friends, reflecting the comparative lack of significance of the social category of 'friends' for manual workers. This was equally true for the wives of manual workers: only 9 per cent said that they visited friends regularly, compared with 35 per cent who said that they visited neighbours, and 56 per cent who said that they visited kin regularly. This was partly the result of the age structure of the population – 'none now' commented one 60-year-old manual worker – and partly, for some non-manual workers, the need to maintain social distance as an aspect of authority within the plant. 'I found my position made me a bit choosy . . . the moment you become a foreman you become staff, whether you like it or not they make you different . . . no personal friends at work, although I looked on personal contacts at the Mills as friendly' (51-year-old redundant line manager). But mostly it stemmed from a heightened consciousness of the desirability of keeping oneself to oneself, and a focus of affiliation upon the family, mentioned by other investigators, for example Hodges and Smith in their investigation of a Sheffield housing estate.[6] This emphasis upon privacy constitutes a longstanding element in the values of the respectable working class; as Mildred, the respectable waitress in Somerset Maugham's *Of Human Bondage*, commented, 'I'm one to keep myself to myself, I'm not one to go about with anybody.' Outsiders, 'acquaintances not friends', were treated with distant friendli-

[6] Liverpool, University of Liverpool Department of Social Science, *Neighbourhood and Community*, Liverpool: Liverpool University Press, 1954.

ness: 'We don't bother with anybody really – say hello to everybody and that's it' (64-year-old power station worker). The community was a noticeably 'friendly' community.

The marginal role of friends for Casterton workers was not a sign of privatisation, of low morale, and did not result in social isolation and lack of participation in communal social activities. The following table shows the major leisure activities of the sample, based upon replies to the question: 'Normally speaking, how do you spend the [time when you are not working]?'

Leisure Activities (Q. 282)

	Manual N	Non-Manual N
Family centred	15	7
House centred	21	22
Watching T.V.	49	24
Hobby	30	46
Visiting kin	15	8
Social with wife	14	10
Social with mates	35	19
Organised social	3	15
Other	8	17

N is number of times a given activity was mentioned: respondents were allowed three responses.

Although the most popular leisure activity for manual workers was watching T.V., as one would expect in view of the Government Social survey finding that watching T.V. was over twice as popular a leisure activity as any other activity, and for non-manual workers was pursuing a hobby of some kind, both presumably solitary activities, 60 per cent of manual workers said that they spent some part of their leisure time with friends, usually at a pub or club, and 72 per cent of non-manual workers mentioned various gregarious activities.[7] Moreover, a substantial number of manual and non-manual workers were members of clubs and societies: 61 per cent of manual workers and 72 per cent of non-manual workers. The most popular types of clubs were social clubs and sports clubs, especially of course for younger workers, although 25 per cent

[7] *Social Trends in Britain*, H.M.S.O., 1970, p. 78.

L

of manual workers who were club members were members of working men's clubs. For some respondents the club was simply a place to meet friends, and 44 per cent of manual workers and 22 per cent of non-manual workers said that they would not be worried if their club closed down. However, for others they formed a major focus of interest: 46 per cent of manual workers and 57 per cent of non-manual workers said that they would be very disappointed if their club were forced to close. '[How would you feel if your club had to close down?] I would not like it to close because it is a focal point for me. I'd have to find an alternative, but it would be difficult' explained a 55-year-old foreman who had been to the local social club once a week for over 20 years. 'Disgusted. I know they have departed a long way from familiar concepts to improve them educationally instead of just filling them with beer and putting bingo cards in their hands. But they do fill a need' (45-year-old foreman on a working man's club). Although the intense emotional attachment to clubs, and the almost phrenetic gregariousness discussed by Jackson in his portrait of the role of working men's clubs in South Yorkshire, was lacking, they clearly played a significant role in the social life of at least a minority of the Casterton Mills workers.[8]

III

There was surprisingly little mention of housing by the Casterton workers in their discussion of the problems involved in geographical mobility; only one or two mentioned housing, and the difficulty of obtaining equivalent housing elsewhere – probably because mobility had not been considered seriously, and practical problems like housing had not emerged. National surveys, summarised by J. B. Cullingworth in his survey of *Housing and Labour Mobility*, suggest that this is a major problem for the mobile, a view repeatedly echoed by government officials on several occasions, publicly and privately.[9] This would have posed a serious problem for Casterton workers.

[8] B. Jackson, *Working Class Community*, Chapter 4.
[9] J. B. Cullingworth, *Housing and Labour Mobility*, Paris: O.E.C.D., 1969.

The majority of Casterton workers owned their own houses – 59 per cent of manual workers and 66 per cent of non-manual workers were owner-occupiers – and a significant minority of manual workers rented accommodation from the Council. Since the average price of houses in the Casterton area, as in other depressed regions, was significantly below the national average it would have been impossible to obtain comparable accommodation elsewhere. Although there are no figures available for the average cost of houses in the area, the prices of houses advertised in the local press were over £1000 below the national average for conventional three-bedroom semi-detached houses, and even more below the level of prices obtaining in areas with substantial job opportunities. Moreover, the problems stemming from the lack of transferability of council house entitlements (or privileges) are notorious; and the absence of immigration into the area meant that the possibility of arranging council house exchanges was negligible.

IV

The effects of inertia, preference for and identification with the area, kinship ties, friends and leisure habits, formal and informal, was cumulative. 'I lived in Casterton all my life: my family and friends are here.' 'I'd miss it all – to some extent I'd miss friends and family. . . . Geographically it is near perfect' (41-year-old foreman). The interdependence of these factors, the size of the sample, and the paucity of the mobile, render it impossible to assess the relative weight of the different factors. However, it is possible to construct an 'ideal-typical' immobile worker and an ideal-typical 'motile' worker (i.e. one who possesses the individual attributes required for mobility).[10] The former is employed in a semi-skilled job, in his late fifties, with elderly relatives in the area, and highly involved, if only at the rank-and-file level, in local activities. The latter is of course the opposite of this: young, skilled, without relatives in the area, and privatised. In Casterton,

[10] Cf. J. Abbott, *Student Life in a Class Society*, Oxford: Pergamon Press, 1971, pp. 410–12.

however, even the 'motile' were not mobile. For example, one 29-year-old motor mechanic, who was unwilling to take any job outside his trade 'because I'm a tradesman', who believed in the importance of changing employers in order to better oneself, and in the need to move out of the area if no work is available, took a makeshift job in Casterton rather than move house. Geographical mobility was outside the range of normal solutions to employment difficulties for Casterton workers: 'I never really have moved, or thought about it' (36-year-old warehouse worker).

However, the redundancy itself contributed to a process of change which had already begun. 'The average Casterton man is not a man for moving about: it is a quiet type of city . . . I think it is part of the Casterton background. It isn't a technical city, its got only a small number of industries and is fairly stable. People lack a real urge to better themselves, and don't move. This was so – it is now changing, and the time is coming when they will move – myself for one' (43-year-old foreman electrician). Others commented on their readiness to move a second time once they had been forced to move a first time: 'I like [my present job]. I won't say I'd stick with it – now I've made one move I'm ready to look out for other jobs that are better. Until then I was a stick-in-the-mud, but now that I've made a move I think I'm better off – better prepared to move' (36-year-old electrician). The numbers involved, and the time of the interviewing, make it impossible to assess how far this feeling resulted in further movement. But it is suggestive: redundancy does not lead to any immediate shift in labour (rather the reverse, because of the immediate uncertainty it causes); but it may lead to an unfreezing of attitudes which, in the long run, results in a closer approach to the classic labour market behaviour of economic man, on the look out for his own best interests, and ready to move where the rewards, whether in financial, status, or other terms, are better. Whether this is good or bad is of course a matter of opinion, and whether it is economically advantageous is a more questionable assumption than recent government policy statements have suggested. But it is in line with the aims of current government employment policy.

164

V

One of the simplifying assumptions involved in the economic analysis of redundancy and unemployment is that there is a national labour market. However, this assumption is a statistical convenience rather than an empirical reality; there is no national labour market, only a number of local labour markets, partially insulated from each other, based upon geography, industry, or occupation.[11] The effect of the redundancy was to force workers to move from one job into another, involving a shift in either industry, occupation, or location. Events showed that the major movement was from one industry to another, rather than from occupation to occupation, or a change in location. Very few workers were geographically mobile, and only a small minority ever considered moving house, mainly because of their general satisfaction with the level of amenities in the area. The redundant were even less likely than the voluntary leavers to take jobs involving movement out of Casterton, only 4 per cent compared with 9 per cent taking jobs more than 25 miles away. The effect of the redundancy payments scheme upon labour mobility was thus negligible: those who received the highest payments, primarily the old, were the least likely to move. Commitment to Casterton and to kin, to a much lesser extent to friends, and custom were the major reasons for the immobility. The redundancy payments provided compensation for workers for the loss of job property rights; but it did not make any contribution to increasing the flexibility of the labour market by stimulating geographical mobility.

[11] Cf. D. Robinson, 'Myths of the Local Labour Market', *Personnel*, Vol. 1, 1969; ed. D. Robinson, *Local Labour Markets and Wage Structures*, Gower Press, 1970.

9 CONCLUSION: REDUNDANCY, SOCIAL POLICY AND SOCIOLOGY

The dominant approach to the study of redundancy has been derived from labour economics, and the analysis of problems of employment and unemployment. The causes of redundancy are seen as changes in the level of aggregate demand, in the direction of demand, in the methods of production, or in government or enterprise policy; unemployment, patterns of labour mobility, and earnings, are the major consequences of redundancy analysed.[1] These factors are, of course, very important, especially to policy makers concerned with broad policy questions and willing to accept simplified assumptions as the necessary price of decision-making in an unsatisfactory world. But, as we hope the preceding chapters have shown, this is far from being the whole story; a fuller and more complex picture is necessary for a full understanding of behaviour during redundancies. Redundancies may be caused primarily by economic problems, or political responses to economic pressures; but other factors, political, cultural, and social, affect their implementation. Nor are their consequences limited to economic behaviour, as Dorothy Wedderburn has shown very clearly in her study of *Redundancy and the Railwaymen*. Unfortunately, viewing redundancy as a sociological rather than an economic problem, and dispensing with the simplifying and often useful assumptions of labour economics, makes the investigation of redundancy complicated, detailed and time consuming; but it also makes it interesting.

Recognising these difficulties, we have adopted a case study approach – partly because of the complexity of the subject matter, partly because of the absence of much of the information that would be required for a macro-analysis (for example

[1] See for example, L. C. Hunter *et al.*, *Labour Problems of Technological Change*, p. 320.

166

on the relationship between changes in productivity and redundancy) and partly because of disciplinary affiliation (to sociology rather than to econometrics), financial resources, and personal preference. We have studied one redundancy, in one place, at one time, in considerable detail. This has obvious disadvantages, especially the difficulty of assessing how typical events at Casterton Mills were; there are few other comparable studies, and no clear criteria to provide a basis for assessing typicality. But the only way to establish the basis for a proper programme of comparative research is by detailed investigation of individual cases, by clarifying the criteria relevant for further comparative investigations. Case studies are necessary, initially as a preliminary. and subsequently as a complement, to comparative research. Moreover, despite many distinctive features, we do not think that the situation at Casterton Mills was unique.

I

Casterton is an isolated, medium-sized industrial town in a mainly rural part of the north of England; since 1900 the population has remained relatively stable, fluctuating between 40,000 and 51,000. At the time of the redundancy Casterton contained a large but fragmented working class, employed primarily in the Mills and in a large number of small workshops in the city, and a substantial petit-bourgeois middle-class, composed mainly of workers in retail distribution and other services, and in public administration. The Mills were the largest employers in the area, occupying a distinctive role in the local social system; they were one of *the* institutions in the area, and exercised a considerable influence upon local political life, both directly and indirectly. The community was highly integrated, and social behaviour highly visible; the boundary between social life and work life was indistinct. The community's isolation, demographic stagnation, social and economic development, and the policy of the Mills created a system of paternalist capitalism, where management adopted an autocratic but benevolent role towards employees, and employees were highly committed to the firm: a classic *Betriebsgemeinschaft* situation. The factors which sustained this structure, and the attitudes which accompanied it, are examined in detail in chapters two, three, and four. This structure survived until the 1960s, given extended life by the boom in consumer demand following the Second World War, and the consequent ease with which management could 'look after' an inflated labour force. The boom collapsed in the early 1960s, and the Mills were forced into a defensive merger with a major rival: the merger led to considerable rationalisation, the disposal of surplus assets and the consolidation of both administration and production at the headquarters of the former rival, in a government development area. This process of rationalisation culminated in the redundancy at Casterton Mills, and the reduction of the labour force there by 1200. The redundancy marked the final collapse of a structure of paternalist capitalism which had been built up in Casterton over a century.

The tightness of the constraints operating upon management during a redundancy depends upon the cause of the redundancy; there is less room for manoeuvre where the causes of the redundancy are external changes in demand (as in Casterton), than where the causes are internal changes in the processes of production (as in the chemical industry redundancies discussed by Hunter and Reid). However, similar constraints operate upon management regardless of the causes of the redundancy, leading to greater or lesser deviations from market rationality, as we argued in Chapter 5. These constraints include the formal and informal obligations built into conceptions of the managerial role; the need to continue to satisfy, at least minimally, managerial goals other than the scheduled reduction of the labour force; the management political system; the plant socio-technical system; the power of the work groups involved; the external market situation; and external social expectations, whether formal like government regulations or informal like general expectations regarding dismissal procedures. Management's ability to act according to the demand of market rationality will vary according to the looseness of these constraints. Management at Casterton Mills had relatively little room for manoeuvre, limited by continuing market uncertainties and by the unpredicted behaviour of its labour force.

The amount and timing of the release of labour on to the labour market will be determined by management policy and by the labour market situation of the employees concerned. Employees in the strongest labour market position will tend to leave as soon as the redundancy is announced, partly because of the general unpleasantness and uncertainty which redundancy involves for all concerned, partly because of doubts about their future with the firm, and partly out of a fear that the best available jobs will be snapped up quickly. Assessment of the impact of redundancy thus involves examining the experience of those who leave of their own accord as well as of those who are declared redundant. The redundant at Casterton Mills were primarily old, long-service employees, many of whom had acquired company specific expertise and authority; the voluntary leavers were predominantly young, short-service workers, especially, amongst manual workers, process workers, and amongst non manual workers, laboratory technicians. The redundant, especially those aged 55 or more, experienced considerable difficulty in finding work; a half of the redundant manual workers, and two-thirds of the redundant non-manual workers in this age group were out of work for three months or more. The voluntary leavers experienced relatively little difficulty, the majority moving directly into new jobs and often (58 per cent of manual workers and 60 per cent of non-manual workers) into new jobs paying higher wages.

Experience of unemployment depends upon personal characteristics (especially age), occupational preferences, methods of job seeking, area of search, and, especially, the structure of available opportunities. The majority of Casterton Mills workers wished to remain in the type of work they had been accustomed to, whether clerical, skilled manual, or process, but had only limied financial aspirations. Both wishes were fulfilled: occupational status was maintained, but at the cost of financial sacrifice for the majority of both manual and non-manual redundant workers. The methods of job seeking used varied between social classes, and between the redundant and the voluntary leavers. Manual workers, especially the redundant, relied upon asking around amongst relatives and friends and, especially the voluntary leavers, upon calling on firms casually:

169

for both groups asking relatives and friends proved the most successful technique. Non-manual workers, especially the voluntary leavers, relied mainly upon replying to newspaper advertisements. The area of search for jobs was restricted. Very few Casterton workers considered taking a job out of the area, partly out of a desire to live within the area, partly because of kinship ties, partly because of housing difficulties, and partly simply because of inertia and custom. There were only limited job oppportunities available in Casterton, the area suffering from economic stagnation even before the redundancy; the majority of workers went into the largest industries in the area: plastics, chemicals, services, and public administration, especially education. Despite local fears that the redundancy would result in a sharp increase in unemployment in the area there was little immediate change in the level, and only the over 50s were out of work for long periods. However, the effect of the redundancy upon the employment structure of Casterton was greater than appeared immediately, for the permanent reduction in the level of labour demand further restricted the already limited openings available locally for school leavers. The redundancy contributed substantially to raising the level of unemployment in the area above the national average; at the time of the redundancy the level was fractionally below the national average, but three years later it had increased to over twice the national average – a grey area had become a black area.

II

There are three major questions of social policy upon which we would like to comment briefly on the basis of our research in Casterton: the effectiveness of the Redundancy Payments Act, especially in increasing the flexibility of the labour force; the length of notice which should be given of redundancy; and the criteria used in assessing the level of government aid to economically depressed areas.

One of the major objectives of the Redundancy Payments Act and derivative schemes is to increase the flexibility of the labour force by facilitating labour mobility. Redundancy pay-

170

ments were seen as, at best, a means of providing for some of the disturbance costs involved in moving house to find a new job, or at worst as a means of reconciling workers to dismissal. Attempts to increase labour mobility imply that payments should be channelled towards potentially mobile workers, especially the young. However, this conflicts with the financial implications of the second objective of government policy, compensation for the loss of property rights in their jobs. The financial implication of this objective is that payments should be made to long-service workers, especially the old, who have lost the most substantial investments in terms of seniority, time, and personal prestige. In practice, of course, the compensation objective receives priority, payments being related to length of service, age and previous earnings rather than to the needs of mobility: the young, who are more willing to make major changes in their mode of life and are thus more likely to be influenced by financial inducements to labour mobility, receive only limited assistance.

The existence of the redundancy payments scheme has made it easier for management to dismiss elderly workers. As Parker *et al.* conclude in their report on *The Effects of the Redundancy Payments Act*: 'There is some evidence to suggest that the Act has influenced the criteria used by employers in the selection of workers for redundancy. Although length of service, efficiency at the job, and skill level continued to be the most important criteria, there is evidence in [our] survey's findings that age and sickness records have become more prominent since the introduction of the Act.'[2] Management knows that older workers are more expensive, and have worse sickness records, and fears that they are less productive than younger workers; consequently redundant workers are older than the non-redundant members of the labour force, even in industries with a relatively young age structure like the West Midlands engineering industry.[3] This is economically beneficial for the firms making men redundant: it helps to maintain a balanced age structure for their labour force. But it is very doubtful

[2] S. R. Parker *et al.*, *op. cit.*, p. 11.
[3] D. I. Mackay, 'After the Shake-out', *Oxford Economic Papers*, 1972, forthcoming.

whether it is beneficial for the economy as a whole; older workers spend longer out of work, have more difficulty in getting jobs, and when they obtain work tend to earn less, as our research in Casterton and other studies have shown.[4] The result is at best considerable labour market friction, and at worst acute personal distress, rather than a flexible labour force. The official report on the workings of the Redundancy Payments Act concludes: 'It was realised that redundancy among older workers often brings with it very severe personal costs, and in this respect the Act contained provisions to compensate for these.'[5] But to suggest that this compensation is adequate is disingenuous in the extreme. Private problems are here inadequately expressed as public issues.

In short, the Redundancy Payments Act has made involuntary dismissal more equitable by providing compensation for the loss of job property rights, although at the cost of increasing the chances of dismissal for elderly workers. There is no evidence, in Casterton or elsewhere, to suggest that the existence of the redundancy payments scheme has had any effect upon labour mobility, especially geographical mobility.

The conflict of interest between management and workers inherent in the structure of the business enterprise becomes sharper during the periods of economic difficulty which customarily precede redundancies. Both management and workers realise that strategies for solving economic difficulties may involve dismissals, and the lines of battle are drawn accordingly. One major issue upon which the conflict focuses is that of the length of notice to be given regarding dismissals. Management wishes to postpone the announcement of a decision, partly because of a general uncertainty, and partly to minimise the disruption of work patterns, and the deterioration in morale which inevitably follow the announcement of impending redundancies. Workers wish to extend the period of notice to allow the maximum period for looking for a new job. Commentators have regarded the desirability of extended periods of notice as axiomatic. Dorothy Wedderburn concludes: 'Provided that a firm decision has been taken to close or to

[4] See above, pp. 131–2.
[5] S. R. Parker, *op. cit.*, p. 11.

dismiss men, we would feel that publication of this decision, or information to the particular men selected for dismissal, is invaluable, however long ahead it is imparted. This not only gives them time to look for new work but also to become adjusted to the situation.'[6] There are obvious advantages in providing lenghy periods of notice: confidence between management and workers is patched up, workers can look around for new jobs. However, there are also considerable disadvantages. Specific announcements are often impossible because of the unpredictability of circumstances, whilst general announcements merely cause insecurity, workers being unsure whether they are to go or not. At Casterton Mills workers with the best prospects of re-employment – and the lowest entitlement to redundancy payments – left of their own accord following the announcement of the run-down, pre-empting the best local vacancies. Hence the comparative success of voluntary leavers in obtaining jobs with higher earnings than those provided by Casterton Mills. Workers in a weaker labour market situation, especially older workers (with or without skills), were placed at an additional disadvantage, being unwilling to leave their relatively high status jobs at the Mills and to surrender their entitlement to redundancy pay unless their personal dismissal was assured. The longer the gap between the general announcement of redundancy and its detailed implementation the greater the polarisation of employees into sharply differentiated groups of 'gaining' voluntary leavers and 'losing' redundant. Moreover, the announcement of a major redundancy has an obviously harmful effect upon morale: feelings of insecurity and suspicion, doubts about the long-term viability of the firm, and incessant jockeying for position, poison the atmosphere of the plant and lead to 'nobody bothering', to declining productivity, and to an obsessive concern with 'who is going to be next'. Prolonging the period allowed for adjusting to redundancy thus has serious disadvantageous consequences, resulting in more insecurity and greater re-employment problems for workers already likely to be facing the greatest employment problems.

[6] D. W. Wedderburn, *Redundancy and the Railwaymen*, p. 181.

Assessment of regional economic policy is obviously a complex and contentious issue in political economy which it is impossible to examine adequately here. However, we would like to make a few brief comments on the subject on the basis of our research in Casterton. Government economic assistance to the regions is currently assessed upon the basis of, firstly, comparative levels of unemployment, and secondly population changes, especially migration. Hence Ulster, Scotland, Wales, Northern England, Furness, Merseyside, and the South West of England – covering a half of Britain's area but only a fifth of the population – are designated as Development Areas because their level of unemployment exceeds a specified level. Such areas, containing a disproportionate concentration of declining extractive and heavy manufacturing industry, with obsolescent capital equipment, and a decaying nineteenth-century infrastructure of inadequate housing and amenities, obviously possess serious economic problems and require substantial government assistance. However, unemployment levels are, at best, an incomplete indicator of regional economic difficulties, and have little predictive value. A more complex indicator of economic development, incorporating indices of comparative rates of economic growth, both in terms of investment achieved and planned, and taking into account the comparative structure of earnings, would be more useful. Hence areas experiencing rates of economic growth significantly below the average, or with a concentration of labour in low earnings industries and occupations, could be watched especially closely and where necessary receive economic assistance before unemployment reaches the level required to justify Development Area status.

Moreover, the division of the country into Development Areas and the rest, the black and the white, with negligible provisions for intermediate areas, creates obvious 'boundary' problems for areas contiguous to Development Areas. Such areas, for example parts of Lancashire, possess pockets of unemployment substantially above the national average, but do not as a whole reach a qualifying level. They inevitably fall further behind national economic development, possessing neither the large markets of the South-East and the Midlands

174

nor the capital investment grants given to firms investing in Development Areas. Their problems would be considerably eased if a more flexible regional policy were adopted, with intermediate grants to intermediate areas, and with a more active reviewing policy, as recommended by the Hunt Committee on The Intermediate Areas in 1969.[7] As Professor A. J. Brown argued in his note of dissent to the report of the Hunt Committee, 'There is a case for four classes of area (excluding the special development areas), namely, development areas with something like their present levels of incentive, intermediate areas with something less, "neutral" areas (i.e. the prosperous but uncongested areas) with no incentives, and, finally, the congested areas – basically the conurbations in prosperous areas and their immediate surroundings where an additional tax, reflecting the cost to the rest of the community of each taxed unit's presence there, would be appropriate. Such a number of zones with different levels of incentive or disincentive is not without precedent; the French system has five.'[8] Unfortunately his note of dissent, like the report as a whole, has been neglected.

III

Our work has been focused upon the problem of redundancy, and the consequences of redundancy for workers involved and for the community. But we hope that our research has a wider significance for sociologists, especially sociologists interested in the sociology of work. Hence, in the final section of this conclusion we would like to place our work in the context of other recent sociological research in Britain, especially, at a substantive level, recent research on manual workers' attitudes towards work and the firm, and at a theoretical level recent work on organisational theory. Obviously we cannot hope to treat either topic in detail; but we feel that a few indications of possible connections would be useful.

[7] *Cmd. 3998. The Intermediate Areas: Report of a Committee under the Chairmanship of Sir Joseph Hunt*, H.M.S.O., 1969.
[8] *Ibid.*, p. 162.

J. H. Goldthorpe, D. Lockwood, and their colleagues in their influential study of *The Affluent Worker* and in a number of related articles have analysed attitudes towards work in terms of three 'ideal-typical' orientations, the instrumental, the bureaucratic, and the solidaristic.[9] Instrumentally oriented workers regard work as a 'means to an end, or ends, external to the work situation; that is, work is regarded as a means of acquiring the income necessary to support a valued way of life of which work itself is not an integral part . . . workers' involvement in the organisation which employs them is primarily a *calculative* one; it will be maintained for so long as the economic return for effort is seen as the best available, but for no other reason'. Work plays a more central role in the concerns of the bureacratically oriented worker: it provides moral and status, as well as financial rewards, and thus creates a strong ego-involvement in the job and the firm. 'The primary meaning of work is as service to an organisation in return for steadily increasing income and social status . . . . Arising from this, the involvement of workers with their organisation contains definite moral elements rather than deriving from a purely market relationship. . . . Work represents a central life interest in so far as the individual's career is crucial to his 'life fate'. Consequently, workers' lives cannot be sharply dichotomised into work and non-work.' Work is also a central life interest for workers with a 'solidaristic' orientation towards work, providing for the satisfaction of expressive needs through membership of the work group (or firm), as well as for the customary satisfaction of material needs. Collective solidarity is regarded as more important than maximising economic rewards, or furthering career prospects.[10]

This threefold typology proved to be a very powerful tool for analysing the attitudes – if not the behaviour, as critics have pointed out – of the affluent workers in the motor car, chemical,

---

[9] J. H. Goldthorpe, D. Lockwood, F. Bechhofer, J. Platt, *The Affluent Worker: Industrial Attitudes and Behaviour*, Cambridge: Cambridge University Press, 1968. See also D. Lockwood, 'Sources of Variation in Working Class Images of Society', *Sociological Review, 1966*.

[10] J. H. Goldthorpe, *et al.*, pp. 38–42.

and metal manufacturing industries in Luton.[11] But it has not proved so successful in other settings. The very term 'orientation' implies a consistency, and a homogeneity of attitudes which was not found in Casterton (or even, on a strict interpretation of the evidence, in Luton).[12] Moreover, it is often difficult to draw the line between the three orientations, for, as the authors point out, all work involves 'an instrumental component'. Bureaucratic and solidaristic workers may be as instrumental in their work behaviour as instrumental workers merely manifesting their instrumentalism in different ways. Hence Mercer and Weir conclude their survey of orientations to work amongst bureaucratic white collar workers in Hull: 'Overall, the picture that begins to emerge is of an orientation to work which, if not

[11] R. Blackburn, 'The Unequal Society', in ed. R. Blackburn and A. Cockburn, *The Incompatibles: Trade Union Militancy and the Consensus*, The Merlin Press, 1967.

[12] See Goldthorpe *et al.*, p. 162, footnote 2: '. . . we have, of course, tended to think of "instrumentalism" as constituting a syndrome of attitudes on the lines indicated in the ideal type. . . . What we in fact discover is that while scores on different [indices of instrumentalism] show a general tendency to be associated, the associations are not, taken individually, of a statistically significant kind. This might be taken to imply that instrumentalism should not be thought of as a single syndrome, which individuals display to a greater or lesser degree, but rather that the various elements in what we have regarded as the instrumental pattern have no particular tendency to coexist'. The authors reject this interpretation on plausible but insubstantial grounds: '. . . it should be remembered that . . . our method of scoring was devised specifically in order to differentiate within a sample in which, collectively, "instrumental" attitudes and behaviour were found to predominate. The distinctions made so as to split the sample up into sizeable sub-divisions had to be relatively fine ones. It might still be the case that the application of more basic distinctions to a less homogeneous sample would in fact confirm the *assumption* of an "instrumental" syndrome. On our reading of the literature of industrial sociology, we would think this result more likely than not. At all events we do not believe that the weak association between the scores on our items is in itself enough to require that such an assumption be abandoned. Finally . . . scores on the different items . . . regularly co-vary in relation to the independent variables we introduce. For example, semi-skilled workers not only have higher total scores than the more skilled men . . . but also come out higher on each of the three component scores' (our italics). Instrumentalism remains a plausible assumption only.

177

entirely instrumental, nonetheless resembles that made familiar by the Luton study at many points. In particular, there is little indication that clerks are less likely than other workers to emphasise the importance of salary, security, and the prospects of achieving a great measure of both, rather than the intrinsic satisfactions to be obtained from the tasks of work.'[13] Similarly, the traditionally solidaristic dockers and ship-builders have shown a complex pattern of both instrumental and solidaristic behaviour, dockers under the casual labour system prevalent before the Devlin Report on the docks constituting one of the most aggressively individualist and instrumental of work groups.[14] R. K. Brown and P. Brannen have analysed the combination of individualism and collectivism characteristic of economic behaviour in the ship-building industry: 'Differentials between trades, and especially between skilled and non-skilled men are closely watched. Within the context of certain restraints each trade tends to secure what it can get . . . this is a situation where the possibility of common action over earnings is slight, and where in fact there can be little common interest over earnings.'[15] In short, it has proved impossible to draw a clear line between instrumental and non-instrumental orientations, for most behaviour and attitudes contain elements of both.

The blurred boundaries of orientations to work and the firm became apparent in our work in Casterton. As we showed in Chapters 2, 3, and 4 the attitudes of Casterton Mills workers towards politics, social class, work and the firm sometimes corresponded with, sometimes overlapped with, and sometimes differed from those found elsewhere: there were traces of all three orientations to work. There were elements of the tradi-

[13] D. E. Mercer and D. T. H. Weir, 'Orientations to Work amongst White Collar Workers', in ed. J. H. Goldthorpe and M. J. Mann, *Proceedings of a Social Science Research Council Conference on Social Stratification and Industrial Relations*, Social Science Research Council, 1969, p. 119.

[14] Liverpool, University of, Department of Social Science, *The Dock Worker*, Liverpool: Liverpool University Press, 1954.

[15] R. K. Brown and P. Brannen, 'Social Relations and Social Perspectives amongst Ship-building Workers, A Preliminary Statement', Part II, *Sociology*, 1970, pp. 199–204.

tional solidaristic working-class orientation: the widespread support for trade union membership; the large number believing that the interests of management and workers were opposed (50 per cent); and the substantial minority who believed that workers had to stick together (45 per cent). There were strong indications of the bureaucratic orientation in the moral significance attached to employment; in the preference for intrinsically interesting jobs, in the case of a large minority at the expense of lower earnings; and, above all, in the strong commitment to the firm. Finally, there were signs of the instrumental orientation in the general agreement with the view that the only reason for changing jobs was to increase earnings, and in the preference of a large minority for a routine job paying £20 rather than an interesting one paying £15.

Non-manual workers show greater homogeneity in their beliefs, the majority holding views consistent with the bureaucratic orientation outlined: in their strong commitment to employment, to hard work, to getting ahead, to the intrinsic rewards to be derived from work, in short to personal fulfilment through work. Moreover, this was associated with a multi-layered conception of the social structure, within which individuals rose or fell according to their efforts and abilities. However, this bureaucratic orientation did not rule out instrumental elements; for example, non-manual workers were more likely than manual workers to mention pay and other extrinsic factors as reasons for preferring, or disliking, jobs.

The attitudes of Casterton Mills workers bore the imprint of the social structure within which they had been socialised, formally and informally: paternalist capitalism. For paternalist capitalism fostered attitudes of commitment and loyalty, of a diffuse particularism, of fatalistic acceptance of limitations – attitudes sometimes alleged to be alien to industrial society. These attitudes were preserved partly because of the lack of an alternative world view, 'It's the way I've been brought up', and partly because of the formal and informal sanctions which dominant groups could bring against deviants. Like the cotton towns of East Lancashire before the collapse of the cotton textile industry in the late 1950s, Casterton was a highly integrated, conformist, yet self-consciously individualist town, its tone set by Casterton Mills and its management. The community had probably changed little between the late nineteenth century, and the time of the redundancy, preserved by geographical isolation, the lack of immigration, the limited local labour market, and the prosperity of the floor-coverings industry. However, attitudes were beginning to change, even before the final announcement of the redundancy, as many respondents commented. Consideration of these changes raises important questions which have been examined in other research: the extent to which full employment and 'affluence' have led to new social attitudes, especially amongst the working class. We were not centrally concerned with this problem, and the inhabitants of Casterton were far from affluent, as the figures for earnings aspirations show (p. 140). However, a fundamental question raised here and elsewhere but not answered satisfactorily is: how far are age-related differences in social attitudes the result of life cycle situation or generation?

J. H. Goldthorpe and his colleagues argue that the first factor explaining the instrumental orientation of the affluent workers they interviewed was life-cycle position. 'In what ways ... is [the instrumental] orientation to work and its associated syndrome of attitudes and behaviour socially generated and sustained? ... The first factor which must be taken into account here is ... the position of our respondents in the life-cycle ... our sample was limited to men who were between the ages of 21 and 46 and who were married ... the large majority (83 per cent) had one or more dependent children. Men who are in this position, we would suggest, are, *ceteris paribus*, more likely than men at either an earlier or a later stage in the life-cycle to take up an instrumental orientation towards their work.'[16] This argument is based upon reasonable assumption, rather than data, for there was little variation according to age within the sample of respondents. There were indeed important differences between older and younger workers at Casterton Mills, some of which are explicable in terms of differences in life-cycle situation: the concern with 'interesting' work revealed by the over-60s was possible because of their reduced financial commitments; the declining interest

[16] J. H. Goldthorpe *et al.*, *op. cit.*, pp. 146–7.

of the over-35s in promotion clearly reflected a process of adjustment to the realities of work life. However, other age related differences are more difficult to relate to position in the life-cycle: differences in commitment to the firm, in the belief in the importance of obedience as a characteristic of the good worker, in the tendency of young workers to blame managerial inefficiency for the redundancy. Such differences may reflect differences in generation, between workers socialised into a culture of work scarcity and those socialised into a more complex world, in which images of plenty are superimposed upon a reality of scarcity, or perhaps may reflect simply shorter exposure to the work situation of paternalist capitalism. We suspect, but cannot demonstrate, the latter. But the respective merits of life-cycle and generational explanations for age-related differences in social attitudes is obviously an important question which would bear further investigation.[17]

IV

Within the last five years there has been a marked revival of interest in social action theory, both in the United States and in Britain. Weber's work on the classification of social action has been discussed extensively, Shutz's essays have been newly translated or republished in more accessible form, and the works of Berger and Luckmann, Garfinkel, Glaser and Strauss, and Goffman have achieved widespread recognition.[18] This revival of interest is probably due partly to the manifest analytical inadequacy of mechanical forms of structural functional theory, and partly to the widespread desire for a voluntaristic social theory, (a desire often associated with hostility to a real or imagined establishment). Structural functional theory, both

[17] There is of course a suggestive analysis of the problem in D. E. Butler and D. Stokes: *Political Change in Britain.*

[18] A. Schutz, *Collected Papers*, The Hague: Martinus Nijhoff, 1964 (Vol. 1), 1971 (Vol. 2); P. L. Berger and T. Luckmann, *The Social Construction of Reality*, New York: Doubleday, 1966; H. Garfinkel, *Studies in Ethnomethodology*, New York: Prentice-Hall, 1967; B. Glaser and A. Strauss, *The Discovery of Grounded Theory*, Weidenfeld and Nicholson, 1968; E. Goffman, *The Presentation of Self in Everyday Life*, New York: Doubleday, 1969.

181

in the strong Parsonian form of analysis in terms of system needs, and in the weak form understood simply as the analysis of behaviour in terms of consequences, has been superseded as the dominant theoretical framework by a more historical, personal, and social psychological approach.

Nowhere is this change more apparent than in the sociology of organisations, especially the sociology of industrial organisations. In the mid-1960s systems theory provided the dominant theoretical paradigm for industrial sociology, exemplified in the work of Katz and Kahn in the United States, and Trist, Miller, and Rice in Britain.[19] Katz and Kahn, drawing explicitly upon Parsonian theory, analysed industrial organisations as open-systems, composed of interdependent sub-systems, and operating through the processing of inputs, throughputs, and outputs. Successive workers at the Tavistock Institute have drawn their inspiration from a different source, from biology directly rather than from biology via structural functionalism, but constructed a similar model. A. K. Rice, for example, wrote: 'This book [*The Enterprise and Its Environment*] treats enterprises as living organisms. . . . [Enterprises], during their existence, employ human beings in a variety of roles, and require an organisation, however transient or primitive, to relate those who work in the enterprise to each other and to the tasks that they perform.'[20] Rice sees enterprises as open-systems, with many of the same characteristics as living organisms, including the tendency to maintain a 'steady state': 'One of the important implications of accepting organisational models based upon open system concepts is that open systems live by the exchange of materials with their environment and have the capacity to reach a time-independent steady state. That is to say, the system itself exerts forces towards the creation and maintenance of fixed relations between its elements in spite of variations in the rate of exchange with the environment. The pattern is that

[19] D. Katz and R. L. Kahn, *The Social Psychology of Organisations*, New York: John Wiley and Son, 1966; A. K. Rice, *The Enterprise and the Environment*, Tavistock Publications, 1963; E. J. Miller and A. K. Rice, *Systems of Organisation*, Tavistock Publications, 1967. Of course much industrial sociology was not guided by any theory at all, to its cost.

[20] A. K. Rice, *op. cit.*, p. 179.

of organic metabolism: increase in the rate of import is followed either by adaptation and increase in the rate of export or by resistance to imports. Once the steady state is disturbed for any reason, external or internal, the system will exert forces to restore it.'[21]

Consultants may find this model adequate for analysing some of the problems faced by their firms, for example problems stemming from malfunctioning communications channels. But the model provides an unsatisfactory basis for an explanatory theory of organisations, for two reasons. Firstly, it involves the transformation of an interesting analogy into an empirical generalisation: a network of relationships, the organisation, is given human characteristics. But, as David Silverman has pointed out in his polemical critique of systems theory, organisations do not act or react: 'Organisations do not react to their environment, their members do.'[22] Secondly, the organic analogy implies a mechanistic view of causation inappropriate to the human sciences; organisations do not automatically respond to stimuli in the same way as the human organism responds to pain. 'Instead of explaining action away, say as a mechanistic reaction to their place in the organisation or as a mere reflection of the nature of class relations, [one must] show how action derives from the definitions of the situation and the ends of the actors as shaped by their prior expectations (associated with their extra organisational statuses) and their historical experiences of past interaction.'[23]

In his *The Theory of Organisations*, David Silverman presents a 'social action' alternative to the systems approach to the theory of organisations. He argues that sociology is primarily concerned with 'understanding action', which 'arises out of meanings which define social reality'. Shared meanings become institutionalised, and are handed down to succeeding generations as social facts, which are reaffirmed and adapted in everyday action. 'It follows that explanations of human actions must take account of the meanings which those concerned

[21] A. K. Rice, *op. cit.*, p. 262.
[22] D. Silverman, *The Theory of Organisations*, Heinemann Educational Books, 1970, p. 37.
[23] *Ibid.*, p. 164.

assign to their acts; the manner in which the everyday world is socially constructed yet perceived as real and routine becomes a crucial concern of sociological analysis. Positivistic explanations which assert that action is determined by external and constraining social and non-social forces, are inadmissible.'[24] This perspective forms the basis for a recommended programme of comparative research into organisations, focusing upon the nature of the 'predominant meaning structure and associated role system . . . the characteristic pattern of involvement . . . the typical strategies used by different actors to attain their ends . . . the relative ability of different actors to impose their definition of the situation upon others . . . [and] the origin and pattern of change of meaning structures'.[25]

This emphasis upon the importance of understanding actors' definitions of the situation, and the manner in which shared definitions and meanings become institutionalised, is important, a valuable corrective to over-deterministic formulations derived from systems theory. It directs attention to the influence of extra-organisational factors, especially cultural norms and values, upon behaviour within organisations, and to the different meanings which may be given to the 'same' phenomena. But concentration upon social action and 'meaning structures' in these terms can be carried to extremes, involving an exaggerated voluntarism, almost Idealism: Silverman's analysis contains clear echoes of Kantian philosophy. The social world is manipulable to a variable, often only limited, extent; some structures of meaning *cannot* be sustained because they conflict with the meaning structures of others, or with external objects. It is erroneous to see social action as an automatic playing out of role expectations, or as a mechanical reaction to situational constraints; but it is equally erroneous to limit sociological concerns to systems of meaning. Social action theory in these terms provides an inadequate basis for explaining *action*, i.e. the behaviour of actors forced to reconcile their interpretations of the situation with those of others, and with the external constraints of geography, of scarce desired objects, etc. As

[24] D. Silverman, *The Theory of Organisations*, Heinemann Educational Books, 1970, p. 127.
[25] *Ibid.*, pp. 171–2.

Weber argued, 'In all the sciences of human action, account must be taken of processes and phenomena which are devoid of subjective meaning, in the role of stimuli, results, favouring or hindering circumstances. . . . Both the actor and the sociologist must accept them as data to be taken into account.'[26] Moreover, definitions of the situation are based in part upon experience of earlier, comparable situations, where actions and outcomes have been determined partially by prior personal definitions, partly by the definitions adopted by others, and partly by external objects like the physical setting. It is likely that present situations will be defined in terms of the most nearly comparable previous situation in which outcomes were favourable, outcomes determined partly by 'non-social' objects.

We have analysed paternalist capitalism, and the redundancy at Casterton Mills, from a social action perspective, broadly conceived; i.e. in terms of actors' definitions of the situation and the way in which such definitions were related to the structure of the community and the plant. Events have been examined in terms of their meanings for the actors involved: the variable attitudes towards politics, social class, work, and the firm have been examined in detail as a way of understanding Casterton, Casterton Mills, and the behaviour of Casterton Mills workers following the redundancy. Social attitudes and behaviour, both before and, to a lesser extent, after the redundancy showed that Casterton Mills workers interpreted the world 'traditionally'; the world was accepted, aspirations were limited. This traditionalism was firmly rooted in a specific pattern of historical development. Social attitudes were conditioned by previous experience, especially previous experience of the local labour market; and the structure of the labour market was largely determined by geographical location and the absence of raw materials in the vicinity. Such factors did not make it inevitable that Casterton Mills workers would adopt a particular set of attitudes; but they did make it very likely.

It is obviously difficult to assess how far the historical development of the economic structure of a community deter-

[26] M. Weber, *Economy and Society*, New York: Bedminster Press, 1968, p. 7.

mines the social attitudes of its inhabitants; the effect is cumulative, 'in the long run', and conditional. But the influence of economic constraints upon behaviour within industrial enterprises in the short run is clearer. During the redundancy itself the market, in the shape of changing consumer preferences, and the socio-technical system, in the form of the variable interdependences between different parts of the plant, set tight limits to individual action. Management had some, but only a small amount, of discretion during the decision making process which preceded the redundancy; the market, socio-technical system, and the behaviour of the labour force were powerful constraining influences. Similarly, Casterton redundant workers were subject to powerful limiting influences from the labour market in their job seeking following the redundancy, and they had little alternative but to define the situation in a certain way: difficult. To emphasise the importance of such situational constraints is not to deny the validity of the social action approach: it is to argue that the social action approach does not require, except in a trivial sense, that explanations in terms of constraints are inadmissible.

V

The study of redundancy is important in its own right: during 1968, before the present sharp increase in redundancies, 264,500 people received payments from the redundancy payments fund, and in 1971 the number rose to over 400,000. The meaning of these figures cannot be understood from national surveys, from global statistics; case study research is necessary to understand the detailed consequences of macro-economic decisions, to see at ground-floor level the economic, social, and sometimes even psychological consequences of large-scale decisions. But the study of redundancy, as we hope this book about events at Casterton Mills has shown, has a wider relevance for industrial sociologists. Substantively, it provides an unusual opportunity to see behaviour under rapidly changing conditions: the constraints, conflicts, and confusions which surround both management and workers attempting to cope with uncertainty and stress; the changeableness, and resilience, of pre-existing attitudes and patterns of behaviour. Methodologically, it provides a unique opportunity to relate work attitudes to labour market behaviour directly, for external pressures force workers to act, confirming or disconfirming their previous expressions; *if* research is started early enough it even provides an opportunity for quasi-experimental social research – but it is an unlikely if.

Redundancy is a time of stress, and sometimes distress, for all concerned: the redundant, the voluntary leavers, and those who stay with the firm. But for the sociologist, able to learn from and thereby help to alleviate the stress, it provides an opportunity: curiosity without attempts to alleviate the problem is mere ghoulishness. We believe that, at the very least, our study will increase general understanding of the problem; but we hope for more.

APPENDIX I
METHODS OF RESEARCH

The major limitations upon our research procedure derived from three sources: the initial formulation of the problem; the resources available, and their organisation; and limited imagination. We are only concerned with the first two in this note; we will no doubt hear enough about the third in due course.

The problem we attempted to investigate was: what are the major causes, processes and consequences of redundancy as exemplified by events at Casterton Mills in 1967 and 1968? Focusing upon redundancy in this way caused two problems: the need to rely upon the memory of respondents; and the need to attempt to reconstruct the system of meanings at Casterton Mills when that system had been seriously disturbed. Almost inevitably sociological research into redundancy only begins when the redundancy situation is either already completed, or near completion. Even very prompt action by researchers cannot eliminate reliance upon memory, hindsight, and bureaucratic records. Memory may be short, or accommodating; hindsight suffers from, or is illuminated by, what McHugh calls 'emergence';[1] and bureaucratic records, especially when made available for researchers, represent the resolution rather than the substance of conflict. These problems loomed especially large when we were attempting to reconstruct the course of the redundancy, and the process of managerial decision-making which preceded it. However, the redundancy was such an important event for the majority of respondents that memories were still clear over twelve months later, and our ability to check sources against each other limited the possibility of a one-sided bias. We cannot say that our reconstruction is accurate; but we believe it to be reasonably so. The dispersal of former employees at Casterton Mills proved to be a less serious problem than we had expected. At a practical level, the small amount of geographical mobility which followed the

[1] P. McHugh, *Defining the Situation*, New York: Bobbs-Merrill, Inc., 1968, p. 31.

188

redundancy meant that we did not have as much difficulty as we expected in contacting respondents, although of course there were a number of respondents whom we failed to contact. The related problem of the fragmentation of the system of meanings shared by employees at the Mills is more complex. We expected that experience of the redundancy would have 'distorted' perceptions of the firm, and of management's handling of the redundancy, leading either to bitter recriminations against the firm, or to a romanticisation of the firm, of the 'golden days' of the past. There were, of course, elements of both reinterpretations. However, we think that the data analysed in the body of our book shows that these tendencies were limited; attitudes towards the firm 'made sense' both in terms of other attitudes, and in themselves. Again, no final assessment is possible; but we believe that we have portrayed accurately the significance of Casterton Mills for its employees.

The major problem, stemming from limitations upon resources, both of men, material, and time, was the need to rely heavily upon the survey questionnaire as a source of data (see below, p. 194). Although one of the authors lived in the community during the period of the field-work, and the other visited frequently, there was no opportunity for participant observation within the plant. Similarly, the size of the sample had to be restricted to what could be managed by one person working in the field for a year; our conclusions are therefore subject to limitations deriving from limitations in the sample (see below pp. 192–3).

We would like to explain our research methods used under three major headings: residence and contact; sources of data; and sample and questionnaire.

Residence and contact

One of the authors lived in the community for fifteen months, in a part of the city where many former employees of Casterton Mills lived; we are grateful to the local authority for making this possible. This period of residence provided the opportunity for widespread informal discussions, and for gathering diverse types of documentary material, about the town, the Mills, and the redundancy. Contact was made with a number of local officials and former employees of the firm, who were able to provide much useful background information about the history of the firm, the role of the Casterton family, and the changes which had occurred in recent years. More formal discussions were held with the local M.P., with local politicians of both parties, with local authority officials, with trade union officials, with the secretaries of local working men's clubs, and with members of the local action committee which was set up following the redundancy in an attempt to attract more industry to the area. All furnished valuable anecdotal and contextual material which enabled us to 'make sense' of the local situation, and to understand the common definitions and myths which were the commonplace assumptions of everyday life in the community.

Sources of Data

More formal and sustained contacts were made with senior managers of the firm, especially the personnel manager, with the manager of the local employment exchange, and with the senior local authority official responsible for trying to attract industry to the area. Each of these, especially the personnel manager and the employment exchange manager, provided detailed information on the work-force of the town and of the Mills. The personnel manager made available to us the names of men who left the firm over a specified period, from which we drew the sample of men to be interviewed. The local employment exchange and the regional office of the Department of Employment and Productivity made available information relating to the pattern of employment, unemployment, and job vacancies in the area, and talked to us generally about local employment problems.

Further data was gathered from the back numbers of the local newspaper, from reports of the Regional Economic Council and the regional Economic Development Association, from the Census, and from other work concerned principally or in passing with the town. These proved especially helpful in Chapters 2 and 7.

Sample and Questionnaire

All of these sources helped to provide the basis for the construction of a long-semi-structured questionnaire, reproduced in full below. This questionnaire was administered to stratified samples of the whole population who left employment at the Mills between 1 February 1967 and 30 November 1968, i.e. to both redundant and voluntary leavers. Where geographical mobility or inconvenience to the interviewee (e.g. shift workers with extensive overtime) prevented a face-to-face interview a postal questionnaire was substituted. This postal questionnaire was an abbreviated version of the full one, and consisted of the questions asterisked in the following schedule. Administered questionnaires normally took between two and two and a half hours to complete, although some took considerably longer, and a few spread over several visits. A number of interviewees, selected randomly, agreed to having their interviews tape-recorded: none who were approached refused. This shortened the time taken by the interview, allowed for considerable flexibility in following up points made by the interviewee, and provided much more information than could be recorded by even the most diligent stenographer.

The Sample

The population from which we drew our samples totalled 564 males, of whom 402 were classified as 'hourly paid' by the company and 162 as 'monthly staff'. With the exception of foremen and charge-hands working on the shop floor, in the engineering section and in the power station, this distinction followed broadly the manual–non-manual dichotomy. It is a measure of the hierarchical structure which had typified the Mills in the past that a third classification of 'weekly staff' had only recently been amalgamaged with the monthly staff. Given the predominance of hourly-paid workers amongst the population we decided to utilise differential sampling fractions for the manual and non-manual group. For the manual the fraction selected was $0·375$ and for the non-manual $0·75$. In addition, we had noted a wide range of occupations and job titles in drawing the population and so we constructed broad bands of occupational or functional groups within the populations of manual and non-manual workers. These groups were based upon task, location, remuneration and level of authority. We further divided each of the populations into 'redundant' and 'voluntary leavers'. With the population thus divided, we drew stratified samples in the proportion already noted.

The tables below show the numbers, occupational distribution and reasons for leaving, of the populations and initial samples and responding samples.

The major reason for non-response was non-contact, although more non-manual than manual workers refused to cooperate. Many of those whom we did contact and interview had to be traced through more than one move of house and this confirmed the company's view and our suspicions that the personnel records were out of date. Those whom we discovered had moved were pursued as far as possible; those whom we presumed to be at the address we had but who were not at home, we visited a maximum of five times. Undoubtedly, some of the sample who were not contacted had moved away from Casterton, but we cannot estimate the numbers.

THE POPULATIONS AND SAMPLES

TABLE 1: Monthly Staff Turnover between 1.2.67 and 30.11.68

	Redundant			Voluntary Leavers*			Males Only — All†		
	Pop.	Initial Sample	Responding Sample	Pop.	Initial Sample	Responding Sample	Pop.	Initial Sample	Responding Sample
White Collar Clerical	24	18	14	24	19	15	48	37	29
White Collar Professional	7	5	5	8	6	3	15	11	8
White Collar Managerial/Supervisory	12	9	6	10	8	5	22	17	11
Laboratory	5	4	2	15	12	10	20	16	12
Line Managerial/Supervisory	18	14	11	2	2	—	20	16	11
Power Managerial/Supervisory	8	6	3	7	6	6	15	12	9
Craft Managerial/Supervisory	9	7	6	5	4	1	14	11	7
Miscellaneous	4	3	2	4	3	2	8	6	4
TOTAL	87	66	49	75	60	42	162	126	91

Sampling Fraction 0·75 (6/8)
Response rate 72·2 per cent

TABLE 2:   *Hourly Paid Turnover between 1.2.67 and 30.11.68.   Males Only*

	Redundant			Voluntary Leavers*			All†		
	Pop.	Initial Sample	Responding Sample	Pop.	Initial Sample	Responding Sample	Pop.	Initial Sample	Responding Sample
Tradesmen/Craftsmen	67	25	21	40	15	10	107	40	31
Mates of Tradesmen/Craftsmen	28	11	8	5	2	2	33	13	10
Process and Allied Workers	51	19	15	124	47	30	175	66	45
Warehouse, Packers and Allied	11	4	4	24	10	8	35	14	12
Power Station Workers	31	12	11	5	2	2	36	14	13
Miscellaneous	8	3	2	8	3	3	16	6	5
	196	74	61	206	79	55	402	153	116

Sampling Fraction 0·375 (3/8)
Response rate 75·8 per cent

* 'Voluntary' are those who left (1) in 'anticipation of redundancy' and (2) for 'better prospects' and 'better jobs'.
† 'All' does not mean all leavers but the aggregation of voluntary and redundant only. Reasons for leaving such as retirement or death are excluded.

Questionnaire

Once the sample had been drawn, letters explaining the aim of the research were posted to the address supplied by the company's records. In all cases the letter was followed by a visit, even where the letter was returned indicating that the member of the sample had 'gone away'. The purpose of the visit was to explain further the aim of the research and to arrange a time for interview or, where the man had gone away, to try to discover his new address. Those who were then contacted personally were interviewed using a lengthy schedule; those who had removed locally were also contacted and interviewed; those who had removed to another part of the country were sent a greatly shortened version of the questionnaire by post. In a very small minority of cases, some locally resident members of the sample who felt unable to give us much of their time, because of family or work commitments, for example, agreed to complete a postal questionnaire. The interviews were, for the most part, undertaken in the respondent's own home, although some were conducted in the researcher's home and a very few in quiet corners of public houses and clubs.

We have included the questionnaire in full, with the exception of a few questions relating to the financial position of friends who had left Casterton Mills which did not work at all (Questions 170–173). We have also excluded instructions to the interviewer with respect to 'filter' questions and such things as thanks. Questions included in the postal questionnaire are marked with an asterisk.

*   1. May I begin by asking how old you are now?

*   2. Are you single
           married
           widowed
      or divorced?

    3. Have you ever done any military service or national service?

    4. Were you ever a 'Regular'?

    5. Did that service take you away from the North of England
                                  the British Isles?

*   6. What is your present occupation?

*   7. Could you tell me in your own words exactly what you do at work?

* 8. What is the name of your present employer?

* 9. Is that in the Casterton area or elsewhere?

* 10. About how many people work on the same site as yourself?

  11. Now, about your own work.
Do you work on your own
           with a mate/assistant
           with a group or gang up to 10
           with a group or gang over 10
           other?

* 12. Do you work at a desk
           on a bench
           on an assembly line or belt
           on a machine
           minding more than one machine
           moving about an office
           moving about a shop/warehouse or store
           other?

* 13. Do you have any intention or hope of changing jobs or obtaining work in the near future?

  14. What job do you hope to change to?

  15. Where would that job be?

  16. Who would your new employer be?

  17. Have you ever thought of changing your present job?

  18. Have you taken any steps towards changing jobs?

  19. What steps have you taken?

  20. How long had you worked at Casterton Mills (C.M.) when you left including any military or National Service?

  21. Had you ever worked at Casterton before this?

  22. When was that?

  23. How long did you work at C.M. then?

  24. What was you job at C.M. then?

  25. Why did you leave on that occasion?

  26. What job did you go to then?

27. Why did you return to work at C.M.?

* 28. (a, b, and c) Now, could we go back over the jobs you did before you (last) worked at C.M., beginning with the job you had immediately before you (last) worked at C.M.

Could you tell me: What the job was?

* 29. The name of your employer?

* 30. How long you worked for that employer?

31. How many people worked on the same site as yourself?

32. Did you work on your own
> with a mate/assistant
> with a group or gang up to 10
> with a group or gang over 10
> other?

33. Did you work at a desk
> on a bench
> on an assembly line/belt
> on a machine
> minding more than one machine
> moving about an office
> moving about a shop/warehouse/store
> other?

* 34. Why did you leave that job?

* 35. And now, could you tell me what jobs you held at C.M. starting with the job you were doing up to the time you left C.M.?

(i)
(ii)
(iii)

36. (iv)
(v)
(vi)

37. Did you work on your own
> with a mate/assistant
> with a group or gang up to 10
> with a group or gang over 10
> other?

38. Did you work at a bench
                  at a desk
                  on an assembly line/belt
                  on a machine
                  minding more than one machine
                  moving about an office
                  moving about a shop/warehouse/store
                  other?

39. Why did you change jobs?
       (i)
       (ii)
       (iii)
       (iv)
       (v)
       (vi)

* 40. And now, since you left C.M. could you tell me
      How many jobs you have had?

* 41. What were those jobs? Could you tell me in your own words
      what those jobs involved?
       (i)
41. (ii)
41. (iii)

42. Did you work on your own
                  with a mate/assistant
                  with a group or gang up to 10
                  with a group or gang over 10
                  other?

43. Did you work at a desk
                  on a bench
                  on an assembly line/belt
                  on a machine
                  minding more than one machine
                  moving about an office
                  moving about a shop/warehouse/store
                  other?

* 44. Why did you leave that job/those jobs?
       (i)
44. (ii)
44. (iii)

* 45. Of all the jobs you have described, which did you like most?

* 46. Why did you like that job most?

* 47. Of all the jobs you have described, which did you like least?

* 48. Why did you like that job least?

* 49. Have you ever been a supervisor
                    section leader
                    foreman
                    manager?

50. Do you think there are any advantages or disadvantages in being   a supervisor
                    section leader
                    foreman
                    manager?

51. Would you like to be/have been a supervisor
                            section leader
                            foreman
                            manager?

52. Why not/why?

* 53. What sort of people do you think become supervisors, etc.?

54. Do you think there are any differences between the type of people who become supervisors, etc., and those who do not or are they the same kind of people?

* 55. Can you tell me why you went to work at C.M. in the first place?

56. How did you get your job at C.M. on that occasion?

* 57. Were jobs easy or difficult to get at C.M. at that time?

58. Why?

* 59. Have/do any of your relations work at C.M.?

* 60. Which ones?

* 61. Are/were they hourly paid
                    monthly staff?

* 62. Have/do any of your wife's relations work/worked at C.M.?

* 63. Which ones?

* 64. Are/were they hourly paid
monthly staff?

* 65. When you left C.M. were you hourly paid
monthly staff?

* 66. Were you ever hourly paid (if monthly staff)
monthly staff (if hourly paid)?

67. Were there any differences between being monthly staff and being hourly paid at C.M.?

68. What were the differences?

69. Were there any differences between the kind of people who were on the monthly staff and those who were hourly paid?

70. What were the differences?

* 71. Do you think that it's a good idea to have a system like that, I mean with hourly paid and monthly staff?

72. Why?

73. Turning now to the run-down itself.
When did you first hear *anything at all* about a reduction of numbers employed or run-down at C.M.?

73a. If official announcement. Had you heard anything before that?

74. How did you hear?

75. What was your reaction to that (rumour, information, etc.)?

* 76. Before you had heard anything at all about a run-down, had you thought of leaving C.M.?

* 77. Why had you thought of leaving?

78. Had you take any steps to get a different job?

79. What steps had you taken?

80. Why did you not take any steps?

81. How did you first hear *officially* that there was to be a run-down at C.M.?

82. What do you think of that way of giving the information?

83. What was your reaction to the official announcement?

84. Do you think the management of C.M. was at all concerned or distressed at the prospect of having to make many men redundant or do you think that they were indifferent?

85. Why do you think that?

86. After the official announcement had been made, did you then think of leaving C.M.?

87. Did you take any steps to get a different job?

88. What steps did you take?

89. Why did you not take any steps?

90. Did you think of staying on at C.M. until you retired?

91. If ever considered leaving C.M.
    Did you consider getting a job away from the Casterton area that would have meant
    (i) travelling some distance to work every day
    (ii) Living away from home during the week
    (iii) moving house?

92. Did you take any steps towards getting such a job?

93. What was that job?

94. Where was that job?

* 95. And so, when you eventually left C.M. was it of your own
                                      accord
                                or because you
                                were declared
                                redundant?

96. How did you first hear that you were to be made redundant?

97. What was your reaction to that news?

98. Have you ever lost your job or been declared redundant before?

99. Where was that?

100. What job did you lose?

101. How were the people to be made redundant at C.M. chosen?

102. How do you feel about that method?

103. Did you leave C.M. before your redundancy notice expired or on the day of expiry?

*104. May I ask how much redundancy payment you received altogether?

*105. May I ask whether you used your redundancy payment for any special purpose or to supplement your income after leaving C.M.?

*106. Following the official announcement there was a protest march and protest meeting at the Casterton Town Hall. Did you go on that march or to the meeting?

*107. Is there any special reason why you did not go on the march or to the meeting?

108. What kind of people did go on the march or to the meeting?

109. What did you think was the aim of the march and meeting?

110. What do you think was the reaction of the people in the Casterton area generally upon hearing of the proposed rundown at C.M.?

111. Why do you think the people in the area reacted in that way?

*112. Did you have a job fixed up before you left C.M.?

113. Did you go to that job immediately
after a short delay (how long)
after a long delay (how long)?

*114. How did you get that job?

115. What was that job?

116. Where was that job?

*117. Were the wages/earnings more or less than you got at C.M.?

*117a. How much more/less per week?

118. Apart from wages, how did that job compare with your job at C.M.?

*119. How long did you stay in that job?

120. Did you have another job fixed up before leaving that job?

*121. Why did you go to the second job?

122. How did you get the second job?

123. When did you start looking for a job. Was it before you left
C.M.
immediately after
you left C.M.
later?

124. How long was it after you left C.M. that you had a job fixed up?

125. What was that job?

126. Where was that job?

127. How did you get that job?

128. Were the wages/earnings more or less than you got at C.M.?

128a. How much more or less per week?

129. Apart from the wages, how did that job compare with your job at C.M.?

130. Did you register with the Employment Exchange immediately after you left C.M.?

131. Why did you not register immediately with the Employment Exchange?

132. Did the Employment Exchange send you to any jobs?

133. How many?

134. Were these the kind of jobs you were looking for?

135. Did you actually apply for any or all of the jobs that the Employment Exchange suggested?

136. Why not?

137. When you were looking or a job, what kind of job did you want?

138. Was there any kind of work you were not prepared to consider?

139. What kind of work?

140. Why were you not prepared, etc.?

*141. What kind of earnings were you looking for?

*141a.How much per week (per month)?

*142. Was there any level of earnings you were not prepared to go below?

*142a.What was that level of earnings (how much per week)?

*143. Were there any jobs that you applied for but were not offered?

144. What were those jobs?

145. Did you really want those jobs?

146. Why did you apply for those jobs that you did not really want?

147. Do you have any idea why you were not offered those jobs?

*148. Were there any jobs that you were offered but turned down?

149. Which jobs did you turn down?

150. Why did you turn those jobs down?

151. Apart from ways you have already mentioned, did you go about looking for a job in any of these ways:

Em/labour Exchange	ask friends or relations
answer newspaper ads.	call at firms on spec.
seek help of T.U./P.A.	answer factory/office gate notices
use T.U./P.A. Journal	or did you seek work in any other
write to friends or relations	way?

*152. Which way do you think is the most effective for finding a job?

153. Why?

154. At the time you started looking for a job, did you think it would be easy or difficult to get the kind of job you wanted?

155. What made you think it would be easy/difficult?

156. Were any of your personal friends made redundant from C.M.?

157. Have they got jobs now?

158. What are those jobs?

159. Where arc these jobs?

160. Does that involve travelling to work daily?

161. Does that involve living away from home during the week?

162. Did that involve moving house?

162. Did any of your personal friends leave C.M. of their own accord?

164. Have they got jobs now?

165. What are those jobs?

166. Where are those jobs?

167. Does that involve travelling some distance to work daily?

168. Does that involve living away from home during the week?

169. Did that involve moving house?

*174. Thinking of yourself, financially speaking, would you say you are better off
worse off
about the same
as five years ago?

*175. Now, thinking ahead, financially speaking, in five years time do you think you will be better off
worse off
about the same
as now?

176. Do you think some people do move about the country when they change jobs?

177. What sort of *people* are they?

178. What sort of jobs do they do?

179. Generally, what are the main reasons for their moving
Prompt   unemployment
more money
time for a change
better job
redundancy
other?

*180. Did C.M. offer you the chance of a transfer to the other factory?

181. Did you go and look round the other factory and think about the offer?

182. What was you decision?
    Was that the feeling of your wife?

183. Why did you not go and look round the other factory?

*184. Would you like to have been offered the chance of a transfer to the other factory?
    Why not?

185. I believe some people did go to the other factory. What kind of people were they?
    What kind of jobs did they do?

186. Now can we talk about unemployment?
    If a man is out of work, do you think he should get an income equivalent to what he would get in a full time job: or some per cent – what per cent?

187. Should everyone who is out of work get this amount or are there some who shouldn't?

188. What sort of people do you have in mind?

189. Why should they not?

190. There are a number of people unemployed at the moment. Why do you think they are out of work?

191. Whose fault do you think it is that you lost your job (and are now out of work)?

192. Do you think you would have lost your job: if you had been younger?

193. If there had not been a merger?

194. Basically whose responsibility is it to find or provide alternative work when people have to change their jobs?

195. What if there is no alternative work in the area, should people:
    share work
    take a less attractive job, with less money
    receive unemployment benefit of the sort you mentioned earlier
    move house
    other?

196. What sort of people have most difficulty in getting new jobs?

197. Why is that?

198. Have you ever thought of applying for entry to a Government Retraining Centre?

I would like now to go on to a rather different kind of question. I will read out some statements and would like you to say whether you agree or disagree, or agree strongly or disagree strongly, or are indifferent.

200. What is good for big business like I.C.I. or British Leyland is good for G.B.?

*201. If you have enough money without working there is no reason for having a job?

*202. The best way to win respect from your superior/bosses is to stick with one firm.
Why?

*203. If a man has a steady job and a reasonable wage then he should be content.
Why?

*204. I greatly admire those who work extremely hard in order to get ahead in their job.

205. The good employee is loyal to his firm even if this means putting himself out.

206. In what ways should the good worker be prepared to put himself out?

207. Managers are there to give orders and those workers who are under them should obey.

208. Are there any occasions when they should not?

*209. Anybody can get to the top if they have got the ability and are prepared to work hard.

210. One of the most important things for a parent to do is to help his children get further in life than himself.
How?

*211. Trade Unions, shop stewards, and other workers' repre-

sentatives only introduce trouble into the co-operation between management and workers.
Why?

*212. Some people are born to be bosses, ordinary people cannot hope to become bosses.

*213. Obedience and respect for authority are the most important characteristics of the good worker.

214. In order for us to do good work our bosses should outline carefully what is to be done and exactly how to do it.

*215. The main reason for voluntarily changing jobs is to improve your wages.

216. Management make the major decisions in industry and the employees/workers should accept them.

217. You will get promotion quicker if you do not join a T.U.
Why?

*218. Although leisure is a good thing, it is hard work that makes life worthwhile.
Why?

I will now read a series of statements. I would like you to choose from each set of two or three statements the statement which comes closest to your opinion. Please say if none of the alternatives comes close to your opinion.

*219. (i) If you stick with one firm and are loyal to them, promotion will come.

(ii) The only way to get promotion is to move around from job to job on the look out to improve your own position.

*220. (i) In Britain today there are basically two main classes, bosses and workers.

(ii) Most people in Britain today belong to the same class.

(iii) There are several classes in Britain.

*220a.If (i) or (iii) where would you place yourself?

*221. (i) Working-class people have got to stick together and stand up for each other.

(ii) Working-class people should strike out on their own. It's no good being held back by the rest.

207

*222. (i) If middle-class people are successful it is because they help each other with their wealth and position.

(ii) If middle-class people are successful it is because they have individual ability and put individual effort into things.

223. (i) Management is only interested in profits.

(ii) Management is interested in the good of the firm and all workers.

(iii) Management is interested in the good of the country and of the firm.

*224. (i) Every worker should join a T.U. because workers should stick together.

(ii) It doesn't really matter whether you join a T.U. or not.

(iii) There is only one reason for joining a T.U. and that's to improve wages and conditions.

*225. (i) A pool of unemployed is essential for the health of the economy.

(ii) The main reason for unemployment is incompetence on the part of the employers and the Government.

(iii) The main reason for unemployment is that many people are too lazy to look for work.

*226. (i) There is no point in making plans in order to get on in life for they only go wrong and make you unhappy.

(ii) If you want to get on in life, you must make plans and try to stick to them.

227. (i) Trade unions have too much power. They are ruining the country and are making things worse for their members.

(ii) Trade unions are not powerful enough. It's about time they started to take a stronger stand against employers and the Government.

(iii) Trade unions have enough power, but not too much power.

*228. (i) I would rather do a fairly routine job with £20 per week.

(ii) I would rather do a very interesting job with £15 per week.

*229. (i) I would rather have a safe job with limited prospects of promotion.

(ii) I would rather have a job with plenty of opportunity of promotion, even if the job was rather insecure.

*230. (i) The reasons for going on strike are to get more money or better conditions.

(ii) You should never go on strike.

(iii) There are several reasons for going on strike; for instance, in support of other unions and members, to get more money, to get 100 per cent membership, to protect your job, to get a grievance settled quickly.

231. (i) Your job is safer if you don't join a T.U.

(ii) Your job is safer if you are a member of a T.U.

232. Finally, do you agree with the statement that:
Workers who hold jobs—particularly those who hold the jobs for a long time—in a sense *own* those jobs and the job becomes part of their property and should not be taken away from them by management.

*233. Do you own this house
          rent it privately
          rent it from the council
other?

234. How long have you lived in this house?

235. Where did you live immediately before?

236. Have you ever lived in any other part of the Casterton area?

237. Do you like living in this part of the Casterton area or would you rather live in another part of the area?

238. Why do you like living in this part of the Casterton area?

239. Where in the Casterton area would you rather live?

240. Why?

241. Have you done anything at all about moving?

*242. Have you ever lived in any other part of the country?

*243. Where abouts was that?
      When was that?

*244. Why did you move (back) to the Casterton area?

O

245. Have you ever thought of living in any other part of the country?

246. Is there any part of the country you would rather live in or would you rather stay in the Casterton area?

247. Why do you like living in the Casterton area?

248. Where abouts in the country would you rather live?

249. Why?

250. Have you done anything about moving?

*251. Where were you born?

*252. Where was your wife born?

*253. Where were your parents born? Father
                                    Mother

*254. Are either of your parents still alive? Father
                                             Mother

*255. Where do they/he/she/ live?

*256. What is or was your father's occupation?

*257. Do you ever visit your mother and/or father or they visit you?

*258. How often   daily
                     per week
                     per month
                     per year?

259. When do you visit them/him/her or they/he/she visit you.
     Is it   during the day
                in the evening
                at the weekend
                holidays or day off
                Christmas, Easter, etc.
                other?

*260. Are either of your wife's parents still alive?

*261. Where do they/he/she live?

*262. What is or was your wife's father's occupation?

*263. Do you ever visit her mother and/or father or they visit you?

*264. How often   daily
                    per week
                    per month
                    per year?

265. When do you visit them/him/her or they he/she visit you.
    Is it   during the day
             in the evening
             at the weekend
             holidays or day off
             Christmas, Easter, etc.
             other?

*266. Do you have any brothers
                    sisters?

*267. What are their occupations? Brothers   Sisters
                                 1   1
                                 2   2
                                 3   3
                                 4   4

*268. Where do they live?   Brothers   Sisters
                                 1   1
                                 2   2
                                 3   3
                                 4   4

269. Do you ever visit them or they visit you?
    How often   daily
                    per week
                    per month
                    per year?

270. When do you visit them or they visit you?
    Is it   during the day
                in the evening
                at the weekend
                holidays or day off
                Christmas, Easter, etc.
                other?

271. Of Wife. Normally speaking might you go to visit anyone or might anyone visit you?

272. Who? Mother/father; neighbour; relative; friend; other.

273. Is this for any special reason or a social visit?

274. Is that during the day
                in the evening
                at weekends?

275. Of Wife.
     May I ask what jobs you (your wife) has done?
     (i)
     (ii)
     (iii)

*276. Of Wife.
      Do you (your wife) have a job at present?

*277. What is that job?

278. Apart from the relatives you have already mentioned do you have any other relatives that you keep in contact with?

279. Which ones?

280. What are their occupations/where do they live?

281. How do you keep in contact?

282. Normally speaking how do you spend your
     Evenings
     weekends
     other days off (e.g. bank holiday)?

*283. Do you belong to any clubs or organisations or societies
      such as   social clubs
                     sports club
                     working men's club
                     British Legion
                     Church or church group
                     other?

284. Do you hold or have you held any post or official position in any club or organisation?

285. Supposing your club(s), etc., had to close down, how would you feel about this?

286. Is there any one public house or hotel where you would usually go for a drink and call your 'regular' or 'local'?

287. When you go out for an evening do you tend to go:
         on your own
         with your wife
         with your wife and family
         with your wife and friends
         with your friends?

288. How often would that be   per week
                         per month?

289. What sort of things would you normally do on these occasions?

290. Do you and your wife have the same friends or do you each have your own friends?

*291. Could you tell me the occupations of your two or three best friends, where they live, how you got to know them, when you see them?
   (i) occupation
      where live
      how live
      how know
      when see
  (ii) occupation
      where live
      how know
      when see
 (iii) occupation
      where live
      how know
      when see.

292. Is there any one of your relatives or friends whom you regard as having done particularly well for himself/herself?

293. Why do you think he/she has done particularly well?

*294. Could you tell me what secondary school you went to and how old you were when you left school?

      School   Age
      F.E.

*295. Could you tell me what secondary school your wife went to and how old she was when she left school?
      School   Age
      F.E.

*296. Do you have any children?

*297. How many?

Boys	Age	Girls	Age
1		1	
2		2	
3		3	
4		4	

298. Of Oldest Child.
What secondary school did/does/would you like X to go to?

299. Would you like/have liked X to take any exams or certificates at school?

300. What kind of job would you like/have liked X to settle down in?

301. If there any kind of job you would not like/have liked X to settle down in?

302. Would you be prepared/have been prepared for X to spend three years away at university or technical college?

303. Supposing you or X knew/had known of a better job that X could get outside the Casterton area would you have wanted X to take it, or would you have preferred X to stay in the Casterton area?

*304. If you had a son about to embark on a career would you rather he became   skilled electrician earning £25 per week
school teacher earning £20 per week?

305. Why would you prefer him to be a skilled electrician/teacher?

*306. Have you ever thought about setting up in business on your own?

*307. Type of Business?

308. Have you discussed this with your wife
other relations
workmates
other friends?

*309. Are you a member of a T.U./P.A.? which one?

*310. Were you a member of a T.U./P.A. at C.M.?

311. Have you ever been a member of a T.U./P.A.?

312. Is there any reason why you are not a member of a T.U./P.A. now?

313. Is there any reason why you were not a member of a T.U./P.A. at C.M.?

314. Is there any reason why you have never been a member of a T.U./P.A.?

315. Do you think white collar workers should be members of a T.U. or do you think they should not? Why?

316. Some people say that the interests of management and workers are opposed, others that they are one and the same, what do you think?

317. Do you normally vote regularly in local elections?

318. Do you consider yourself a consistent supporter of the
    Conservative party
    Labour party
    Liberal party
  or any other party
    someone who switches his vote
    according to circumstances?

319. What would be those circumstances?

320. Do you think it makes a great deal of difference to you which party wins the General Election?

321. Why?

*322. If you could have your life over again what job would you choose to go into?

*323. Why?

324. Looking back now, with the move from C.M. behind you, do you regret having to leave/having left or are you glad that you left?

325. Why?

*326. Had you moved/now you have moved from the Casterton area what would you have missed/what do you miss about living in the Casterton area?

APPENDIX II
REDUNDANCY AND PUBLIC POLICY*

by BOB FRYER

Labour Law and Industrial Sociology

Despite the earlier advocacy of a sociologically informed study and practice of the law by such scholars as Weber, Ehrlich, Gurvitch and Pound,[1] a little under twenty years ago a leading labour lawyer was able to observe in a manifest understatement that 'the lawyer's approach to the problem of industrial relations differs in some respects from that of the sociologist'.[2] Today, however, it is possible that one of the less dramatic consequences of the Industrial Relations Act, 1971 will be a greater interpenetration of sociology and the law. Much of the behaviour which has long since commanded the attention of students of sociology has now been brought more directly within the ambit of the law than hitherto. Obvious examples are industrial conflict – especially strikes[3] – and the closed shop,[4] but equally important are the level of bargaining and method of

---

* This paper was first given to the July 1972 Conference of the Industrial Law Society at St Johns College, Oxford.

[1] See: Max Rheinstein (ed.), *Max Weber on Law in Economy and Society* (Cambridge, Mass: Harvard U.P., 1966); Eugen Ehrlich, *Fundamental Principles of the Sociology of Law* (New York: Russell and Russell, 1962); Georges Gurvitch, *Sociology of Law* (London: Kegan Paul, 1947) and Roscoe Pound, *An Introduction to the Philosophy of Law* (New Haven: Yale U.P., 1922), *Outline of Lectures on Jurisprudence* (Cambridge: Harvard U.P., 1928).

[2] Otto Kahn-Freund, 'The Legal Framework' in Allan Flanders and H. A. Clegg (eds.), *The System of Industrial Relations in Great Britain* (Oxford: Basil Blackwell, 1954), p. 42.

[3] For an incisive survey see Richard Hyman, *Strikes* (London: Fontana, 1972); also J. E. T. Eldridge, *Industrial Disputes* (London: Routledge and Kegan Paul, 1968).

[4] W. E. J. McCarthy, *The Closed Shop in Britain* (Oxford: Basil Blackwell, 1964); M. Olson, *The Logic of Collective Action* (Cambridge, Mass: Harvard U.P., 1965).

dispute settlement,[5] the strategies used by employers and employees alike to enforce their own norms in respect of trade union membership and activities[6] and the vexed question of trade union government.[7] No longer does it suffice to make the simple distinction between the sociologist's interest in the 'normal relations between employers and employees' and the lawyer's concern with the 'sanctions by which that conduct can be made to conform to a postulated standard':[8] under the provisions of the Industrial Relations Act, the subject matter of sociology and the law becomes inextricably intertwined.

Although the Industrial Relations Act marks the most significant break with the traditional 'abstentionist' role of the law in British labour relations, it is true to say that during the last ten years the development of public policy has entailed a growing involvement of lawyers and the law in the world of work. As Professor Kahn-Freund has written:

'It is undeniable that within a short period of four or five years British labour legislation has already taken a new turn. What has happened since 1963 by way of legislative regulation of labour conditions exceeds in volume and in significance what in previous years happened in decades'.[9]

The enactment of such 'regulatory' legislation,[10] it has been argued, has been not so much in accordance with an orderly and

---

[5] For example, J. W. Kuhn, *Bargaining in Grievance Settlement* (New York: Columbia U.P., 1961); A. I. Marsh, *Disputes Procedures in British Industry* (London: H.M.S.O., 1966) and H. A. Clegg, *The System of Industrial Relations in Great Britain* (Oxford: Basil Blackwell, 1970).

[6] See, for example, George Sayers Bain, *Trade Union Growth and Recognition* (London: H.M.S.O., 1967); A. J. M. Sykes, 'Union Workshop Organisation in the Printing Industry', *Human Relations*, 1960, and 'Unity and Restrictive Practices in the British Printing Industry', *Sociological Review*, 1960; and T. Lupton, *On the Shop Floor* (Oxford: Pergamon, 1963).

[7] B. C. Roberts, *Trade Union Government and Administration* (London: Bell & Sons, 1956); H. A. Turner, *Trade Union Growth, Structure and Policy* (London: Allen & Unwin, 1962); John Hughes, *Trade Union Structure and Government* (London: H.M.S.O., 1967).

[8] Kahn-Freund, *op. cit.*

[9] Otto Kahn-Freund, *Labour Law: Old Traditions and New Developments* (Toronto: Clarke, Irwin, 1968), p. 52.

[10] Otto Kahn-Freund, *Labour and the Law* (London: Stevens and Sons, 1972), especially pp. 29–41.

gradually unfolding plan for labour law as in 'reponse to needs as they arise'.[11] Hence, public policy has been prompted by the inadequate resolution of industrial relations problems through the institutions and provisions of collective bargaining. Redundancy is a case in point. As Sir James Dunnet said to the Donovan Commission:

'I think to some extent one could say, if collective bargaining in this country had at an earlier stage put more emphasis on things like redundancy and the rest of it, it might not have been necessary for the government to pass legislation. . . . Whatever the reasons, the trade unions have chosen to give priorities to certain things in collective bargaining and not to others. . . . I think the State now perhaps more than in the past is looking at the end result and saying, here are gaps where we think something has to be done.'[12]

Since the implementation of the Redundancy Payments Act, 1965 the law has become closely involved in the problem of redundancy and the Act which, amongst other provisions, lays down a scale of severance payments for certain workers dismissed by reason of redundancy, has provided much interpretative work for the tribunals and courts.[13]

The problem of redundancy has also attracted the attention of sociologists.[14] Indeed, the sociological study of redundancy ought to provide a signal illustration of the link between 'personal troubles' and 'public issues' which, according to C. Wright Mills, is the distinctive character of the sociological imagination.[15] There can be little doubt that the problem of redundancy satisfies both elements of Mills' celebrated prescription, but the precise way in which these

[11] *Labour Law: Old Traditions and New Developments*, p. 30.

[12] Royal Commission on Trade Unions and Employers' Associations, *Minutes of Evidence 2 and 3* (Ministry of Labour) (London: H.M.S.O., 1966), pp. 45–46.

[13] See, Cyril Grunfeld, *The Law of Redundancy* (London: Sweet and Maxwell, 1971); R. W. Rideout, *Reforming the Redundancy Payments Act* (London: IPM, 1969); and K. W. Wedderburn and P. L. Davies, *Employment Grievances and Disputes Procedures in Great Britain* (Berkeley: University of California Press, 1969).

[14] Notably Hilda Kahn, *Repercussions of Redundancy* (London: Allen & Unwin, 1964); Dorothy Wedderburn, *White Collar Redundancy* (Cambridge: University Press, 1964) and *Redundancy and the Railwaymen* (Cambridge: University Press, 1965); Alan Fox, *The Milton Plan* (London: I.P.M., 1965).

[15] C. Wright Mills, *The Sociological Imagination* (New York: Oxford University Press, 1959).

'public' and 'private' problems are defined vitally affects the response to them and the remedies that those concerned with public policy are prepared to consider. Public policy and legislative regulation at once imply a view of what is wrong with the world and represent a prescription for its correction. In both its diagnostic and prescriptive form, public policy entails models of social structure and the norms that guide behaviour in social life, the very area with which sociologists properly concern themselves. Furthermore, both the law and sociology have to do with the question of values:

> 'Sociology is concerned with the preferences and evaluations that underlie basic structural arrangements in society. Many of these values are embodied in law.'[16]

Thus, far from operating in separate territories, lawyers and sociologists hold much of their subject matter in common. Where industry and industrial relations are concerned, that common subject matter includes the structural arrangements which produce and the evaluations which accompany the problems of the work-a-day world.

Whose Redundancy Problem?

Ten years ago, one commentator observed (in tones that have contemporary relevance) 'almost every day now we can read in the newspapers about a fresh outbreak of what has become known, perhaps euphemistically, as "The Redundancy Problem"'.[17] As indicated earlier, this problem has attracted much attention from sociologists and an O.E.C.D. report in 1966 declared:

> 'There is now a spate of reports emanating from universities, government departments and international organisations that examine specific and frequently rather narrow aspects of the "redundancy problem" in an attempt to throw light on the best ways of dealing with it.'[18]

Now, when social processes and social actions are defined as 'problems' and, by implication, in need of some sort of 'reform' or 'remedy' it is crucially important to examine the perspectives that promote such definitions and to enquire closely into the assumptions that underpin both diagnosis and prescription. Plainly, not every

[16] Vilhelm Aubert (ed.), *Sociology of Law* (Harmondsworth: Penguin, 1969), p. 11.

[17] Geoffrey Goodman, *Redundancy in the Affluent Society*, Fabian Tract, 340 (London: Fabian Society, 1962).

[18] A. D. Smith, *Redundancy Practices in Four Industries* (Paris: O.E.C.D., 1966).

aspect of industrial life that causes harm or difficulty is elevated to the status of a 'social problem' or deemed to be deserving of legislative regulation. Even those features of employment that today all agree should be restricted – such as a dangerous and squalid work environment – in the past did not constitute a 'problem' which as a matter of course called for remedial public policy. The mere existence of an objective state of affairs is not in itself a condition sufficient to merit the label of 'problem'. Consider, for example, the very severe losses to production caused by lumbago or influenza[19] which attract far less attention than the 'problem' of unofficial strikes.[20] For some phenomenon of social life to qualify as social problem requires that someone should both pick it out and identify it as undesirable and, further, be able to mobilise public policy with a view to migrating the 'harm' caused by the problem.[21] As one sociologist has remarked:

'A social problem consists not only of a fixed and given condition, but the perception by certain people that this condition poses a threat which is against their interests and that something should be done about it.'[22]

Where redundancy is concerned, public policy has defined the problem largely in *managerial* terms. That is to say, that the 'threat' that has been discerned is the threat of economic and technological stagnation caused by the undue restriction of managerial initiative and the unwillingness of workers to adapt to change. The assumption has *not* been that redundancy as such is undesirable and should therefore be eliminated. On the contrary, the very legitimacy of redundancy has been underlined and the problem defined in terms of how best to facilitate managerial decision-making and encourage workers to accept the inevitability, indeed, desirability of redundancy.

[19] Between 1963 and 1968 the national average total of working days lost through certified sickness was 302·54 millions; for influenza the figure was 11·98 millions; D.H. & S.S., *Digest of Statistics for England and Wales* (London: H.M.S.O., 1971). See also, Office of Health Economics, *Work Lost Through Sickness* (London: O.H.E., 1965).

[20] For an illuminating analysis of the strike 'problem', see Hyman, *op. cit.*

[21] Herbert Blumer argues that there are five stages in the development of social problems: emergence, legitimation, mobilisation of action, formation of official plan and implementation of the plan. 'Social Problems as Collective Behaviour', *Social Problems*, 18, 1971.

[22] Stanley Cohen (ed.), *Images of Deviance* (Harmondsworth: Penguin, 1971), p. 14.

220

Management's Problem

As a consequence of this managerial view of redundancy, the 'need' for redundancy and the kind of social and industrial structure in which redundancy has become an everyday phenomenon have been simply taken for granted. Occasionally, this has meant a mere fatalistic recognition of the probability of more redundancies, but more often, especially amongst policy makers, the attitude has represented a positive endorsement of the necessity of redundancy. For example, Mr Ray Gunter, the (then) Minister of Labour recommended the Redundancy Payments Bill by pointing out that the proposed legislation was:

'An active policy to make it easier for workers to change their jobs in accordance with the needs of technological progress . . . to ensure the planned use of resources, expecially our reserves of manpower . . . an important complement to our efforts to develop the science-based industries and to deploy our manpower resources where they can make the most effective contribution to the economy.'[23]

Standing in the way of such a 'rational' manpower policy were the restrictive activities and postures of trade unions and workers on the shop floor neither of whom appeared to appreciate the fundamental economic case for an end to what labour economists, with their disarming feel for a catchword, had labelled 'featherbedding'.[24] As the Minister continued:

'One of our most urgent needs is to use our manpower efficiently. We have far too many restrictive practices and far too much overmanning and under-employment of labour.'[25]

Although the case for an active policy for redundancy rested upon a managerial definition of the problems faced, the advocates of such a course of action, in common with those who recommended the path to greater managerial control by way of productivity bargaining,[26] did not exonerate management for its contribution to the threat of stagnation. In this sense, redundancy was as much a problem *of* management as *for* management. 'The concept of the

---

[23] *Hansard*, 26 April 1965, Volume 711, column 33.

[24] See, for example, Paul A. Weinstein (ed.), *Featherbedding and Technological Change* (Boston: D. C. Heath, 1965).

[25] *Hansard*, 26 April 1965, Volume 711, column 36.

[26] For example, Allan Flanders, *The Fawley Productivity Agreements* (London: Faber and Faber, 1964), especially Chapter six.

221

good employer', wrote one commentator who was later to become closely involved in the operations of the Department of Economic Affairs, 'has now tended to come to mean an employer who never sacks anybody . . . the employer who has to lay workers off is almost as much a figure of shame as the Victorian bankrupt. "Yes, I'm afraid we had some redundancies last year" an executive will mutter shame-facedly; or proudly, "we went through the last two recessions without laying off a man".'[27] In view of this problem 'the first need . . . is for the unions as a whole to accept the necessity for some redundancy'[28] coupled with an encouragement to employers to abandon labour-hoarding for 'the important point of policy here is not to make it too expensive for employers to dismiss their workers'.[29]

Such a diagnosis of the main features of the problem has been expanded by the authors of *Effects of the Redundancy Payments Act*[30] who declare that 'by the early 1960's there was a growing awareness that the malutilisation of manpower constituted a major barrier to long-term economic expansion'.[31] As Parker and his colleagues have written (though with different intent) 'the Act was based upon certain assumptions about redundancy',[32] namely that the efficient use of labour requires both the acceptance of the inevitability of redundancy and the abandonment of the 'non-rational' norm of last-in-first-out which it is widely thought workers attempt to enforce at times of redundancy. The reviewers of the Act write:

'In order to bring about a more effective utilisation of manpower within the internal labour market, management has to be able to pursue a manpower policy which is consistent with the economic

[27] Michael Shanks, *The Stagnant Society: A Warning* (Harmondsworth: Penguin, 1961), p. 49.   [28] *ibid.*, p. 146.

[29] *ibid.*, pp. 147–8. In a later work, *The Innovators*, Shanks has a section on 'How to De-Man'.

[30] S. R. Parker, C. G. Thomas, N. D. Ellis and W. E. J. McCarthy, *Effects of the Redundancy Payments Act* (London: H.M.S.O., 1971). In view of the fact that I criticise parts of this study, it is only fair to point out that most of my criticisms centre upon the first part, 'Introduction and Interpretation', written by the last two authors. For convenience I shall refer to 'Parker and his colleagues' when quoting from any part of the publication. It is probable that this study was published with great difficulty in view of the Conservative Government's opposition to the Redundancy Payments Act, and this should be borne in mind during the following discussion.

[31] *ibid.*, p. 3.   [32] *ibid.*, p. 7.

objectives of the firm. . . . An effective manpower policy which is consistent with the economic objectives of the firm requires flexibility in the deployment of labour, and this means that employees may have to be willing to accept both the need for redundancies in those circumstances where they are an inevitable consequence of economic or technological change and, in addition, the application of criteria which are related to the economic objectives of the firm in the selection of those workers to be made redundant.'[33]

Thus, the legislation was aimed at breaking down 'non-rational' resistance to the demands of technical rationality and 'unreal' opposition to the realities of economics. In short, the Act was 'aimed at securing a greater acceptance by employees of the need for more economic, organisational and technological change'.[34]

Such a point of view has been echoed from other quarters. In 1958 the authors of the Acton Society Trust's pamphlet on *Redundancy* wrote:

'*Realistically*, it can be argued that the workers' collective organisations, the trade unions, have a major responsibility; a responsibility . . . for accepting the inevitability of redundancy (especially where a forward wage policy has enforced an economy of increasingly costly manpower). . . . Some Trade Unionists maintain that redundancies ought not to occur, that no-one should be put out of a job until another has been found for him. This *impractical* view is, however, rejected by most of the trade union movement.'[35]

In similar vein, Clegg wrote at the time of the parliamentary consideration of the Redundancy Payments Bill, that 'most trade union leaders, however, being reasonable men, acknowledge that redundancies must occur'.[36] The pay-off for these 'reasonable' and 'practical' attitudes is said to be that an explicit acceptance of redundancy enables trade unions to embark upon vigorous negotiations to limit the extent and improve the terms of redundancy. However, no evidence is adduced to prove that unions did so limit a redundancy or that members actually preferred better terms to no

[33] *ibid.*, p. 10. [34] *ibid.*, p. 20.
[35] J. S. Hutchinson and Nancy Wansbrough, *Redundancy: A Survey of Problems and Practices* (Acton Society Trust, 1958), p. 3, my emphasis.
[36] H. A. Clegg, 'Mobility of Labour', *National Provincial Bank Review*, No. 70, May 1965.

redundancy at all. It is simply thought to be sufficient condemnation of the (then) A.E.U.'s 'no redundancy' policy to pronounce that 'the union is indeed hampered by a resolution of its annual conference upholding a policy of no redundancy' and that 'on balance . . . there is little doubt that it has done more harm than good to the A.E.U.'s own members as well as to the industry as a whole'.[37]

It is by reference to what is implied in this notion of the 'industry as a whole' that we can best understand the real definition of what constitutes the main problem of redundancy according to many commentators. When Parker and his colleagues write that 'it was recognised at the outset that the provisions of the Redundancy Payments Act would not fit all the varying circumstances of redundancy equally well'[38] they are referring not to the greater vulnerability of workers in some industries but to employers' responses to the question 'how well does the Redundancy Payments Act fit the conditions of your business?'[39] This recognition of the *primacy* of business considerations and the purely *secondary* nature of the question of employment security is made plain in the Code of Industrial Relations Practice which recommends that management should 'provide stable employment including reasonable job security . . . as far as is consistent with the operational efficiency and the success of the undertaking.'[40] And, in rather more uncharacteristic fashion, the Code deals unequivocally with the question of decision-making prerogatives declaring baldly that 'responsibility for deciding the size of the workforce rests with management'.[41]

It is, of course, plain that the corollary of this need for workers to accept the economic and technical rationality of both the fact and the composition of redundancies is the strategic importance of underpinning management control. As the reviewers of the effects of the Redundancy Payments Act put it:

'An effective manpower policy in the internal labour market

---

[37] Clegg, 'Mobility of Labour', p. 9; Shanks, *op. cit.*, p. 144. For a quite different evaluation of this policy see Goodman, *op. cit.*, p. 27.

[38] *op. cit.*, p. 19.

[39] *ibid.*, p. 218. The priorities of the policy are well illustrated in the distinction Grunfeld draws between the '*paramount* policy of the Act to enable British management . . . to achieve needed economics in the use of labour' and the '*subsidiary* effect of the drafting of the Act to provide certain employees in certain limited circumstances with compensation', *op. cit.*, p. 8, my emphasis.

[40] *Industrial Relations Code of Practice* (London: H.M.S.O., no date), p. 11. [41] *ibid.*, pp. 11–12.

involving redundancies necessitates decisions based on criteria of efficiency about whom to retain and whom to dismiss.'[42]

Parker and his colleagues certainly recognised the logic of their position, as did those who advocated productivity bargaining in the 1960s. As Allan Flanders put it:

'Management's primary commitment is to efficiency; its job is to organise the use of human and material resources to produce the best results with an economy of effort. Working practices which are grossly inefficient are a challenge to management that it can only ignore at the price of professional incompetence.'[43]

The fundamental importance of protecting managerial rights has also been recognised by the Courts. As Sachs L. J. commented in the notorious case of *Hindle v. Percival Boats Ltd:*

'(The Redundancy Payments Act) does not provide for any case where an employer wishes to see if someone else can do the job better: it could indeed be industrially disastrous if it puts the brake on employers seeking to get the best man for any given job. Nor does it provide for any case where an employer simply wishes not to continue to employ a particular employee.'[44]

Similarly, the High Court in reversing the decision of the tribunal in *North Riding Garages Ltd. v Butterwick* declared:

'For the purpose of this Act an employee who remains in the same kind of work is expected to adapt himself to new methods and techniques and cannot complain if his employer insists on higher standards of efficiency than those previously required.'[45]

This deference to the hard-headed norms of economic rationality and to the subjective managerial definition of efficiency[46] is not confined to those who formulate, evaluate and interpret public policy. As a lay trade union official at Rolls Royce remarked when

[42] *op. cit.*, p. 10.
[43] *op. cit.*, p. 235.   [44] Cited in Grunfeld, *op. cit.*, p. 7.
[45] Cited in Wedderburn and Davies, *op. cit.*, p. 268.
[46] The recent case of *Rev. P. Nicolson v. Imperial Chemical Industries, Ltd.* is instructive. It seems that neither regular pay increments nor nomination for promotion is sufficient to counter-balance employer claims of inefficiency.

P   225

asked why his Branch did not press for a greater say in the numbers and selection of the redundant.

'Admittedly at times of redundancy management will want to get rid of the "deadwood" first. This is a difficult one. Last-in-first-out may be fairest for those who go, but is it honestly in the best interests of the company and those who stay?'[47]

The view that the so-called 'deadwood' should go first – thus creating a new under-class of 'undesirable unemployed' – was echoed in the findings of Robert Slater's research on redundancy practice. Amongst personnel managers 72 per cent considered it fairest to dismiss those workers with a poor work record first and 65 per cent believed that this was already the practice in industry.[48] Similarly, 72 per cent of a volunteer panel of 545 subjects thought that the first to go in a redundancy should be employees with a bad work record.[49] Unfortunately Slater's research did not pursue the question of *who* should decide which people had a poor record but, by implication, took it for granted that it should be those whose positions in the hierarchy of power gave them control over the workforce.

Reification of the Problem

Some commentators on redundancy, rather than defining it in blunt managerial terms, have attempted to portray redundancy as part of the 'logic' of historical development and the 'needs' of industrial organisation and have, in so doing, *depersonalised* both history and the social structure of industry. Such writers have, for example portrayed both redundancy and the enactment of the Redundancy Payments Act as fulfilling the 'needs' of the 'economy' or meeting the 'needs' of 'society'. Thus, Professor Kahn-Freund has written, in reference to the Redundancy Payments Act:

'Mobility of labour, in both its aspects, geographical as well as occupational, is one of the most urgent needs of our economy, one of the most urgent needs of a country which has the advantage,

[47] Author's field notes taken in connection with a study of the Rolls Royce Redundancy by Dorothy Wedderburn and myself. To be published by Davis Poynter.
[48] Robert Slater, 'Who Goes First', *Personnel Management*, December 1969.
[49] Robert Slater, 'Last in-Third Out', *Personnel Management*, May 1971.

or disadvantage, of having developed its industry earlier than anyone else and which now to remain competitive must transform its economic structure at a fairly rapid pace.'[50]

In like fashion Alan Fox, in his description of the Milton closure as a 'success' argued that:

'A society seeking to maximise its economic wealth either to consume or to produce or to give to others less fortunate must pursue industrial efficiency.'[51]

Presented in this way, it is relatively easy to ignore or avoid an explicit recognition of a conflict of interests as the distinguishing characteristic of both the employment relationship itself and, more especially of its termination, redundancy.[52] In tones implying the shared nature of the redundancy problem, the question of industrial efficiency can, in Professor Grunfeld's words, be seen as 'a central national problem'.[53] It follows from this definition of the nature of the redundancy problem that the intervention of the law can be portrayed not as the furtherance of any one sectional interest but, on the contrary, in Roscoe Pound's words as a 'social institution to satisfy social wants',[54] a kind of impartial hand which acts to resolve questions of national interest in which statutory provision gradually achieves 'a more embracing and more effective securing of social interests'[55] in such a way as 'to give effect to the greatest total of

---

[50] *Labour Law: Old Traditions and New Developments*, p. 39.

[51] Alan Fox, *op. cit.*, p. 45. The author continues, with a clear implication of the shared nature of the redundancy problem: 'Advance in industry like advance in war, sometimes provides a casualty list'. The analogy is in some ways apt for, cynically, it may be noted that 'public' concern about the rate of casualties seems to grow markedly when the names of 'senior officers' as well as 'other ranks' appear on the casualty list!

[52] At first it may seem inconsistent that these two authors, both of whom are noted for their insistence on conflict and divergences of interest in industry, should overlook such conflict in the problem of redundancy. However, it is their analysis of conflict in terms of pluralistic frame of reference that explains this paradox. Pluralism embraces conflict within a higher order framework of co-operation. The best critique of pluralism is Alan Fox's own most recent contribution to the analysis of industrial conflict: 'Industrial Relations: A Social Critique of Pluralist Ideology' in J. Child (ed.), *Man and Organisation: The Search for Understanding and Relevance* (London: Allen & Unwin, forthcoming).

[53] *op. cit.*, p. 1.

[54] *An Introduction to the Philosophy of Law*, p. 98.   [55] *ibid.*, p. 99.

interests or to the interests that weigh most in our civilisation, with the least sacrifice of the scheme of interests as a whole'.[56]

The validity of such a formulation of the role of the law turns on the precise meaning of such phrases as 'the interests that weigh most in our civilisation' and exactly which interests are granted legitimacy in the 'scheme of interests as a whole'. For example, just how are the claims of different social groups to be balanced and assessed? More importantly, references to notions such as the 'economy' or 'country' or 'nation' or 'our civilisation' or 'society' and the attribution of 'wants' and 'needs' to thise abstractions are excellent examples of what the sociologist, in his jargon, calls, *reification*. By reification the sociologist means the ascription of essentially *human* characteristics to abstractions or to social structures in such a way as to obscure the fundamental part played by human agencies and human values in social processes. The paradox of reification is that in ascribing human motivations to social processes, the very products of human activity are apprehended '*as if* they were something other than human products – such as facts of nature, results of cosmic laws, manifestations of divine will',[57] the dictates of a logic of industrialism or 'the need for the high rate of change demanded by a modern economy'.[58] For those who thus reify the social world 'a definite social relation between men . . . assumes, in their eyes, the fantastic form of a relation between things'.[59] By challenging the validity of such reified concepts and their consequent assumption of an achievable commonality of interest, the sociologist emphasises the role of men and their norms and values in social life and is prepared to consider the possibility of a real divergence of interests in industry. Where redundancy is concerned, the *supposed* needs of 'the economy' may be revealed in truth as the *actual* needs of one particular group in industry – a conclusion that depends upon asking the relatively simple-minded but analytically fundamental questions obfuscated by reification – 'Effective *for whom*?' 'Successful *for whom*?' 'Urgent *for whom*?' 'A problem *for whom*?' As the T.U.C. put it in their evidence to Donovan:

'The interests of different individuals and groups diverge in many

[56] Roscoe Pound, 'A Survey of Social Interests', *Harvard Law Review*, 57, October 1943, p. 39. Cited in R. Quinney, *The Social Reality of Crime* (Boston: Little Brown, 1970).

[57] Peter L. Berger and Thomas Luckman, *The Social Construction of Reality* (Harmondsworth: Penguin, 1971), p. 106.

[58] Parker *et al.*, *op. cit.*, p. 3.

[59] Karl Marx, *Capital*, Vol. I (London: Swan Sonnenschein, 1887), p. 43.

228

respects. Where this is so, some groups clearly think it is effective propaganda to claim that their policy corresponds to, or reflects, the national interest and that other groups ought likewise to take account of the national interest. However successful in the propaganda battle such advocacy might be, it is almost invariably based on myths and a few moments' consideration would convince the disinterested observer, if such could be found, that this was so. Trade unionists therefore take a somewhat jaundiced view of those whose interests are different to their own lecturing them on their social responsibilities, with the real intention of producing a result which is favourable to their own interests'.[60]

'Job security and redundancy provide the best example of this. Observers whose perspective is different to that of most workpeople cite the national interest and argue that this implies or demands certain actions on the part of groups and individuals. Yet there can be no national interest divorced from individual interests. People in employment, whose status was described at the beginning of this part of the evidence, comprise a large part of the nation. Therefore, when workpeople demand certain safeguards or otherwise refuse to do this or that, the argument that they are acting against the national interest often begs important questions. The argument from the national interest is but one of a rich repertoire employed by those whose interests are different to those of trade unionists.'[61]

Two Rationalities

It might, of course, be argued that even accepting the different kinds of problems which redundancy poses for managers and workers, there is still a *common* interest in introducing change into industry in an orderly fashion. This variant of the 'joint' problem approach explains the Redundancy Payments Act as the intervention of the 'law' to promote more 'order' in industrial change, thus:

'The Redundancy Payments Act, 1965 is a small piece in a giant national jigsaw puzzle which government and both sides of industry

[60] Trades Union Congress, *Trade Unionism*, Evidence to the Royal Commission on Trade Unions and Employers' Associations (London: TUC, 1966), p. 61.

[61] *ibid.*, pp. 35–65. As two students of mergers put it: 'the employee interest does not appear so frequently in the press as the national interest or even "public (consumer) interest".' R. Smith and D. Brooks, *Mergers: Past and Present* (London: Acton Society Trust, 1963), p. 56.

have been trying to solve in recent years, the puzzle has been how to transform Britain . . .'[62]

Thus the fact that all three groups were party to the N.E.D.C. report of 1963 'which did much to set the legislative machinery in motion'[63] is cited as evidence of the shared nature of the problem. But there are two objections to such reasoning: firstly, the acceptance by trade union leaders of the 'need' for redundancy cannot necessarily be taken as a fair reflection of the attitudes of rank and file members. Secondly, the N.E.D.C. report had a first priority which was blatantly absent from the legislative action: 'the main object of a redundancy policy must be to provide jobs for the displaced workers'.[64]

Furthermore, the validity of this assumption of a common interest in orderly change depends on showing not only that orderly change is *in fact* shared by management and workers, but also on how far the definitions of 'order' and 'disorder' held by either side of industry are indeed compatible. There are good reasons for doubting any such shared perspective, especially where redundancy is concerned. As Robert Dubin, an American industrial sociologist has noted:

'Industrial disorder has special meanings for management and workers in an enterprise. . . . To management the business firm operates in an orderly fashion when it exhibits (1) continuity with its past, (2) controlled direction and amount of change in the present and (3) predictability in the future . . . . The employees' view of industrial disorder differs significantly from that of management . . . the very evidence of his daily work brings home to the manual worker the degree to which he is directed in his behaviour with only limited free choice available. From the worker's standpoint, many sources of instability in his work environment are either a consequence of managerial action or are presumed as originating with management. Obviously things like technical change and changes in work schedule originate with management.'[65]

[62] Grunfeld, *op. cit.*, p. 1.

[63] Kahn-Freund, *Labour Law: Old Traditions and New Developments*, p. 39.

[64] National Economic Development Council, *Conditions Favourable to Faster Growth* (London: H.M.S.O., 1963), p. 10. The recent rejection of the 'Jones-Aldington' Interim Report by dockers illustrates the first objection.

[65] Robert Dubin, 'Constructive Aspects of Conflict' in Allan Flanders (ed.), *Collective Bargaining* (Harmondsworth: Penguin, 1969), pp. 48–51.

It is true that redundancy – especially prior to the Redundancy Payments Act – has often entailed a degree of 'disorder' for both sides in the shape of strike action by workers. Clegg pointed out that 'some of our bitterest strikes in recent years have arisen out of redundancy'.[66] The reduction of such 'disorder' and lowering of days lost through 'redundancy strikes' has been deemed to be one of the valuable by-products of the Redundancy Payments Act. It was hoped that the Act 'might have a generally beneficial effect in this sphere', and Parker and his colleagues conclude that the legislation might have helped 'to reduce some of the tensions and conflicts inherent in the redundancy situation by creating a *more relaxed and favourable climate*'.[67] Again, it must be asked, whose definition of 'beneficial' and favourable' is in question? For whom does the more relaxed climate mean more 'order'? This same question has been asked by a sociologist in a different context:

'Is order in workplace relations so obviously a good thing, desirable, in the interests of the rank and file workers . . .? The concept of order has never in (industrial relations) literature been looked at closely; *order* – from whose point of view?'[68]

In other words, rather than simply adopting the managerial definition of redundancy or obscuring human action behind the smoke screen of reification, it has to be asked whether management and workers do not each have their own definition of order and disorder and the 'problem' of redundancy. Nor should it simply be assumed that the managerial definition of the problem is more 'rational' than that of the workers, as is implied in reference to 'reasonable' 'realistic' and 'practical' approaches to the problem of redundancy. As Eldridge has observed:

'One may talk meaningfully about the existence of competing rationalities: since strong logical arguments are advanced on the basis of different value assumptions. The implication is that one cannot speak of 'pure rationality'. Each system of rationality is bounded by evaluative considerations of what is the desirable end(s) to achieve and by normative considerations of what are the appropriate means to utilise in attaining such end(s)'.[69]

[66] 'Mobility of Labour', p. 9.   [67] *op. cit.*, p. 12. My emphasis.
[68] John Goldthorpe, 'A Comment on Mr Fox's Paper' in J. Floud, P. Lewis and R. Stuart (eds.), *Proceedings of a Seminar: Problems and Prospects of Socio-Legal Research* (Oxford: Nuffield College, 1972), p. 212.
[69] 'Redundancy' in *op. cit.*, p. 225. In 'Mobility of Labour' Clegg counterposes two ethics, one of the economist and the other of the shopfloor. This parallels Eldridge's two rationalities to some extent but not

Recognition of the divergent and equally valid bases of managerial and shop floor rationality is vital for the development of public policy. The weakness of current public policy with respect to redundancy is that it has largely neglected this conflicting rationality of management and workers and, even worse, has assumed that management's definitions are inspired by rationality while workers' definitions owe more to sentiment. Thus, 'enterprise rationality' is contrasted with 'human non-rationality':

'The testing ground of rationality is typically held to be the market-place. Rationality derives its coercive power over the behaviour of the enterprise from the economic life-and-death judgments presumably rendered by market forces. In the absence of an effective convenient market for registering the precise degree of rationality, a market judgement is simulated largely on the basis of managerial folk-wisdom.

Human non-rationality is meant to describe the security reponses of the human objects of rationality – the reactions of the order-takers to the order-givers. The order-givers try to get the order-takers to conform to a discipline made necessary by the rationality objectives of the enterprise, and the latter by various means try to shape the discipline in a way to make it tolerable.'[70]

The usual implication of the classic human relations formulation of the different perspectives from the boardroom and the shop floor is that the workers' 'logic of sentiment' is amenable to certain techniques which encourage the abandonment of restrictive attitudes and the development of a more co-operative spirit. Typically this involves shifting the basis of managerial rule from coercive power to government by consent so that subordinates come to accept the legitimacy of decisions taken by super-ordinates[71] How far the Redundancy Payments Act, for example, can be ajudged a 'success' depends on its ability to induce 'changes in workers' attitudes (which) allowed management greater freedom in its decisions'.[72] It was

entirely. Clegg's analysis focuses upon the paralysing dilemma for management torn between 'economic argument' and 'humanitarian instincts' and so portrays the problem in two different ways from one point of view rather than from two opposing positions.

[70] Jack Barbash, 'Elements of Industrial Relations', *British Journal of Industrial Relations*, Vol. II, No. 1, March 1964.

[71] For an excellent discussion of power and authority see Alan Fox, *A Sociology of Work in Industry* (London: Collier: MacMillan, 1971), pp. 34–37.

[72] Parker *et al.*, *op. cit.*, p. 9.

recognised that this greater freedom could not be ensured merely by reiterating the importance of managerial prerogatives in economic matters, and so the legislation 'was intended to create a situation where those affected are more likely to accept the implications of these economic conditions'.[73] In short, the authors of *Effects of the Redundancy Payments Act* define the problem of redundancy as how best to underpin the 'economic rationality' of management by modifying the 'emotive non-rationality' of workers. Consequently, this approach never gives serious consideration to workers' own definitions of the problem of redundancy.

The Workers' Problem

It must be admitted that for some workers the problem of redundancy accords, at first sight, more or less with management's definition and with the perspective upon which public policy rests. Such workers appear either to accept the legitimacy of management control, to recognise the 'logic' of economic rationality or, more likely, consider themselves beyond the danger of dismissal by virtue of redundancy. Why such attitudes should prevail is in itself problematic and requires analysis of the forms of domination and the patterning of systems of belief in our society. However, these questions are usually ignored and the response of such workers is labelled 'realistic' or 'reasonable' and taken as sufficient evidence of the rationality of the managerial definition or redundancy. Worse still, the considerable evidence that many workers regard redundancy as 'inevitable'[74] is construed as evidence of the logic of both managerial and reified definitions. But closer inspection of such pessimistic expectations reveal that *inevitability* cannot simply be taken to mean *desirability*. Even where workers accept the 'need' for redundancy, they are likely to contest the timing, extent and procedures of the redundancy as well as to assert their own definition of their post-redundancy employment needs.

In contrast to the assumption that workers either already accept or could be made to accept the desirability of redundancy, it is evident that many workers define the problem of redundancy quite differently to managers and those who formulate public policy. W. W. Daniel, in his work on the Woolwich redundancies, found that there was no relationship between the amount of severance payment

---

[73] Parker *et al.*, *op. cit.*, p. 9.

[74] See for example Kahn, *op. cit.*, p. 226, and Wedderburn, *White Collar Redundancy*, p. 34.

received and a predisposition to look favourably upon redundancy: 'far from it being the case that the higher the lump sum received the less concerned people were about the prospect of redundancy, the opposite was the case'.[75] The above case study of redundancy in the floorcoverings industry showed that only 23 per cent of workers – both redundant and 'voluntary leavers' – had thought of leaving the firm before the redundancy and 70 per cent of the redundant had intended staying with the company until retirement. Only 2 per cent of the redundant workers had thought of moving to another part of the country to find employment and almost threequarters of both redundant and voluntary leavers had no desire whatsoever to live elsewhere in the country; every one of the 34 per cent non-manual and 7 per cent manual workers offered the chance of a transfer to the firm's Scottish plant declined and only 12 per cent manual and 7 per cent non-manual workers not offered a transfer said they would have welcomed such an offer. Similarly in Rolls Royce,[76] despite their relative youth, 59 per cent of a sample of redundant white collar workers had not even thought of leaving the company prior to the redundancy. Indeed, the Rolls Royce redundancy represented a particularly rude interruption of the career plans of some workers: four-fifths of the foremen made redundant had no intention of leaving the firm before the redundancy. Such figures are confirmed by the Parker survey which reported that only '12 per cent of the paid and 19 per cent of the unpaid redundant had thought about leaving the firm before they got to know they might be redundant there'.[77]

It might be argued that such views were wrong-headed, short-term and typical of the restrictionism which the Act sought to break down. However, it must be borne in mind that a great deal of managerial strategy and government exhortation is given over to engineering the commitment of workers to their employment: labour turnover, it is constantly emphasised, is both a financial and social problem. It is not unusual for high labour turnover to be equated with low morale.[78] As it happens, experience often vindicates

[75] W. W. Daniel, *Whatever Happened to the Workers in Woolwich?* (London: P.E.P., 1972), p. 102.

[76] Dorothy Wedderburn and Bob Fryer, *ASTMS – Rolls Royce Study: Report on First Stage*, January 1972, unpublished. See also Wedderburn and Fryer, *Rolls Royce Redundancy* (London: Davis Poynter, forthcoming). [77] *op. cit.*, p. 75.

[78] See, for example, the discussion by G. K. Ingham, *Size of Industrial Organization and Worker Behaviour* (Cambridge: University Press, 1970); also W. H. Scott *et al.*, *Coal and Conflict* (Liverpool: University Press, 1963).

the apparent conservatism of workers: in the floorcoverings industry, transferees were reported to be unsettled and some returned home disillusioned; two thirds of the Rolls Royce workers were unemployed for two months and over, and, in the Parker survey, redundancy marked the end of employment for no less than 15 per cent of the paid redundant.[79] In any case, there is good reason for groups of workers to resist redundancy where there is the likelihood or possibility of hardship being caused to a few:

'To a group of workers, however, the likelihood that redundancy will bring serious hardship to a few is enough to justify resistance. In the first place, since no one knows beforehand on whom the hardship will fall, and whose turn it will be to go next, even this means insecurity for all. Secondly, solidarity is still a potent sentiment among British trade unionists. An injury to one is an injury to all. Thirdly, the group as a whole can only lose by the change. The dismissals mean decimation of its numbers and breaking up some of the relationships which bind it together; and they demonstrate the limits of its ability to protect its members.'[80]

In such circumstances and with such motivation it is not only pointless but also inappropriate to appeal to considerations of the national interest or the precepts of economic rationality. Even if certain trade union leaders find it expedient to see eye to eye with public policy at the expense of their members, it is open to members to initiate their own response to redundancy, as has been clearly demonstrated by the recent emergence of the strategies of the 'work-in' and occupation to fight closures. As Flanders has noted:

'When unions are asked to co-operate in introducing measures that will raise productivity, they cannot decide their attitude on general grounds of national interest or economic theory. They must weigh up the *immediate* gains and losses that are likely to accrue to their *own* members. When the balance is unfavourable their opposition is assured. The weaker their internal democracy the easier it is for their leaders to be 'statesmanlike' and to take a longer and a broader view, but there are limits to the extent to which they can ignore membership pressures, as was seen during the period of 'wage restraint'. It is pointless to condemn the unions' attitude as selfish when they take a cool, hard look at what is in it for their members. That is a law of their being which they can never deny in practice, whatever may be said in propaganda. They exist to

[79] *op. cit.*, p. 89. [80] Clegg, 'Mobility of Labour', p. 10.

represent a sectional interest and if they fail to put this first they forfeit their claim to support.'[81]

The A.E.U. put the point forcefully in its evidence to the Donovan Commission arguing that 'it is vain, cruel, and unthinking to expect a man to consider national, social and economic interests of an abstract nature when pressures force him to fight for the very existence of his family and himself by preserving the job, the trade, the firm, and the way of life he knows so well'.

Thus, if public policy is not to define the redundancy problem from a managerial or reified perspective as the need for certain managements in some parts of the country to be rid of workers and for certain other managements elsewhere to obtain workers, then, seen from the workers' point of view, the problem is how to continue present employment, in the same plant and for the foreseeable future. As Dorothy Wedderburn wrote of the railway workshop redundancies:

'The news of the closure hit an extremely stable community where the men looked forward to doing the jobs they had always done in the company of other men, whom they knew very well, not just because they had worked together for many years, but also because they were the sons or brothers of old "so and so".'[82]

What is lacking in the managerial basis of the problem for public policy is an appreciation of the very real and legitimate attachment of workers to their occupational and social communities.[83] Even where the existence of such 'communities' may be doubted, the problem for the worker is not so much acceptance of the 'need' for more redundancy but how to protect himself from the vagaries of both management decision-making and the labour market. As one redundant car worker succinctly put it:

'It's outdated, this idea of employers getting all the work out of them and then throwing them on the scrap-heap.'[84]

Of course, when it comes to an assessment of 'poor work record,' then, seen from the worker's perspective, the performance of management may leave a lot to be desired. Indeed the position of super-ordinate and sub-ordinate might even be reversed as at Fisher-Bendix when the convenor of shop stewards is reported to have told

[81] op cit., p. 240.   [82] Redundancy and the Railwaymen, p. 50.
[83] See also Michael Barrett Brown, 'What Will the Miners do Now?' New Society, 23 November 1967, and F. Cottrell, 'Death by Dieselization', American Sociological Review, 16, 1951.
[84] Kahn, op. cit., pp. 227–8.

a senior manager 'the best thing you can do is get your coat on and leave these premises'.[85] Needless to say, both the opposition to managerial decisions about redundancy and the counter evaluation of managerial performance by workers challenge what Meyers, in his comparative study of ownership of jobs, called:

'The "cherished prerogative" of British management to dismiss (which) has traditionally extended to the right both to reduce forces and to select those workers to be separated in the event of a reduction.'[86]

However, as Meyers observed, despite the failure of the institutions of collective bargaining to deal adequately with the workers' redundancy problem and in the face of trade union officers' view that redundancy is unavoidable,[87]

'Paradoxically, it was in the period of full-employment that plant level reaction to reductions in force made it apparent that many British workers were not satisfied with alternative job opportunities; they sought continued tenure in the jobs they held.'[88]

As many of the earlier references to the Parker survey indicate, it is precisely this parodox which most puzzles those who advocate a 'shake-out' of labour. Fear of unemployment is only one of a number of reasons for workers having their own perspective upon changes that may entail redundancy. Even if unemployment were the sole source of worker opposition there would, as Fox has argued, be a great deal more to say about the rationality of such a stance than those who rush to criticise are prepared to allow:

'Who enjoys being forced out of his job even when there is another available? To protect oneself against imposed and unwanted change is a rational enough response and if increases in output, more apprentices, abandonment of demarcation rules or reductions

---

[85] *7 Days*, 19 January 1972, p. 14.

[86] Fredcrick Meyers, *Ownership of Jobs* (Los Angeles: University of California Institute of Industrial Relations, 1964), p. 31.

[87] Parker and his colleagues report 47 per cent trade union officers saying redundancies among their members were 'entirely unavoidable' in the short term. Similarly 49 per cent thought that they were 'entirely unavoidable' in the long term. In stark contrast, the numbers of officers thinking the redundancies were entirely avoidable were 6 per cent and 5 per cent respectively (p. 140). [88] Meyers, *op. cit.*, p. 31.

in "manning ratios" seem likely to cause redundancy then restrictions will have appeal even when new jobs lie to hand.'[89]

But, if full employment was the source of a demand for no redundancy, something less than a full-employment situation has been the major occasion of its application. Even in the floor-coverings firm characterised by paternalist domination, weak unionism and a high degree of loyalty to the firm, no less than 36 per cent took the view that workers have a right in their jobs which should not be taken away from them by management. Elsewhere the announcement of redundancy has called forth what in recent times has been arguably the most significant development in labour strategy, the work-in and occupation.

If public policy is to confront a definition of the redundancy problem which contradicts the way the problem has been construed so far, then doubt must be cast over the opinions of those 'experts who will claim that redundancy is really the mark of a healthy vigorous economy'.[90] Manpower policy and conflicts about manpower policy cannot be treated simply as the final consideration in business strategy. Even those who have asserted the problem of overmanning have paid lip service to the importance of regarding manpower policy as an integral part of the organisation of production and not merely as a residue function of that activity. Of course, explicit recognition of the centrality of manpower to industrial organisation may carry with it implications that those who shape public policy either fail to recognise or, finding them unpalatable, choose to ignore. These implications are that public policy must recognise that employment (and dismissal) has much more to do with the question of power in industrial organisation than with what is largely the political fiction of the 'national interest'. Such a conclusion about manpower policy is thrown into sharp relief by the problem of redundancy for it must be recognised that 'redundancy, like any other problem of industrial conflict, is closely related to the ownership and control of industry.'[91]

[89] Alan Fox, 'Labour Utilization and Industrial Relations', in D. Pym (ed.), *Industrial Society* (Harmondsworth: Penguin, 1968), p. 45.

[90] Goodman, *op. cit.*, p. 1.

[91] *ibid.*, p. 30. One of the few publications dealing with redundancy to make this explicit is R. Thomas (ed.), *Redundancy?* A study by a Bristol Trade Union Group, 1971. For a critical reaction to 'expert' opinion see also H. Kahn, 'Labour Mobility: Some Critical reflections', *District Bank Review*, March 1966.

However, recognition of the centrality of labour to productive processes and acceptance of the importance of power in this connection does not of necessity entail invoking public policy in support of workers' definitions of the need for more restrictions upon managerial discretion. On the contrary, the development of public policy with regard to redundancy has emphasised the fundamental aim of freeing management from the constraints of shopfloor opposition to the euphemisms of 'shake-out', 'rationalisation' and 'streamlining'. As Professor Wedderburn has observed, where employment security and redundancy are concerned 'we have to decide to whom, in a modern society, jobs really "belong" '.[92] Despite the muddle-headed views of many commentators upon the British scene and the frequent use of misleading analogies of 'property rights' in jobs, the decision incorporated into public policy is that jobs certainly do not belong to workers.

Humanitarianism and Formalisation

It might be objected that accusations of muddle-headed and misleading commentaries upon British employment policy ill befit an analysis that, in concentrating upon the managerial definition of redundancy, has neglected the obvious concern for the displaced worker manifest in public policy, particularly in the provisions of the Redundancy Payments Act. After all, since the inception of the Act redundant workers have shared the not inconsiderable sum of more than £400 million in redundancy payments. Prior to the legislation, provision for severance payments was scant indeed: in 1963 out of a total of 371 redundancy schemes in private industry, only 192 (covering 1,149,000 workers) included arrangements for redundancy payments[93] and the Act provides for a 'level of compensation which was generous in comparison to most existing voluntary arrangements at that time'.[94] For his part, Mr Gunter declared that

[92] K. W. Wedderburn, *The Worker and the Law* (Harmondsworth: Penquin, 1971), p. 155.

[93] Ministry of Labour, *Security and Change: Progress in Provision for Redundancy* (London: H.M.S.O., 1961), gives the first survey by the Ministry of Labour and N.J.A.C. The statistics cited come from 'Redundancy in Great Britain', *Ministry of Labour Gazette*, February 1963, pp. 50–55.

[94] Parker *et al., op. cit.*, p. 4. However, it should be pointed out that the terms of the 1965 Act were no more generous than those envisaged in Mr John (now Lord) Diamond's proposals in 1962. In his evidence to the Donovan Commission Prof. K. W. Wedderburn recommended

'the compensation of an employee for the loss of his job marks a very significant step forward in the way we think about the status of the industrial worker'.[95] Under the legislation, severance pay for the displaced worker would not be contingent on his post-redundancy situation for he would be 'compensated for loss of job irrespective of whether that leads to unemployment'.[96] Taken together – as they often are – redundancy payments and earnings related unemployment benefit are often cited as clear evidence of a greater commitment in public policy to reduce hardship.

It might be further objected that concentration upon the managerial definition of redundancy has entailed overlooking the emphasis in public policy upon the importance of forward planning of manpower and consultation with employees or their representatives, of keeping redundancies to a minimum, of full information and as long a notice of redundancy as possible and, the key to it all, of the advance preparation of a redundancy agreement.[97] For example *Security and Change* declares:

'The individual appreciates knowing what his position will be if his job is threatened. Plans for dealing with possible redundancy in the future should be regarded as a normal part of the responsibility of management, even in firms which have good reason for hoping that they will never have to operate a redundancy procedure. Improved working relationships can be established by the existence of such a scheme and serious trouble at the time of redundancy can be averted if the plans for dealing with it are known in advance, particularly if the scheme has been agreed with the workers likely to be affected.'[98]

Dealing first with this second set of objections to the predominant theme of 'managerial' definitions, it is plain that even if the policies advocated ever got beyond exhortation, they would not represent a *negation* of the principle of redundancy. Their major impact, if implemented, would be the formalisation of redundancy in such a way as to 'take redundancy out of industrial conflict' by contributing to what the Donovan Commission referred to as the effective

that the qualification period be reduced from 2 years to 3 months; a change which would have brought far more of those declared redundant within the scope of the Act. See below, pp. 255–6.

[95] *loc. cit.* [96] *loc. cit.*

[97] See, *Security and Change, op. cit.; Code of Industrial Relations Practice, op. cit.*, and Department of Employment and Productivity, *Dealing with Redundancies* (London, 1968). [98] *op. cit.*, p. 31.

regulation of industrial relations, or what the Parker survey called a more relaxed climate. In this way trade unions can become, in the words of one who negotiated the celebrated Delta Rod Redundancy Agreement 'a mere arm of the personnel department'.[99]

The case for formalisation has been made by both Donovan and the Commission on Industrial Relations. Donovan argued that one of the major underlying causes of unofficial strikes was 'the confusion which so often surrounds the exercise by management of its "rights" (which can be) resolved by the settlement of clear rules and procedures'.[100] The CIR argued for formalisation believing that it 'does contribute to effective industrial relations by adding clarity and certainty in changing situations'.[101] However, as it happens, despite all the public exhortation, very little of this additional formalisation has yet been achieved where redundancy is concerned. The formalisation seems to be limited largely to the legislation itself and Parker reports that 'the Redundancy Payments Act appears to have had no influence upon manpower planning',[102] that less than a tenth of employers have redundancy agreements with trade unions,[103] and indeed, that there are grounds to believe that 'there has been an increase in the frequency of redundancy since the Act'.[104]

Turning to the objection that the analysis so far has overlooked what the Parker survey called the 'social objectives' of public policy, it is plain that here change has marked a step forward from exhortation. Undoubtedly, the receipt of unemployment benefit and redundancy payments has done something to alleviate some of the financial difficulties of a minority proportion of the workers who are declared redundant. In this limited sense it would be foolish to deny the improvement made in public policy. However, this so-called 'new thinking' about the status of the industrial worker does nothing to contradict either the legitimacy of redundancy or the importance of

---

[99] Author's field notes. It is instructive to set this view against that of the Deputy Chairman of Delta Rod. Writing of the value of a redundancy agreement he points out that 'if it exists, management will find it immeasurably easier to deal in a relevant and confident manner with the inevitable personal and industrial relations problems which arise from redundancy'. Richard O'Brien, 'Points of Procedure', *Personnel Management*, August 1972, p. 25.

[100] Royal Commission on Trade Unions and Employers' Associations 1965–1968, *Report* (London: H.M.S.O., 1968), p. 121.

[101] Commission on Industrial Relations, Report No. 17, *Facilities Afforded to Shop Stewards* (London: H.M.S.O., 1971), p. 42.

[102] *op. cit.*, p. 29.   [103] *ibid.*, p. 50.   [104] *ibid.*, p. 14.

managerial discretion and control. On the contrary, the declared aim of the policy is to persuade workers to give up unilateral job control: 'The Act', said the Tribunal's President, 'is to encourage workers to accept redundancy without damaging industrial relations'.[105] Further, in implementing what, in effect, is a fixed scale of compulsory purchase prices, the Act did nothing at all to modify the commodity and object-like view of labour evident in references to manpower 'resources' and 'reserves' within the managerial definition of the problem. Indeed, a more plausible view of the legislation and its financial provisions is that it reinforced not only the commodity view of labour, but also served to facilitate an approach which regards workers as quite properly the most easily varied factor of production.

This interpretation of public policy as a way of making it 'easier for managers to do their duty by diminishing the workers' opposition to redundancy',[106] accords well not only with received opinion about the advantages of formalisation, but also with the precepts of both humanitarianism and the Human Relations Approach. In a redundancy situation each of these last two philosophies simultaneously denies any fundamental conflict of interests and emphasises the importance of 'methods of assisting employees to adjust to changes within the enterprise'.[107] The latest development in this approach to redundancy is the technique of counselling which aims to get redundant employees 'working towards a realistic adaptation to their situation',[108] In short, the primary concern of both philosophies is not so much to validate the worker's own definition of the problem of redundancy but rather to encourage him to adapt himself to the managerial definition which, in turn, redefines the worker's problem to what happens to him *after* he has been declared redundant. Thus, the humanitarian rationale behind the public policy of severance payments is neither a mere expression of conscience nor simply an assembly of fine but empty phrases: there is undoubtedly a possible benefit for management, even if the worth of redundancy payments can easily be exaggerated and even though they do not satisfy the worker's won definition of the problem:

'In so far as they reduce the hardship of dismissal they may also be

[105] Cited in Grunfeld, *op. cit.*, p. 8.

[106] Clegg, *Mobility of Labour*, p. 11.

[107] A. D. Smith, *op. cit.*, p. 7.

[108] Pamela Pocock, 'Softening the Blow of Redundancy', *Personnel Management*, June 1972, p. 25.

expected to diminish hostility to redundancy, but that is not to say they constitute an adequate solution, for workers want security, and these palliatives do not more than begin to diminish insecurity. ... But even handsome payments do not put an end to objections to redundancy, for the best form of security is the knowledge that the worker's present employment will continue as long as he wants it.'[109]

It is possible that the failure to recognise the real function of humanitarian concern in public policy owes something to the notion of a 'floor of rights' which has been applied to the Redundancy Payments Act. Thus it may be thought that in thinking differently about workers and their jobs, public policy had made life more difficult for managers. However, Parker and his colleagues report that 'the Act had made it easier for many employers to discharge workers'.[110] Indeed only 11 per cent of managers thought the Act had made it more difficult to dismiss workers while three times as many thought it had made dismissal easier.[111] After all, there is plenty of scope for manoeuvre within the provisions of the legislation as it operates in industry, for while the Act lays down detailed substantive rules to govern the compensation of those declared redundant, its procedural rules are largely concerned with question of notice and are confined to those that guide the tribunals and courts in assessing appeals. Complaints about 'legalistic' interpretations of the legislation apply to the tiny minority of cases that come to the tribunals and courts. The Act says nothing about the method of selection of the redundant and the provisions under the Industrial Relations Act (Section 24 (5)(b)) that 'redundancy' dismissals shall be unfair where they are 'in contravention of a customary arrangement or agreed procedure relating to redundancy' are weakened first by the rider of 'special reasons justifying a departure from that arrangement' (e.g. 'bumping'),[112] secondly by the fact that a good many criteria for selection such as skill, efficiency, and work record,[113] overlap the criteria for 'fair' dismissal under Section 24(2) (a) and thirdly by the fact that only 15 per cent of all establishments surveyed by Parker had 'an agreement on understanding with trade unions about redundancy'.[114]

---

[109] Clegg, 'Mobility of Labour', p. 12.
[110] op. cit., p. 29. [111] ibid., p. 62.
[112] Parker reports that 'two thirds of employers with experience of redundancy said they made exceptions to their general rules', ibid., p. 28.
[113] ibid., p. 49. [114] ibid., p. 50.

The point was well illustrated in the floorcoverings redundancy where the management had a fivefold plan for the scheduled run-down of the plant in which redundancy payments were to play a very important role in maintaining control over the workforce throughout the reduction and in shaping the workforce at the end of the redundancy. Management aimed to retain key employees until such time as they could be released in line with the company's plans; to shed from the workforce the 'inefficient', 'trouble-makers', 'poor time-keepers' and 'inflexible'; to reduce the average age of the workforce; to reward 'loyal' company servants and generally to prune the workforce in accordance with the firm's traditional policy of beneficence.[115] Thus 'success' for the firm meant keeping certain men out of the labour market to suit management's goals; dismissing men with a poor work record; declaring a high proportion of older men redundant; releasing sick men and fitting in with the personal plans and projects of a small privileged group.

It is nonsense to call this 'abuse' of the legislation,[116] for such a use by management of redundancy payments in the main accords closely with the priorities given in public policy to 'operational efficiency' and 'criteria of efficiency about whom to retain and whom to dismiss'. Of course, the Act is *defective* if seen from the perspective of all but the privileged few whose plans were furthered by the fact and timing of their redundancy. The 'problem' for most of those whom management wished most to dismiss needs hardly to be laboured, but in almost all respects it contradicts the fantasy world which declares that public policy has 'broadly achieved its objectives'.[117] Those who cannot wait upon management's convenience leave 'voluntarily' and forfeit their payments; employees with a poor work record are scarcely the most sought-after labour; older workers find getting work and adapting to new jobs especially hard; the sick seek withdrawal from the work situation. Indeed the social reality of redundancy flies in the face of the fantasy world of public policy. The difficulty is that a whole myriad of myths has been erected around redundancy which obscures public debate.[118] These myths owe something partly to the way that public policy was shaped,

[115] This is argued in more detail in Bob Fryer and R. Martin, 'Redundancy Payments and the Social Reality of Law', forthcoming.

[116] See W. W. Daniel, 'Redundant Act?', *New Society*, 23 September 1971.   [117] Parker, *op. cit.*, p. 21.

[118] I have analysed some of these myths in 'Unemployment, Myths and Science', *New Scientist*, 16 December 1971.

are further perpetuated by the way that public policy has been evaluated and endure partly because of the consuming interest that lawyers have shown in the law in court rather than the law in action.

The Myths of Redundancy

Because shopfloor practices and, to some extent, trade union attitudes have been portrayed as central to the (managerial) problems of redundancy, public policy in respect of the redundancy problem has been cast in such a fashion as to eliminate opposition and secure cooperation amongst trade union officials and workers. Engineering this consent, as has been indicated already, has thus entailed emphasising the shared nature of the need for greater manpower flexibility, underlining the humanitarian concern for displaced workers and exhorting managers to consult more with their employees about manpower reductions and to conclude redundancy agreements. An indication of the impact of this approach to the redundancy problem is given in the 'success' accorded to the 'economic', 'social' and 'industrial relations' effects of the Redundancy Payments Act.[119] But this 'success' also owes much to the mythology which surrounds the phenomenon of redundancy in general and the provisions of the Redundancy Payments Act in particular. This mythology portrays public policy as having wrought fundamental changes in the nature of employment relations and dismissal by reason of redundancy and, by virtue of such a portrayal, succeeds in obscuring the reality of redundancy.

The myths of the Redundancy Payments Act are sixfold: namely, that the legislation provides an element of employment security; that it gives some sort of job 'property rights' to workers; that, by regulating redundancy, it restricts managerial discretion; that it compensates workers for their loss of job; that redundancy payments act as a disincentive to find alternative work and that, irrespective of other advantages or disadvantages, it at least affords minimum cover to all who lose their job because of redundancy. Taken together, these six myths add up to a belief that what the Webbs called the 'method of legal enactment' has done something, even too much, to redress the gross imbalance between capital and labour.[120]

The belief that the Redundancy Payments Act has to do with

[119] Parker et al., op. cit.

[120] For a discussion of law and power, see Kahn-Freund, *Labour and the Law, op. cit.*

employment security is reflected by the inclusion of the legislation under this heading in legal text books. This mistaken classification is perhaps understandable in view of the fact that the reviewers of the statute have declared that:

> 'It was recognised at the outset that the "restrictive" attitudes and practices of workers were a legacy of years of economic insecurity, and *that these could only be reduced by tackling their source*'.[121]

As has already been argued, economic insecurity, although a powerful stimulus to shopfloor resistance, is not the only reason for opposition to redundancy. Collective reactions to managerial decisions are based on more than just the individual fear of being out of work subsequent to being declared redundant. But even accepting this restricted view of the reason for hostility to redundancy, it would be most difficult to contend that the Redundancy Payments Act actually did tackle the *source* of economic insecurity or even its manifestation in dismissal and unemployment.[122] Such a task would have entailed the minimum requirement of a restriction upon managerial power and the implementation of a 'right to work' (which had to do not with freedom *not* to be a trade union member but with freedom from insecurity of employment). In point of fact, by its negative relationship to security of employment, the legislation has become a positive inducement to insecurity in work: public policy encourages managers, trade union officers and workers alike to abandon their 'protective' attitudes which put too great a premium on job security and too little emphasis upon over-manning and low productivity.[123] Thus, to claim that the provisions of the statute amount to an improvement in employment security is akin to arguing that legislating for insurance cover for a proportion of road

---

[121] Parker *et al.*, *op. cit.*, p. 3, my emphasis.

[122] Kahn-Freund refers to the 'imprecise' characterisation of the legislation as job security. *Labour Law: Old Traditions and New Developments*, *op. cit.*, p. 37. Grunfeld, also observes that 'one purpose or effect the Act does not have is to confer on employees job security', *op. cit.*, p. 9.

[123] An American economist puts the point succinctly when comparing European and U.S. Labour market behaviour: 'It would be unfortunate, in my opinion, if what one European economist calls "an allergy to risk-taking" should spread among American workers as it has among European workers. The experience of this decade will provide a critical test of the relative social values attributed by workers to risk-taking versus economic security . . .' Gladys L. Palmer, 'Social Values in Labor Mobility', in E. Wight Bakke *et al.*, *Labor Mobility and Economic Opportunity* (Cambridge, Mass: M.I.T. Press), pp. 115–16.

users would be about road safety.[124] Just as such insurance would be a clear recognition of the carnage we tolerate upon our roads, so too the Redundancy Payments Act is a straight-forward acceptance of the centrality of the phenomenon of redundancy to contemporary capitalist development and to the everyday world of the worker.

The second myth of the Redundancy Payments Act is linked to the first and holds that the legislation confers some sort of job property rights upon workers. Wedderburn and Davies note that 'such a concept of "property" in *the* job and in a *particular* job has become widespread'.[125] As if to validate such a statement, the Industrial Tribunal's President has argued:

'Just as a property owner has a right in his property . . . so a long term employee is considered to have a right analogous to a right of property in his job'.[126]

Some commentators have seen grave dangers in this principle, fearing that universal recognition of any such job rights will eventually mean providing workers with 'further monetary inducement not to resist industrial change'[127] for 'it seems possible that the recognition of such property rights may actually increase inflexibility of labour, and strengthen opposition to change of a less dramatic kind than that involved in the loss of a job'.[128] These arguments

[124] This is by no means the most remarkable claim about the impact of the legislation. Grunfeld, for example, has argued that the Act may be said to be concerned with the 'equitable distribution of wealth', *op. cit.*, p. 1. Ironically, this view was reflected in what a senior academic connected with the formulation of public policy has claimed was the main reason for continuing with the Act at a time when the Conservative government wished to change it: the Treasury, he says, argued for the Act's retention on the grounds that it was a useful way of 'pumping money into the economy'!

[125] *op. cit.*, p. 41. See also H. A. Turner's evidence to the Donovan Commission.

[126] Cited in Grunfeld, *op. cit.*, p. 8. See also Parker *et al.*, *op. cit.*, p. 4.

[127] Grunfeld, *op. cit.*, p. 9.

[128] Dorothy Wedderburn, 'Redundancy' in Pym (ed.), *op. cit.*, p. 74. For a case against the principle of granting property rights in work see Simon Rottenberg, 'Property in Work', *Industrial and Labor Relations Review*, Vol. 15, No. 3, April 1962. On a slightly different note Lord Robens has argued that the Redundancy Payments Act counteracted the N.C.B.'s plans for redeployment: 'by 1968, it had reduced the flow of transferring workers to a trickle'. Lord Robens has no difficulty in perceiving for whom this is a problem: 'the real moral is that Governments might find it useful to discuss rather more fully than they do now, employment

closely parallel the view that one effect of productivity bargaining is to make workers fabricate 'restrictive practices', yet no evidence is produced to show that this is so and, as the Donovan Secretariat noted, there is good reason to doubt the validity of the claim in that it misunderstands the genesis and rationale of these so-called restrictive labour practices.[129]

Allusions to property rights in work probably owe their appeal in part to the centrality of property-as-a-value in the development of capitalist mores and institutions. Independence, individuality, worth, thrift and humanity are all positive attributes associated with the notion of property: 'property is in its nature a kind of limited sovereignty'.[130] Furthermore, 'the classes who own little or no property may reverence it because it is security'.[131] But just as redundancy payments bear little relation to employment security, so too they are far from implying recognition of workers' job property rights. The notion of property rights first of all entails some degree of control and the restricted ability to dispense with one's property at one's own leisure and to enjoy the fruits of one's property. Thus, where employment is concerned, the property owner ought at least to be able to say

legislation with employers before they introduce it'. *Ten Year Stint* (London: Cassell, 1972), pp. 105–106. Martin Bulmer has set out the conflict inherent in the rundown of the mines: 'the response of employees faced with the closure of their place of work and the offer of alternative work need not, however, coincide with the management view of what is desirable. . . . The immediate effect of the Act is thus to create a built-in conflict between the N.C.B. and the miners over closure because, whereas it is in the N.C.B.'s interests to transfer as many miners as possible to other pits, the men want, if possible, to be made redundant and qualify for the lump sum payment . . . It thus seems reasonable to speak . . . of "competing rationalities". Strong logical arguments can be put forward in favour of both the employer's and the employees' point of view.' 'Mining Redundancy: a case study of the workings of the Redundancy Payments Act in the Durham Coalfield', *Industrial Relations Journal*, Vol. 2, No. 4, pp. 10, 11 and 12.

[129] Royal Commission on Trade Unions and Employers' Associations, Research Papers 4: *Productivity Bargaining and Restrictive Practices* (London: H.M.S.O., 1966), p. 40. See also Alan Fox, 'Labour Utilisation and Industrial Relations', *op. cit.*, National Board for Prices and Incomes, *Report No. 123 Productivity Agreements*, p. 33, and William Brown, 'A Consideration of "Custom and Practice" ', *British Journal of Industrial Relations*, Vol. X, No. 1, March 1972.

[130] R. H. Tawney, *The Acquisitive Society* (London: Fontana, 1961), p. 77.   [131] *ibid.*, p. 73.

whether or not there ought to be a redundancy and, if so, just when that redundancy ought to occur. Even the financial compensation for redundancy bears little relation to compensation for the 'compulsory purchase' of property, for it takes no account of fluctuations in the market (i.e. does not increase when jobs are scarce), has an arbitrarily restricted upper limit and does not provide the dispossessed worker with the wherewithal to 'purchase' property comparable to that which he has lost in terms not only of income but also of job interest, authority, seniority, familiarity, utilisation of skills and so on; nor are there provisions in public policy for appeal against redundancy.[132]

However, while it may be admitted that this relatively 'hard' definition of property has no validity, nevertheless a 'softer' definition is more appropriate in which property rights in work are really analogous to rights of access acquired by unrestrained trespass and restricted simply to use. In this sense, frequently implied in the analysis of productivity bargaining,[133] the rights of workers are not so much dependent upon their own proprietorship as upon the tacit agreement of the real (or proxy) owners, management. But even this analogy is doubtful, for once rights of way have been established, the former owner cannot repossess them in the face of opposition from whomsoever has gained the easement and if owners are to prevent such easement being gained in the first place, they must follow certain specified procedures annually for a given number of years.

Even supposing, for one moment, that the property analogy has some value, when it comes to a conflict of property rights exercised by management on the one hand and workers on the other, it is plain that some sorts of property confer more rights than others, thus contradicting 'the naïve philosophy which would treat all such rights as equal in sanctity merely because they are equal in name'.[134] In short, claims that public policy for redundancy recognises property in work are no less misleading than the analysis which seeks to show that the Redundancy Payments Act confers security of employment.

The third myth of the Redundancy Payments Act is closely related to the first two and this is that the legislation imposes some restriction upon managerial power. Indeed, it has even been speculated

---

[132] See above, p. 243, for a criticism of the provisions made in the Industrial Relations Act.

[133] See also William Brown, *op. cit.*

[134] R. H. Tawney, *op. cit.*, p. 79.

that as a result of recognising the logic of the Act, management has come to impose these restrictions upon itself:

'In other words, because the Act makes it quite explicit that workers do accumulate "rights" in the jobs they hold, it is possible that this has come to be accepted by management in a rather wider sense than is implied by direct money compensation'.[135]

This point of view rests upon the plausible argument that rules, by their very nature, reduce discretion and introduce a uniform standard of action: 'one of the effects of rules is to establish rights and obligations which together define status'.[136] This regulation might be expected to be bolstered by the development of collective agreements in respect of redundancy which would have the additional effect of eliminating some of the uncertainty which surrounds redundancy. Of course, the Redundancy Payments Act imposes no obligation to bargain with trade unions or workers' representatives: 58 per cent of trade union officers surveyed by Parker felt the Act had made no difference to employers' willingness to sign redundancy agreements,[137] and we have already seen how few employers have concluded such agreements. Further, it has been shown that, in effect, management's freedom to select whomsoever they please for redundancy is not limited by public policy: indeed, three times as many employers felt the Redundancy Payments Act had actually made it easier to dismiss workers as thought the reverse and two thirds of employers felt the Act suited the conditions of their business well or fairly well.[138]

Added to this, more than threequarters of trade union officers in the Parker survey thought that the Redundancy Payments Act had helped management to get workers to accept manpower changes.[139] Thus, the regulatory effect of the Redundancy Payments Act, such as it is, rather than restricting management, has been to take redundancy out of both conflict and the area of collective action and control by workers.

The fourth element in the Redundancy Payments Act myth also

[135] Parker *et al.*, *op. cit.*, p. 16. 36 per cent of employers thought the Act overprotected workers, *ibid.*, p. 69.

[136] Allan Flanders, *Industrial Relations: What is Wrong with the System?* (London: Faber, 1965), p. 11. For a most illuminating analysis of the function of bureaucratic rules see Alvin Gouldner, *Patterns of Industrial Bureaucracy* (New York: Free Press, 1964), pp. 157–180.

[137] *op. cit.*, p. 139.   [138] *ibid.*, p. 67.

touches upon 'security', 'property rights' and the substantive rules which cover dismissal by reason of redundancy. This fourth myth holds that the substantive rules for compensating displaced workers were drawn up more or less correctly:

> 'The survey has shown that the criteria which determined eligibility and the size of the statutory payment have been more or less correctly defined. In general, age, length of service, and level of earnings in the redundant job were found to be positively related to the extent of social and economic costs incurred by the individual as a consequence of redundancy.'[140]

Thus, in so far as 'the purpose of redundancy pay was to provide compensation to the worker for the loss of job',[141] the Redundancy Payments Act has 'broadly achieved'[142] its 'principal social objective'[143]. Parker and his colleagues argue that these social objectives were more specific than the economic objectives of the legislation, namely 'to provide financial compensation for the *social and economic costs* incurred by the individual as a consequence of his involuntary redundancy'.[144] Now Parker and his colleagues report that, 'generally speaking, redundant workers tended to lose income, pension rights, fringe benefits and job satisfaction'.[145] Hence, the provisions of the Act seek to set a money value on the loss of a job, firstly, where any such monetary value can be only a financial fiction (a further exemplification of the crude commodity view of labour) and, secondly, without even dealing explicitly with those elements of a job – such as future income and pension rights – which may be said to be primarily material and more immediately amenable to financial calculation. Nor is it sufficient to point to the positive association between size of redundancy payment and deprivations as measured by simple rank ordering.[146] Such an association tells us nothing about the appropriateness or adequacy of the compensation but only about the correctness of the direction of association. For example, if redundant workers received only £1 for each year of service so that a man with 30 years' service received £30 compensation, there would still be the same positive association between social and economic costs and the size of the lump sum. A further

---

[139] *ibid.*, p. 138.   [140] *ibid.*, p. 21.   [141] *ibid.*, p. 5.
[142] *ibid.*, p. 21.   [143] *ibid.*, p. 7.   [144] *ibid.*, p. 7, my emphasis.
[145] *ibid.*, p. 7.   [146] *ibid.*, p. 8.

problem with this crude rank ordering is that there is no necessary relation between the intervals on a scale of deprivation and those on the scale of compensation: in other words, does the shift from (say) small loss of satisfaction to great loss of satisfaction actually correspond with the rank number allocated to the associated increase in redundancy payment? On a simple rank ordering each of these changes may be arbitrarily indicated by the movement from one ordinal number to the next, but such a crude transposition of qualitative changes into quantitative values can highlight only gross discrepancies in the association between the two scales. The remarkable conclusion by Parker and his colleagues owes less to their invaluable research than to their simplistic and arbitrary method of measuring the 'losses' suffered by redundant workers.

In any case, two further facts contradict this complacent assessment of the effects of the Redundancy Payments Act. Firstly, as I will show below, the statute covers no more than a sizable minority of workers who lose their job because of redundancy and says nothing about the so-called voluntary leavers who quit under the impact of redundancy and who might better be called 'constructively redundant'. Secondly, Parker's research shows that only 47 per cent of the most redundancy-prone group – those between 60 and 64 – succeeded in finding another job of any sort,[147] and as Parker and his colleagues observe, 'it would be misleading to assume that success in obtaining any new job'[148] is an indication of the correctness of the criteria for compensation. All studies of redundancy have demonstrated the particular vulnerability of older workers: in the floorcoverings study, 32 per cent of the shopfloor redundant and 20 per cent of the staff redundant were aged 60 and over; in the Rolls Royce study 81 per cent of those workers aged 50 and over were still out of work two months after the redundancy. It might be argued that the plight of these older workers should be the proper concern of unemployment benefit, but consider the findings of McKay's work on West Midland engineering redundancies after the July 1966 'shake-out': 18·3 per cent were unemployed for 26 weeks or more, the period which marks the termination of earnings related unemployment benefit.[149] In Rolls Royce 26 per cent were still out of work six months after being declared redundant. Even those who had found jobs were hardly ecstatic about them:

[147] *ibid.*, p. 89.　　　　　　　　　　　　　　　[148] *ibid.*, p. 5.
[149] D. I. McKay, 'After the "Shake-out" ', *Oxford Economic Papers*, Vol. 24, No. 1, March 1972.

54 per cent said they had taken the employment because it was just a job,[150] 40 per cent thought their skills underutilised, 41 per cent had further to travel to work, 63 per cent had lost holiday entitlement and 33 per cent had dropped more than a fifth on their earnings at Rolls Royce.[151] It needs a fairly accommodating method of assessment to label such social effects of redundancy and the Redundancy Payments Act as 'broadly successful'.

However, by arguing that the degree of unemployment consequent upon redundancy must be taken into account in evaluating the Redundancy Payments Act, one myth may have been demolished only at the expense of providing support for another, namely that what the *Economist* called 'hefty redundancy payments'[152] have a disincentive effect upon the intensity of job-seeking after redundancy and thus inflate the unemployment statistics. Both Parker and his his colleagues and the *Economist* give credence to the claim that there has been a shift in the meaning of the unemployment figures which is due partly to the financial cushion of redundancy payments.[153] Of course, one of the intentions of the legislation was to give redundant workers greater leisure to look round for suitable alternative work and so a slight increase in the period between jobs might be expected. In addition, given the recognition of the possible adverse psychological impact of redundancy, it would be hard to fault redundant workers for using some of their redundancy payment to finance a short break between jobs.

In considering this myth it should first be noted that the average redundancy payments of £292 during 1971[154] and of £370 received by the 60–64 age group of the paid redundant in the Parker survey hardly justify the epithet 'hefty'.[155] Moreover, if this part of the

[150] Another study of redundancy reports this as the main reason given for taking the first job after dismissal 'despite the size of lump sum payments received'. W. W. Daniel, *Whatever Happened to the Workers in Woolwich?* (London: P.E.P., 1972), p. 104.

[151] Comparison with national average earnings showed the earnings of our sample to be slightly below average.

[152] 24 July 1971, p. 75.

[153] Parker *et al.*, *op. cit.*, p. 108, and *The Economist*, 24 April 1971, pp. 62–63.

[154] Data computed from the D.E. *Gazette* quarterly reports of redundancy payments.

[155] For a much more accurate description of hefty severance payments see the evidence cited in *Redundancy?*, *op. cit.*, pp. 28–29, where it is reported that one director received ' "the bulk" of £59,000 in compensation' while two other directors shared £110,000, another received £41,000 another £65,000 and another £25,000.

myth is valid it would be hard to explain the fact that both paid and unpaid redundant workers have the same average length of post redundancy unemployment, eight weeks.[156] Even amongst the paid redundant when age is held constant, there is no variation in length of unemployment according to size of lump sum compensation.[157] Other research by Daniel[158] and McKay[159] reinforces the view that redundancy payments do not have their alleged disincentive effects either upon job seeking behaviour or upon the length of time between jobs. The detailed research conducted by Daniel found 'no tendency . . . for the size of the lump-sum payment to be associated with the delaying of job seeking . . . no indication that redundancy payments made people turn down suitable jobs . . . (and) no tendency for unemployment to increase with size of payment'.[160] Similarly, McKay found that the correlation coefficient between length of unemployment and size of redundancy payment was a mere 0·12: many of those who had received small sums in redundancy payments had experienced long periods of unemployment and *vice versa*. In the Rolls Royce study, even without allowing for the distorting effect of age,[161] there was no simple relationship between size of redundancy payment and intensity of job search: 55 per cent of those who had received less than £200 had applied for six or more jobs by the time we first interviewed[162] compared with 77 per cent who had received between £200 and £399, 52 per cent who had received between £400 and £599, 48 per cent who had received £600–799 and 60 per cent who had received £800 or more.[163] Thus there is little evidence of the disincentive impact of redundancy payments upon intensity of job-search, for there is no marked reduction in job applications with the increase in compensation. Of course, faced with such data, those who prefer the comfort of myths to the reality of evidence may choose their myths according to the occasion, sometimes arguing that large redundancy payments deter workers from seeking jobs and sometimes arguing the reverse that workers do not 'need' redundancy payments because they can

---

[156] Parker *et al., op. cit.,* p. 108.   [157] *ibid.,* p. 109.   [158] *op. cit.*

[159] 'Redundancy, Unemployment and Manpower Policy', *Economic Journal,* December 1972.

[160] *op. cit.,* pp. 99–100.

[161] Age would both inflate the redundancy payments and reduce the number of job opportunities.

[162] Interviews were conducted between two and four months after the redundancy.

[163] The mean for redundancy payments was £320.

simply cross the street and obtain immediate re-employment.[164] Where the first argument is not supported by the findings of research, the second rests upon a misunderstanding of the nature of redundancy payments. Compensation is payable irrespective of whether redundancy leads to unemployment: 'It is not unemployment pay. I repeat "not". Even if the worker gets another job straight away, he nevertheless is entitled to full redundancy payment'.[165]

The sixth and final myth of the Redundancy Payments Act maintains that no matter what the precise effects or even intentions of the Act might be, at least it offers statutory cover to most workers where none existed before. Those workers who lose their jobs through no fault of their own are now entitled to compensation; hence, the legislation is said to provide 'financial compensation for the great majority of workers who lose their job as a result of redundancy'.[166] If this claim is true, then all that need be noted is that there has been almost a threefold increase in the annual numbers being declared redundant since the Act has been in operation. The figures in the table below show two large jumps in the numbers receiving redundancy payments; between 1966 and 1967 and again between 1970 and 1971. The first of these increases is accounted for partly by the 'take-off' of the legislation and partly by the impact in 1967 of the July 1966 measures. The second increase marks 1971 as the Year of Redundancy, although already there are signs that 1972 might provide yet another increase; for the first quarter 90,625 received payments which represented more than 20 per cent increase on the comparable figure for 1971 which was itself a 10 per cent increase on the figure for the first quarter of the previous year.

TABLE

Numbers Receiving Statutory Redundancy Payments[167]

Year	Number of Payments	Average Payment
1966	137,208	£193
1967	241,581	£207·6
1968	264,500	£233·8
1969	250,764	£246·8
1970	275,563	£263·2
1971	370,221	£292·3
First quarter 1972	90,625	£310·1

[164] Parker and his colleagues provide evidence that some employers believe that payments should only be made where unemployment follows redundancy, *op. cit.*, p. 69.

[165] Lord Denning in *Lloyd v. Brassey*, cited in Grunfeld *op. cit.*, p. 7.

[166] Dorothy Wedderburn, 'Redundancy', in Pym (ed.), *op. cit.*, p. 65.

[167] Table computed from quarterly statistics published in the D.E. *Gazette.*

But of course, not all those declared redundant receive statutory redundancy payments: some do not qualify by virtue of their age; some because of inadequate unbroken service; some because they are excluded from the provisions of the Act and some because they leave their employment before receiving notice or refuse offers of 'suitable' alternative work. It is impossible to estimate exactly how many unpaid redundancies there are every year, but in 1967 the Ministry of Labour put the annual number of dismissals attributable to redundancy at between 750,000 and 1,000,000,[168] so it can be seen that unpaid redundancies for 1967 were calculated at between half and threequarters of a million. In 1968 a D.E.P. estimate put the annual number of unpaid redundancies at between 500,000 and 750,000 and Parker and his colleagues agree that on any reasonably inclusive definition of unpaid redundancy, the estimate of a minimum of half a million is probably correct (although it should be pointed out that this does not include so-called 'voluntary leavers').

Now, at the time of the two government departments' estimates, *paid* redundancies were running at around a quarter of a million annually. Parker and his colleagues report that the unpaid group as a whole seemed more redundancy-prone than the paid redundant, so that, with the increase to 370,000 in 1971, it seems reasonable to conclude that unpaid redundancies have increased *at least* in direct proportion and probably at a faster rate than paid redundancies. Furthermore, given that Parker and his colleagues report an increase in redundancies, it is most unlikely that the total paid and unpaid redundant for 1971 fell below the 1967 estimates of up to one million; indeed, it is more than likely that that figure was very much exceeded. In other words, the total unpaid redundancies last year was certainly no less than three quarters of a million and probably more than topped the million mark.

A number of important considerations flow even from these approximations. Firstly, the calculations show that even on the most optimistic (i.e. lowest) totals for 1971, only one third of those dismissed by reason of redundancy received statutory payments and, in fact, the proportion may have fallen to 25 per cent or less. This is serious enough in itself but concern must be heightened by the finding that:

'Where redundancy involved making statutory payments, those employees affected generally received better treatment from their employers than the unpaid redundant workers. On average they

---

[168] Report of the Working Group on the Redundancy Payments Act, cited in Parker *et al.*, *op. cit.*, p. 145.

received longer advanced warning of redundancy and longer periods of formal notice. Also the paid redundant workers regarded the action of their employers in the redundancy situation more favourably. . . . '[169]

Furthermore the financial position of the paid redundant at the time of their termination is considerably better (if still unsatisfactory) than that of their unpaid redundant colleagues: on average paid redundant left their employer with a total of £380 made up of statutory redundancy payments, employer's supplementary severance pay and other emoluments compared with an average of £30 for the unpaid redundant.[170]

Even leaving aside the question of non-cover for 'voluntary leavers' who quit under the impact of redundancy, these findings show the dangers of complacently assuming that the great majority of workers are covered by the provisions of the Act. In addition, as the period of operation of the Act lengthens and workers find themselves being declared redundant for a second or third time,[171] so the proportion excluded by the two-year qualifying period might be expected to increase. It is illustrative of whose definition of the problems prevailed when the legislation was drafted that Parker and his colleagues report two main reasons for limiting payments to those with two years' service: firstly, this was thought to be a minimum period in which the worker could prove his worth 'in the eyes of his employer' and secondly, that with any shorter qualifying period workers 'might have been tempted to stay on for an extra month or so in order to "try on" a case before the tribunal. Such actions could have overburdened (the) machinery and brought the scheme generally into disrepute'.[172] In short, the problems that had to be faced were mainly managerial, but also partly bureaucratic.[173]

[169] Parker *et al.*, *op. cit.*, p. 15.   [170] *ibid.*, p. 84.
[171] W. W. Daniel found that 'ten per cent of those who managed to find jobs had been made redundant again between the time of their dismissal and their interview, on average a two-year period', *Whatever Happened to the Workers in Woolwich?*, *op. cit.*, p. 50.
[172] *op. cit.*, p. 6.
[173] A senior academic connected with the formulation of public policy has argued that the bureaucratic consideration was uppermost in setting limits for qualification for unfair dismissal claims. First, it was estimated what number of cases could be dealt with annually by the tribunals; this was then set against the findings of surveys on unfair dismissals so that those variables which would restrict the number of cases to a tolerable case-load could be built-in to the qualification.

R   257

A second consideration that flows from our rough and ready statistics is the impact of redundancy upon the numbers of working days lost. At the time of the Parker survey the average unemployment of both paid and unpaid redundant was eight weeks; since then employment opportunities have deteriorated and it seems unlikely that the average length of post-redundancy unemployment has declined: during the last quarter of 1968, 68·8 per cent of the wholly unemployed had been unemployed for between four and twenty-six weeks and 24·7 per cent for between eight and twenty-six weeks compared with 71·6 per cent and 28·2 per cent respectively for the last quarter of 1971.[174] Confining calculations to the paid redundant alone and using the same basis of 6 working days per week as used in the calculation of losses through accidents and prescribed diseases, it can be seen that over seventeen and three quarter million working days were lost because of redundancy during 1971. To this figure can be added, on the basis of my minimum calculations, the working days lost by a further 750,000 unpaid redundant, that is an additional thirty-six million working days. Taken together it can be seen on minimum calculations that just short of fifty-four million working days, or more than four times the number lost through strikes, were lost through unemployment consequent upon redundancy during 1971.

The comparison with the number of days lost through strikes illustrates the point made earlier about the nature of 'problems': there is no debate about the 'nature of Britain's redundancy problem' to parallel that between Turner and McCarthy in respect of the strike problem.[175] The words of the Robens' report about the question of health and safety might be applied with equal value to the redundancy problem:

'We should like to see it eventually command something like the degree of interest and attention commonly accorded to other subjects – such as industrial relations – where the problems may be more controversial but are often less real and important in terms of human well-being.'[176]

[174] Figures computed from data published in the D.E. *Gazette*.

[175] H. A. Turner, *Is Britain Really Strike Prone?* (Cambridge: University Press, 1969), and W. E. J. McCarthy, 'The Nature of Britain's Strike Problem', *British Journal of Industrial Relations*, Vol. VIII, No. 2, July 1970.

[176] *Safety and Health at Work*, Report on the Committee 1970–72 (London: H.M.S.O., 1972), p. 2.

Comparison of the losses occasioned by redundancy and by strikes has further value: despite the hue and cry about strikes, it is recognised that a proportion of the time lost through strikes can be made up afterwards by increased effort, overtime, speeding up tracks and so on, and that, in any case, some of the lost time attributed to strikes would have been lost through inadequate production scheduling. Furthermore, one of the benefits of strikes is said to be the 'safety-valve' effect whereby strike action clears the air. The same considerations by no means apply to time lost through redundancy, indeed the loss is likely to be increased firstly by a general drop in morale and production after the announcement of redundancy but prior to its implementation and secondly, by the time taken by workers to adjust and acclimatise in their post-redundancy jobs.

Hence, *pace* the obfuscation created by the mythology of public policy, even within the managerial definition of the problem – losses to production, working days lost etc. – the redundancy problem demands far more serious attention than it has been customarily paid. From the workers' perspective mythology needs to be substituted by reality: a correction that can only be achieved by first examining the validity of the kind of myths that are perpetrated about the Redundancy Payments Act.

Conclusion

This paper began with an indication that both lawyers and sociologists should concern themselves with the question of values in society. For the sociologist, a concern with values leads to enquiring into the definition, origin and proposed mediation of social problems. Central to such an enquiry must be an analysis of the kind of social structure, the type of work organisation and the form of industrial authority under which redundancy occurs and is defined as a more or less acceptable way of achieving other social goals such as economic growth or technical change. For the lawyer, a concern with values is more immediately connected with the formulation and evaluation of public policy but also with the wider, and essentially philosophical and political question, 'what kind of society do we want?'. Where redundancy is in question the choice is between continuing with a variant of the present managerial definition of the problem (as, for example, in making the Redundancy Payments Act more selective[177]) and giving more serious consideration to the

[177] In accordance with the changes sought by employers reported in Parker *et al.*, *op. cit.*, pp. 69–70.

workers' redundancy problem. If the former path is chosen, then the precise form of legislation will depend upon a combination of expedience and appropriateness. If the latter course of action is preferred, then the way forward can be either toward more restrictions upon managerial discretion in the internal labour market and a much more comprehensive strategy in the external labour market[178] or toward a situation in which certain of the current myths of redundancy policy gain considerably in substance and are transformed into reality, especially those to do with job security and property in work. In other words there is a second choice between making the present structure more humanely efficient and radically altering the values on which that structure rests. Each of these last two developments depends initially upon listening to the workers' point of view, but the first does so with a view to engineering 'men's adaption to the idea of redundancy',[179] while the second recognises that 'the worker exists in a subordinate position to the property owner and (that) his demands involve an inherent challenge to the nature and justification of the property system itself'[180] and that those demands are legitimate.

At bottom, public policy is inescapably a question of values, however well or ill articulated. As Milton Derber has noted, most labour research 'has been based upon the assumption that the prevailing values of the society and of its chief components – government, corporations, unions – are intrinsically sound and that the problems are primarily technical in nature. . . . It is vital however, to any scientific field that its underlying assumptions should always be subject to critical appraisal and, if necessary, challenge'.[181] This paper has sought to indicate not only how, in respect of redundancy, those values may simply be taken for granted but also that they may be challenged by other equally semi-articulated values. It is a question of choice but that choice cannot be separated from the distribution of power in society.

[178] See, for example, Santosh Mukherjee, *Making Labour Markets Work* (London: P.E.P., 1972); W. W. Daniel, *Strategies for the Displaced Worker* (London: P.E.P., 1970); and Dorothy Wedderburn, 'Redundancy', *op. cit.*

[179] W. W. Daniel, *Strategies for the Displaced Worker, op. cit.*, p. 10.

[180] Daniel Bell, 'Industrial Conflict and Public Opinion' in A. Kornhauser *et al.* (eds.), *Industrial Conflict* (New York: McGraw-Hill, 1954), p. 242.

[181] Milton Derber, *Research in Labor Problems in the United States*, (New York: Random House, 1967) p. 158.

BIBLIOGRAPHY

The place of publication is London unless otherwise stated

Abbot, J., *Student Life in a Class Society*, Oxford: Pergamon Press 1971.

Acton Society Trust, *Redundancy: Three Studies of Redundant Workers*, Acton Society Trust, 1959.

Acton Society Trust, *Redundancy II*, Acton Society Trust, 1962.

Almond, G. A., and Verba, S., *The Civic Culture*, Princeton: Princeton University Press, 1963.

Anderman, S. K., ed., *Trade Unions and Technological Change*, George Allen and Unwin, 1967.

Anderson, M., *Family Structure in Nineteenth Century Lancashire*, Cambridge: Cambridge University Press, 1971.

Arendt, H., *The Human Condition*, Chicago: Chicago University Press, 1958.

Argyris, C., *Integrating the Individual and the Organisation*, New York: John Wiley and Son, Inc., 1964.

Berger, P. L., and Luckmann, T., *The Social Construction of Reality*, New York: Doubleday and Co., Inc., 1966.

Beveridge, W. H., *Unemployment – A Problem of Industry*, 2nd edn,. Longmans, 1930.

Blackburn, R., 'The Unequal Society', in ed. Blackburn, R., and Cockburn, P., *The Incompatibles: Trade Union Militancy and the Consensus*, Harmondsworth: Penguin Books Ltd., 1967.

Blau, P. M., *The Dynamics of Bureaucracy*, Chicago: Chicago University Press, 1955.

Bottomore, T. B., and Reubel, M., eds, *Selections from Marx: Sociology and Social Philosophy*, Harmondsworth: Penguin Books Ltd., 1961.

Broom, L., and Smith, J. H., 'Bridging Occupations', *British Journal of Sociology*, Vol. 14, 1963.

Brown, R. K., and Brannen, P., 'Social Relations and Social Perspectives amongst Shipbuilding Workers', a Preliminary Statement', *Sociology*, Vol. 4, 1970.

Bulmer, M. I. A., 'Mining Redundancy: A Case Study of the Workings of the Redundancy Payments Act in the Durham Coalfield', *Industrial Relations Journal*, Vol. 1, 1971.

Burns, T., and Stalker, G. M., *The Management of Innovation*, Tavistock Publications, 1961.

Butler, D. E., and Stokes, D., *Political Change in Britain: Forces Shaping Electoral Choice*, Macmillan, 1969.

Child, J., *British Management Thought: A Critical Analysis*, George Allen and Unwin, 1969.

Child, J., 'Organisational Structure, Environment, and Performance: The Role of Strategic Choice', *Sociology*, Vol. 6, 1972.

Chinoy, E., *Automobile Workers and the American Dream*, New York: Doubleday and Co., Inc., 1955.

Clarke, P. F., 'British Politics and Blackburn Politics', 1900–10, *Historical Journal*, Vol. 12, 1969.

Clarke, P. F., *Lancashire and the New Liberalism*, Cambridge: Cambridge University Press, 1971.

Cochran, T. C., *The Puerto-Rican Businessman*, Philadelphia: University of Pennsylvania Press, 1959.

Cotgrove, S., and Box, S., *Science, Industry, and Society*, George Allen and Unwin, 1970.

Cotgrove, S., Dunham, J., and Vamplew, C., *The Nylon Spinners: A Case Study in Productivity Bargaining and Job Enlargement*, George Allen and Unwin, 1971.

Cowling, K., Dean, M., Pyatt, G., and Wabe, S., *An Investigation into the Demand for Manpower and Its Supply in the Engineering Industry*, Coventry: University of Warwick Papers in Social and Economic Research, n.d.

Crozier, M., *The Bureaucratic Phenomenon*, Chicago: University of Chicago Press, 1964.

Cullingworth, J. B., *Housing and Labour Mobility*, Paris: O.E.C.D., 1969.

Cunnison, S., *Wages and Work Allocation*, Tavistock Publications, 1966.

Dalton, M., *Men Who Manage*, New York: John Wiley and Son, Inc., 1959.

Dennis, N., Henriques, F., and Slaughter, C., *Coal is our Life*, 2nd edn, Tavistock Publications, 1969.

Dow, J. C. R., *The Management of the British Economy, 1945–60*, Cambridge: Cambridge University Press, 1964.

Dubin, R., 'Industrial Workers' Worlds: A Study of the Central Life Interests of Industrial Workers', *Social Problems*, Vol. 3, 1955.

Dumont, L., *Homo Hierarchicus*, Weidenfeld and Nicolson, 1970.

Durkheim, E., *Suicide: A Study in Sociology*, trans. Spaulding and Simpson, Routledge and Kegan Paul, 1952.

Economic Affairs, Department of, *The North West: A Regional Study*, H.M.S.O., 1965.

Eldridge, J. E. T., *Industrial Disputes*, Routledge and Kegan Paul, 1968.

Eldridge, J. E. T., *Max Weber: The Interpretation of Social Reality*, Michael Joseph, 1971.

Employment and Productivity Gazette, 1967 and 1968.

Employment and Productivity, Department of, *The Redundancy Payments Scheme, A Revised Guide*, H.M.S.O., 1970.

Festinger, L., *A Theory of Cognitive Dissonance*, Tavistock Publications, 1962.

Foltman, F. F., *White and Blue Collars in a Mill Shut-down*, Ithaca: New York School of Industrial and Labour Relations, 1968.

Ford, J., and Box, S., 'Sociological Theory and Occupational Choice', *Sociological Review*, Vol. 16, 1968.

Fowler, R. F., *Duration of Unemployment Based on the Register of the Wholly Unemployed*, H.M.S.O., 1968.

Fox, A., *The Milton Plan*, Institute of Personnel Management, 1965.

Fox, A., *Industrial Sociology and Industrial Relations*, H.M.S.O., 1967.

Fox, A., *A Sociology of Work in Industry*, Collier-Macmillan, 1971.

Friedmann, G., *Industrial Society: The Emergence of the Human Problems of Automation*, Glencoe: The Free Press, 1955.

Garfinkel, H., *Studies in Ethnomethodology*, Englewood Cliffs: Prentice-Hall, Inc., 1967.

Gilpatrick, E. G., *Structural Unemployment and Aggregate Demand, A Study of Employment and Unemployment in the United States, 1948–64*, Baltimore: The Johns Hopkins Press, 1966.

Glaser, B., and Strauss, A., *The Discovery of Grounded Theory*, Weidenfeld and Nicolson, 1968.

Gluckmann, M., *Analysis of a Social Situation in Modern Zululand, Rhodes–Livingstone Paper No. 28*, Manchester: Manchester University Press, 1958.

Goffman, E., *The Presentation of Self in Everyday Life*, New York: Doubleday and Co., Inc., 1959.

Goffman, E., *Stigma*, Englewood Cliffs: Prentice-Hall, Inc., 1963.

Goldthorpe J. H. Lockwood D. Platt J. Bechhofer, F., *The Affluent Worker: Industrial Attitudes and Behaviour*, Cambridge: Cambridge University Press, 1968.

Goldthorpe, J. H., Lockwood, D., Platt, J., Bechhofer, F., *The Affluent Worker: Political Attitudes and Behaviour*, Cambridge: Cambridge University Press, 1968.

Goldthorpe, J. H., Lockwood, D., Platt, J., Bechhofer, F., *The Affluent Worker in the Class Structure*, Cambridge: Cambridge University Press, 1969.

Gouldner, A. W., *Patterns of Industrial Bureaucracy*, Glencoe: The Free Press, 1954.

Grunfeld, C., *The Law of Redundancy*, Sweet and Maxwell, 1971.

Haire, M., Ghisseli, E. E., and Porter, L. W., *Managerial Thinking: An International Study*, New York: John Wiley and Son, Inc., 1966.

Hanham, H. J., *Elections and Party Management in the Age of Gladstone and Disraeli*, Longmans, 1959.

Harris, A. I., and Clausen, G., *Labour Mobility in Britain, 1953–63*, H.M.S.O., 1966.

Harrison, T., *Britain Revisited*, Victor Gollancz, 1961.

Herzberg, F., *Work and the Nature of Man*, Staples Press, 1968.

Herzberg, F., Mauser, B., Peterson, R. O., and Capwell, D. F., *Job Attitudes: Review of Research and Opinion*, Pittsburgh: Psychological Services of Pittsburgh, 1957.

Hoggart, R., *The Uses of Literacy*, Chatto and Windus, 1957.

Hollowell, P. G., *The Lorry Driver*, Routledge and Kegan Paul, 1968.

Homans, G. C., *Social Behaviour: Its Elementary Forms*, Routledge and Kegan Paul, 1961.

Hunter, L. C., and Reid, G. L., *Urban Worker Mobility*, Paris: O.E.C.D., 1968.

Hunter, L. C., Reid, G. L., and Boddy, D., *Labour Problems of Techological Change*, George Allen and Unwin, 1970.

Iden, G., 'Industrial Growth and Areas of Chronic Unemployment', *Monthly Labour Review*, 1966.

Ingham, G. K., *Size of Industrial Organisation and Worker Behaviour*, Cambridge: Cambridge University Press, 1970.

Intermediate Areas: Report of a Committee under the Chairmanship of Sir John Hunt, Cmd 3998, H.M.S.O., 1969.

Jackson, B., *Working-Class Community: Some General Notions Raised by a Series of Studies in Northern England*, Routledge and Kegan Paul, 1968.

Jacobs, P., 'Unemployment as a Way of Life', in ed. Ross, A. M.,

Employment Policy and the Labour Market, Berkeley and Los Angeles, University of California Press, 1966.

Kahn, H. R., *Repercussions of Redundancy*, George Allen and Unwin, 1964.

Karpik, L., 'Urbanisation et satisfactions au travail', *Sociologie du travail*, Vol. 8, 1966.

Katz, D., and Kahn, R. L., *The Social Psychology of Organisations*, New York: John Wiley and Son, Inc., 1966.

Kerr, C., Dunlop, J., Harbison, F., and Myers, C. A., *Industrialism and Industrial Man*, Heinemann Educational Books, 1962.

Kohn, M. L., *Class and Conformity*, Homewood: The Dorsey Press, 1969.

Krupp, S., *Pattern in Organisational Analysis: A Critical Examination*, New York: Holt, Rinehart and Winston, Inc., 1961.

Labour, Ministry of, 'Redundancy in Great Britain', *Ministry of Labour Gazette*, 1963.

Lane, A., and Roberts, K., *Strike at Pilkingtons*, Collins/Fontana, 1971.

Lee, J. M., *Social Leaders and Public Persons*, Oxford: Oxford University Press, 1963.

Liverpool, University of, Department of Social Science, *The Dock Worker*, Liverpool: Liverpool University Press, 1954.

Liverpool, University of, Department of Social Science, *Neighbourhood and Community*, Liverpool: Liverpool University Press, 1954.

Mackay, D. I., 'After the Shakeout', *Oxford Economic Papers*, 1972.

Mackay, D. I., Boddy, D., Brack, J., Diack, J. A., and Jones, N., *Labour Markers under Different Employment Conditions*, George Allen and Unwin, 1971.

Mann, M. J., *Sociological Aspects of Factory Relocation: A Case Study*, Unpublished D.Phil. thesis, Oxford, 1970.

Marris, R., *The Economic Theory of Managerial Capitalism*, Macmillan, 1966.

Martin, R., 'The "Rational Maximising" Model of Labour Mobility', in ed. Loveridge, R., *Industrial Relations and Manpower Planning*, Heinemann Educational Books, forthcoming.

Martin, R., and Fryer, R. H., 'Management and Redundancy: An Analysis of Planned Organisational Change', *British Journal of Industrial Relations*, Vol. 8, 1970.

Maslow, A. H., *Motivation and Personality*, New York: Harper and Row, Inc., 1954.

Matthews, R. C. O., 'Why Britain has had Full Employment since the War', *Economic Journal*, Vol. 78, 1968.

265

McCrone, G., *Regional Policy in Britain*, George Allen and Unwin, 1969.

McHugh, P., *Defining the Situation: the Organisation of Meaning in Social Interaction*, New York: Bobbs-Merrill, Inc., 1968.

Mercer, D. E., and Weir, D. T. H., 'Orientations to Work amongst White Collar Workers', in eds. Goldthorpe, J. H., and Mann, M. J., *Social Science Research Council Conference on Social Stratification and Industrial Relations*, Social Science Research Council, 1969.

Meissner, M., *Technology and the Worker*, San Francisco: Chandler Publishing Corporation, 1969.

Miller, E. J., and Rice, A. K., *Systems of Organisation*, Tavistock Publications, 1967.

Mills, C. Wright, *White Collar: the American Middle Class*, New York: Oxford University Press, 1956.

Mills, C. Wright, *The Sociological Imagination*, New York: Oxford University Press, 1959.

Mitchell, J. C., *The Kalela Dance: Rhodes–Livingstone Paper no. 27*, Manchester: Manchester University Press, 1956.

Morse, N. C., and Weiss, R. S., 'The Function and Meaning of Work and the Job', *American Sociological Review*, Vol. 20, 1955.

Neff, W. S., *Work and Human Behaviour*, New York: The Atherton Press, 1968.

Nichols, T., *Ownership, Control, and Ideology*, George Allen and Unwin, 1970.

Nosow, S., and Form, W. H., *Man, Work, and Society: A Reader in the Sociology of Occupations*, New York: Basic Books, Inc., 1962.

Ossowski, S., *Class Structure in the Social Consciousness*, Routledge and Kegan Paul, 1963.

Parker, S. R., Thomas, C. A., Ellis, N. D., and McCarthy, W. E. J., *Effects of the Redundancy Payments Act*, H.M.S.O., 1971.

Perrow, C., *Organisational Analysis: A Sociological View*, Tavistock Publications, 1970.

Piepe, A., Prior, R., and Box, A., 'The Location of the Proletarian and Deferential Worker', *Sociology*, Vol. 3, 1969.

Pilgrim Trust, *Men Without Work*, Cambridge: Cambridge University Press, 1938.

Rice, A. K., *The Organisation and the Environment*, Tavistock Publications, 1963.

Robinson, D., ed., *Local Labour Markets and Wage Structures*, Gower Press, 1970.

Rosenberg, M., *Occupations and Values*, Glencoe: The Free Press, 1957.

Ross, A. M., ed., *Unemployment and the American Economy*, New York: John Wiley and Son, Inc., 1964.

Runciman, W. G., *Relative Deprivation and Social Justice*, Routledge and Kegan Paul, 1966.

Sams, K. I., and Simpson, J. V., 'A Case Study of a Ship-building Redundancy in Northern Ireland', *Scottish Journal of Political Economy*, Vol. 15, 1968.

Sayles, L., *Managerial Behaviour*, New York: McGraw-Hill, 1964.

Sayles, L., and Strauss, G., *Human Behaviour in Organisations*, Englewood Cliffs: Prentice-Hall, Inc., 1966.

Schutz, A., *Collected Papers*, The Hague: Martinus Nijhoff, 1964 (vol. 1), 1971 (vol. 2).

Shinwell, E., *The Britain I Want*, Macdonald and Co., 1943.

Silverman, D., *The Theory of Organisations*, Heinemann Educational Books, 1970.

Simon, H. A., *Administrative Behaviour*, 2nd edn, New York: The Free Press, 1965.

Simon, H. A., and March, J. G., *Organisations*, New York: John Wiley and Son, Inc., 1958.

Smith, A. D., *Redundancy Practices in Four Industries*, Paris: O.E.C.D., 1966.

Social Trends in Britain, H.M.S.O., 1972.

Stedman-Jones, G., *Outcast London: A Study in the Relationship between Social Classes in Victorian London*, Oxford: Oxford University Press, 1971.

Sykes, A. J. M., 'Some Differences in the Attitudes of Clerical and Manual workers', *Sociological Review*, Vol. 13, 1965.

Taylor, R. C., 'Migration and Motivation', in ed. Jackson, J. A., *Migration*, Cambridge: Cambridge University Press, 1970.

Thompson, J. D., *Organisations in Action*, New York: McGraw-Hill, 1967.

Tourraine, A., and Ragazzi, O., *Ouvriers d'origine agricole*, Paris: Editions du Seuil, 1961.

Turner, B. A., *Exploring the Industrial Subculture*, Macmillan, 1971.

Turner, H. A., *Trade Union Growth, Structure, and Policy: A Comparative Study of the Cotton Unions*, George Allen and Unwin, 1962.

Turner, A. N., and Lawrence, P. R., *Industrial Jobs and the Worker*, Boston: Division of Research: Harvard Business School, 1965.

Vroom, V. H., *Work and Motivation*, New York: John Wiley and Son, Inc., 1964.

Warner, W. L., and Low, J. O., *The Modern Factory: The Strike: A Social Analysis*, New Haven: Yale University Press, 1947.

Webb, S., and Webb, B., *Industrial Democracy*, 2nd edn, Longmans, 1920.

Weber, M., *The Methodology of the Social Sciences*, Glencoe: The Free Press, 1949.

Weber, M., *Economy and Society*, New York: Bedminster Press, 1968.

Wedderburn, D., *White Collar Redundancy: A Case Study*, Cambridge: Cambridge University Press, 1964.

Wedderburn, D., *Redundancy and the Railwaymen*, Cambridge: Cambridge University Press, 1965.

Wedderburn, D., 'Redundancy', in ed. Pym, D., *Industrial Society: Social Sciences in Management*, Harmondsworth: Penguin Books Ltd., 1968.

Whyte, W. F., *Men at Work*, Homewood: Richard D. Irwin, Inc., 1961.

Willner, A., 'L'ouvrier et l'Organisation', *Sociologie due Travail*, Vol. 4, 1962.

Woodward, J., *Industrial Organisation: Theory and Practice*, Oxford: Oxford University Press, 1965.

Woodward, J., ed, *Industrial Organisation: Behaviour and Control*, Oxford University Press, 1970.

Wootton, B., *The Social Foundations of Wage Policy*, 2nd edn, George Allen and Unwin, 1962.

Youngson, A. J., *The British Economy, 1920–57*, George Allen and Unwin, 1960.

INDEX

S